THE BATTLE
OF THE
ATLANTIC

THE BATTLE OF THE ATLANTIC

ANDREW WILLIAMS

For Chook, Lachlan and Finn

Published to accompany the television series *The Battle of the Atlantic*, first broadcast on BBC2 in 2002.
Executive producer: Laurence Rees
Writer and producer: Andrew Williams
Associate producers: Dominic Sutherland and Dr Frank Stucke

Published by BBC Worldwide Ltd, Woodlands, 80 Wood Lane, London W12 0TT

First published in 2002 © Andrew Williams 2002
The moral right of the author has been asserted.

ISBN 0 563 53429 X

Commissioning editor: Sally Potter
Project editor: Rhianwen Bailey
Copy editor: Esther Jagger
Art director: Linda Blakemore
Designer: Martin Hendry
Picture researchers: Anne-Marie Ehrlich and David Cottingham
Production controller: Kenneth McKay
Cartographer: Olive Pearson

Set in Plantin
Printed in Great Britain by Butler and Tanner Ltd, Frome
Jacket and plate sections printed by Lawrence-Allen Ltd, Weston-super-Mare

CONTENTS

FOREWORD

THE BATTLE OF THE ATLANTIC was the decisive naval battle of the Second World War. Without victory by the Western Allies, it is probable that Britain would have been forced out of the war: German power would have been supreme throughout Western Europe; the Mediterranean would have become an Axis lake; there would have been no Allied aid to Russia and it would have been impossible for the Western Allies to invade France in 1944 and defeat the German armies in Western Europe. The effects of a victory over the Western Allies in this conflict are thus almost beyond calculation and comprehension.

Beginning on 3 September 1939 and lasting until VE Day in 1945, the Battle of the Atlantic was the longest, largest and most complex naval battle in history. During the course of this huge sprawling conflict, hundreds of Allied and German sailors were either killed, wounded or posted missing.

This was a battle that the Germans might have won, but in the harsh light of hindsight, they lost because of superior Allied strategy, tactics, intelligence, technology and material resources. However, during the struggle itself, nothing was clear to the men who manned Allied ships and aircraft. For them, the outline of the conflict was obscured by endless images of sinking ships, exploding depth charges, and ever so rarely a U-boat being blasted to the surface and sunk by gunfire. To the Germans who manned the U-boats, the Battle of the Atlantic was equally cloudy. Although they sank thousands of Allied merchant ships, their own losses of U-boats steadily rose for reasons that even the German high command never fully understood.

Comprehending this conflict at the time was probably an impossible task; nearly as impossible is the task of making sense of the battle's immense complexities today. Yet this is where the importance of Andrew Williams's book lies: by thoughtfully leading his interviewees through the difficult phases of the battle, he gives us an effective, evocative yet lucid account of these momentous events. He accomplishes this task by offering us a wealth of new information, crucial to understanding the flow of events; through new eye-witness accounts from both sides of the battle, as they occurred, both from the German and the Allied sides, as well as the complexity of the Allied final victory.

In a field that is already rich in historiography, Andrew Williams has made an important and lasting contribution, providing a vivid, yet fully-documented account, aiding an understanding of the depth of struggle involved in one of the greatest battles of the 20th century.

PROFESSOR DAVID SYRETT
Queens College, City University of New York

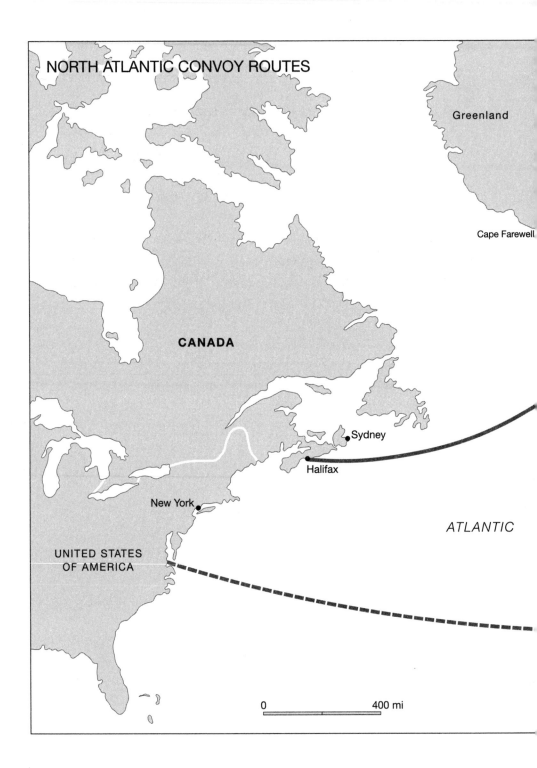

NORTH ATLANTIC CONVOY ROUTES

Greenland

Cape Farewell

CANADA

Sydney

Halifax

New York

UNITED STATES
OF AMERICA

ATLANTIC

0   400 mi

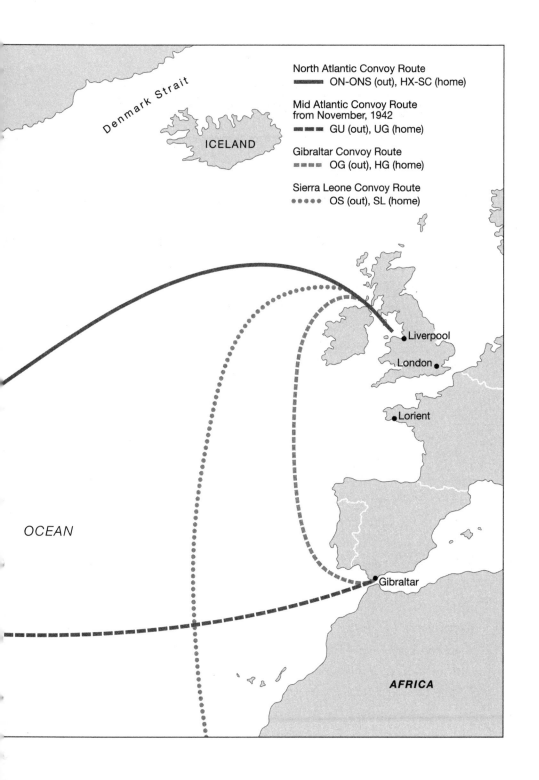

North Atlantic Convoy Route
━━━ ON-ONS (out), HX-SC (home)

Mid Atlantic Convoy Route
from November, 1942
━ ━ ━ GU (out), UG (home)

Gibraltar Convoy Route
▪▪▪▪ OG (out), HG (home)

Sierra Leone Convoy Route
●●●●● OS (out), SL (home)

Denmark Strait

ICELAND

OCEAN

Liverpool

London

Lorient

Gibraltar

AFRICA

AUTHOR'S NOTE

THE THOUSANDS OF SIGHTSEERS that hurry every day from the underground to join the queues outside the Tower of London pass, almost unnoticed, a large, dusty, white stone memorial that lists the names of the British and Empire seamen who died in two World Wars. On 3 September 2001 I stood at this memorial with a veteran who had come to remember friends lost sixty years ago, almost to the day. John Wright's ship the *Empire Wave* was sunk in 1941; he spent his 19th birthday in a lifeboat in the icy waters between Greenland and Iceland. Not everyone in the boat survived this fourteen-day ordeal, some of those that did lost hands and feet to frostbite. For John it is still very raw; once a year he makes this personal act of remembrance and stands before the names of the 30 comrades who have no grave.

The Battle of the Atlantic was, in Winston Churchill's words, 'the dominating factor all through the war'; everything depended on its outcome. Yet whilst the story of 'the few' pilots who fought the Battle of Britain in the summer of 1940 has been told often on television, surprisingly little has been made of the struggle to protect the country's vital trade routes across the North Atlantic. It was the longest campaign of World War II, thousands of people played their part in protecting Britain's 'lifeline' and yet in many respects it was, in the words of one of the contributors to this book, 'an unseen war with nothing to show for what had been lost; it had all been lost at sea'. Battles known only by a convoy number, but of first importance to the outcome of the war, were fought every few months. Little was reported of these at the time; even less is known of them today. I hope the television series and this book play some small part in redressing this balance. The story told here concentrates almost entirely on the U-boat war in the North Atlantic. I have taken my cue from the Royal Navy's official historian: 'We knew beyond doubt', he wrote of the U-boat, 'that the peril in which our nation so long stood, derived mainly from those utterly ruthless enemies, and that only by destroying them could we survive'.

First and foremost I am grateful to the men and women who were prepared to be interviewed for the series, and whose recollections form the core of this book. I also owe a special debt of gratitude to the Creative Director of BBC History, Laurence Rees, for the opportunity to make the series and for the support he has given me throughout. This project, like so many before it, has benefited immeasurably from his sure editorial touch. Both the Series Consultants, Dr Axel Niestlé and Professor David Syrett read this book in draft form and I am grateful for their guidance. Dr Niestlé helped me to develop my ideas for both the book and the series at the research stage and since then he has been an honest, much-valued critic, upon whose judgement I have depended. I would also like to thank Jock Gardner of the Naval Historical Branch and Dr Alan Scarth of the Merseyside Maritime Museum for their help, and Ralph Erskine for his advice on all matters relating to British and German naval ciphers.

Of the many people involved in the production of the television series on which this book is based I would particularly like to thank my colleagues Dominic Sutherland and Dr Frank Stucke. They played an equal part in the research and the interviews that are at the heart of the series and this book, and I am greatly in their debt. My thanks are due to: production manager Jane Johnston who was enormously supportive and as efficient as ever; Victoria Brignell and David List for their help with the research; Anne-Marie Ehrlich who found the wonderful photographic images in this book; the History Unit's production executive Ann Cattini for her support and help with the budget; film editor Alan Lygo for his craftsmanship and sound editorial advice, and to cameraman Fred Fabre for his wonderful 'eye' and boundless enthusiasm. I would also like to mention Jesse Stoecker who worked as a soundman on the series and who died in tragic circumstances before it was finished. All those who worked with him will remember him fondly.

I am grateful to Sally Potter at BBC Worldwide who commissioned the book and was always supportive; Esther Jagger who edited the manuscript in record time and improved it in the process; and Rhianwen Bailey who coolly and professionally saw the whole thing through to production.

Finally a few words of thanks to my family: Kate, Lachlan and Finn – without whose support, good humour and patience this book would never have been finished. It was written in their time: in the early mornings and the evenings, at weekends and in the holidays. When I began to flag, my wife Kate was there to encourage me on, confident, even when I was not, that I would get there in the end. In exile at the top of the house, my sanity was sometimes in the balance; it was always saved by Lachlan or Finn who would pad upstairs to insist that it was now time for 'Daddy' to play a game. This book is dedicated to Kate and the boys.

CHAPTER ONE

THE FREIKORPS DÖNITZ

THE RADIO had been humming with traffic all morning. No one stopped to think about it. If it happened, it happened. There were still the usual tasks to perform: the U-boat to be cleaned, the torpedoes greased, and breakfast prepared for the middle watch, just off duty. Its commander Fritz-Julius Lemp joined the new watch on *U-30*'s conning tower; it was a fine, clear day with just a gentle Atlantic swell, and for once life below was almost comfortable. The boat was, in Lemp's estimation, some 250 miles off the northwest coast of Scotland, well within its designated patrol area. Its orders were simply to await an urgent signal; and be ready for immediate action. That morning, Sunday, 3 September 1939, it looked as if that was how the waiting would end. There would be war.

It had all begun to bubble up the month before. No one on *U-30* had taken it too seriously at first. The German navy, the Kriegsmarine, had placed its U-boats on alert three times in the last year; each time they had been stood down again.[1] Were Britain and France prepared to go to war over Poland? Lemp thought not. He had sent one of his radio operators, Georg Högel, home on leave to Munich. Högel remembers: 'Lemp said to me, "Högel, listen, perhaps this whole business that's starting in Poland will end up like the *Hornberger Schiessen*," by which he meant that it would all come to nothing. "You may as well take your leave, but you must promise me that it will be possible to contact you within two hours." So I went on leave. I got home on Wednesday morning. Saturday lunchtime, the doorbell rang and my mother went out. When she came back her hands were trembling – she was holding a telegram from the commander. "Return Wilhelmshaven 21 August, 2400 hours at the latest." I said to my father, "Now it's starting."

The nineteen-year-old Högel reached the naval dockyard just in time. *U-30* was preparing to put to sea, but he found a sailor from his own boat and asked what was happening:

> "'We're leaving at four.'"
>
> "What's the cargo? Mines or torpedoes?" That was the next question, of course.
>
> "Torpedoes."

After the usual checks on the boat, the crew had time for a last beer in the mess; Högel remembers tears on the face of the steward's wife as she said goodbye to them all. It was still dark when *U-30* slipped out of the harbour. The journey across the North Sea into the Atlantic was uneventful, but for one heart-racing moment. One night the bridge watch were surprised by an enormous shape that rose black and menacing out of the Atlantic. Högel recalls: 'We dived and came up again, and it was only then we saw what it was: a rock. What they had taken for a steamer was in fact the barren thumb of rock that sticks out of the ocean some 280 miles west of Scotland, known appropriately as Rockall.

It was the seventh day *U-30* had spent waiting, discreetly cruising the box of sea allocated to her. The boat's watch had observed a good number of ships on the horizon but all of these were allowed to pass unmolested. By 3 September everyone on board felt anxious, tense. When the signal came it was bald, unambiguous, deeply shocking: 'Britain and France have declared war on Germany. Battle-stations immediate.' No one on board *U-30* had wanted this. Georg Högel remembers: 'I was lying on my bunk, still sleepy from the middle watch. My comrades came in and gave me a poke, saying, "England has declared war on us." Eleven in the morning. I looked at my watch; it was twelve o'clock in Germany. We felt a certain tension, curiosity, but there was no enthusiasm.'

The German counter-declaration came at one o'clock: 'Hostilities with England effective immediately.' It mentioned only England; what of France? Lemp and his crew had no way of knowing it but their Führer, Adolf Hitler, still hoped to coax France away from the brink. Hitler had already imposed severe restrictions on U-boat operations. It was his view that, for now, Germany's war at sea should be fought within the international agreements it had signed. He had chosen to pursue this uncharacteristically cautious course in the hope that it might all be brought to a swift conclusion. If Britain and France could not be won round, then the neutrality of the United States would be of first importance. Before sailing, all U-boats had been issued with strict orders to operate within the Prize Rules, the international agreements governing the conduct of war at sea. Merchant ships were to be stopped and searched; if found to be carrying enemy cargo they could be sunk, but only after the crew had been seen safely into the lifeboats. These restrictions made a nonsense of submarine warfare. The U-boat's chief weapon was surprise; the undetected rush of a high-explosive torpedo. Stop and search was a lengthy business; the U-boat ran the risk of being caught on the surface in daylight, and it was not equipped to fight artillery duels with enemy warships.

At two o'clock on that first afternoon of the war the Führer der U-Boote, Karl Dönitz, sent a message to his forces reminding them of these restrictions. The signal certainly reached *U-30*, for Högel himself had taken it. If anyone could make sense of all this, Högel thought, the commander could. The twenty-six-year-old Lemp had been in command of *U-30* for almost a year; in that time he had impressed the staff at U-boat Command with his ability to act coolly and decisively under pressure. The crew respected him and had confidence in his judgement. He was a stickler for discipline; the safety of the boat required every man to do his duty quickly and without question, and no excuse was accepted for failure to do so. Yet Lemp's discipline was tempered by humour and compassion; you could laugh with 'the old man'.

After days spent avoiding traffic, *U-30* was now patrolling the shipping lanes off the northwest coast of Ireland in search of its first target. At about 4.30pm the watch picked up the outline of a large ship on the horizon on a course that suggested she was outbound from the British Isles. Lemp decided on pursuit. Georg Högel remembers: 'While the commander was unsure what he was supposed to do we remained at a distance, so that we always had the ship on the horizon. He waited until dusk fell, and then we moved closer.'

Through the periscope Lemp noted that she was blacked out and zigzagging on a defensive course; she must, he concluded, be a British merchant cruiser. If so, she was armed and fair game under the Prize Rules. No warning was necessary.

At 7.40pm Lemp gave the order to fire two torpedoes. One found its target: it exploded amidships, ripping open the bulkhead between the engine and boiler rooms. Lemp had struck the first blow in the Battle of the Atlantic, although it was not one in which he would be able to take pride. Through the gloom he could see the ship had begun to list; she was finished. Yet there was something about her that troubled him; he decided to take *U-30* closer.

Högel was at his post in the radio room below: 'I tuned into the shipping wavelength, and then I heard the distress call. I realized straightaway that it couldn't be a troop transport but that they had passengers on board. I knew her name from the call sign, the *Athenia*. Then the commander came to the radio room and asked for the *Lloyds Register*, which showed the silhouettes of the various types of ship; his finger came to rest on the *Athenia*. He was, of course, shocked.'

It was a ghastly mistake. She was an ocean liner, bound for Canada with 13,581 passengers and crew on board, including more than 300 Americans. Lemp had made a ghastly mistake. He had not taken enough time to check the target. Later he admitted that he had been just too 'over-excited by the declaration of war'.[2] Högel recalls: 'The petty officer responsible for radio came and said, "Do you want to go up top?" I was curious so I went up and saw the *Athenia* lying there with something of a list; it was easy to imagine what was happening on her. I thought, of course, about other maritime disasters, but what were we supposed to do? We couldn't give them any help. It was a submarine and we couldn't take people on board. We could only stop attacking and leave the ship alone and…well, the boat slipped away in the darkness.'

Lemp had disobeyed all orders. His failure to offer any help to the ship's passengers had made matters worse. Fortunately, there had been time enough to take to the lifeboats; the survivors were picked up the following morning by the ships sent to answer the *Athenia*'s call: 'SSS' – attacked by submarine. Most of the 118 people lost had been trapped below deck in the third- and tourist-class dining rooms when the torpedo struck. Among the dead were twenty-eight citizens of the United States.

Within twenty-four hours, news of this German 'outrage' had been reported around the world. British and American newspapers carried graphic accounts of the dying ship. One eyewitness spoke of bodies scattered across the upper deck; another of children trapped in cabins below. It was difficult not to draw the conclusion that on day one of the war Germany had broken all the international agreements she had signed. This was an act of 'total war'; civilians the target. The leader writers on both sides of the Atlantic were quick to draw parallels with Germany's unrestricted U-boat campaign of World War I. Then the U-boat had been the crafty, brutal, invisible enemy; an object of almost universal public loathing. Nothing appeared to have changed. Lemp's ill-judged attack was a propaganda gift. The new First Lord of the Admiralty, Winston Churchill, told the War Cabinet as much the morning after the sinking; the whole affair, he said, could not fail to have 'a helpful effect' on public opinion in America.[3]

Its significance was instantly recognized by Hitler. The first step was to deny responsibility. In the version of events issued by Propaganda Minister Joseph Goebbels, it was a British torpedo that had sunk the *Athenia*; Churchill had planned it all in a desperate attempt to bring the United States into the war. The second step was a further tightening of restrictions on U-boat operations. The Kriegsmarine issued a new order to its commanders: 'The Führer has forbidden attacks on passenger ships sailing independently or in convoy.' This went even further than Germany was required to do under her international obligations.

While still at sea, Lemp had made his crew promise not to breathe a word of the affair. The same promise was wrung from them when they returned to Wilhelmshaven at the end of the month. 'We were assembled in the bow compartment, apart from the officers,' Högel recalls, 'and then we were sworn to secrecy. Not only were we not to discuss it, but we were not to betray anything by sign or gesture.'

This was not easy, for *U-30* had sailed back into Wilhelmshaven with three victory pennants flying from her periscope, representing three ships sunk. Painted on one was the figure '14,000', the approximate tonnage of the *Athenia*; that was quite a claim – one bound to attract comment from U-boat comrades. Yet the official version of events was that drafted in the Ministry of Propaganda. Dönitz and his staff played their part in this elaborate deception; The U-boat Command War Diary made no mention of the affair, and *U-30*'s log was rewritten to remove any mention of the *Athenia*. Georg Högel was personally involved: 'Lemp went to see the Flotilla chief with the boat's war diary. He had written it by hand on board and I had typed it up on the appropriate form. Lemp then signed each entry. When he came back from Flotilla HQ we went to the officers' accommodation block, and there the two of us rewrote a double page of this war diary. He altered the first page, which dealt with the *Athenia* – he drafted it and I retyped it. Then it was put back with the rest of the diary.'

It had not been an auspicious start. Germany's first blow in the war at sea had only succeeded in embarrassing the Führer. The U-boat had once again established itself as a terror weapon and a gift to the propagandists of both sides; it was a long way from demonstrating its importance to Germany's war effort. Few shared Dönitz's conviction that the U-boat was capable of challenging the supremacy of the Royal Navy, capable of defeating Great Britain at sea.

Dönitz's supreme confidence was born of four hard years building and training the fledgling U-boat arm. It was not a role he had at first welcomed. His appointment as Captain 1st U-Flotilla had marked the end of a rewarding year in command of a light cruiser. It was clearly something of a sacrifice; first priority in the Kriegsmarine was given to the construction of a surface fleet made up of big ships with big guns. Dönitz believed that, at the age of forty-three, he was being 'pushed into a backwater'. No one, least of all the man himself, could have predicted how momentous his appointment would prove to be.

The Führer der U-Boote was every inch a military man, somewhat stiff and Prussian in the way he carried himself. Although he was of only average height, his thin, birdlike appearance gave the impression of a taller man. He was from a solid middle-class family with no naval traditions, yet from the first it was apparent to his superiors that he was a gifted young officer. He is described variously in official reports as tough, brisk, ambitious, industrious and duty-conscious. Some also observed a restless impatience, which made it difficult for him to accept the judgement of others.[4] He had a wife and three children, but the navy was his life.

Dönitz was familiar with the cramped, clattering world of the submarine and the very particular camaraderie of its crews. He had commanded his own U-boat during World War I and played his part in sinking nearly 13 million tons of Allied shipping. His boat had been lost in the Mediterranean in the last weeks of the war; commander and crew were rescued from the water but were obliged to spend the best part of a year in British captivity. He had been one of the lucky few retained in the post-war German navy; his career advanced with a series of sea and staff appointments through the 1920s and 1930s. Then in 1935 came the disappointment of his new post with the 1st U-Flotilla.[5]

For Germany, the bitter disappointment of defeat in World War I had been sharpened by the humiliating terms of the victors' peace. Her navy had been effectively dismantled by the Versailles Treaty; whilst a token force of warships was permitted, there was an absolute ban on the construction and deployment of U-boats. Although Germany was only officially released from this ban in June 1935, the month before Dönitz's appointment to the U-boat arm, planning for a new submarine service had begun almost before the ink was dry on the Versailles Treaty. A chosen few were secretly trained for submarine warfare; among their number was Hans-Rudolf Rösing. 'Even before the first U-boats were built', he recalls, ' we had carried out attack exercises using surface vessels fitted with a small periscope.'

Dönitz threw himself into his new role with characteristic zeal; 'body and soul, I was once more a submariner', he later wrote.[6] His command consisted of just six small 250-ton boats; so small that their crews referred to them as 'dug-outs' or 'ducks'. Within days of his appointment these boats had embarked on a punishing six-month training schedule designed to bring them up to combat-readiness. Dönitz drew up a timetable of targets; every boat had to complete sixty-six simulated sur-face attacks and the same number submerged before it could proceed to the next stage, the first torpedo-firing exercise. Rösing, the thirty-year-old commander of *U-11*, knew something of this thoroughness; he had served as a midshipman under Dönitz on the light cruiser *Nymphe*. In those first months Dönitz's energetic leadership drove them forward at a punishing pace: 'He trained us personally,' Rösing recalls. 'He organized the training exercises, he would sail with each one of us, and he observed how we did things. After we had done one part of our training, he would call us together and then every action would be discussed in detail. He would ask our opinion – it was a very lively exchange of ideas, and through this we all learned from each other.'

By the end of the first year's training Dönitz had made his mark. In recognition of his work he was given the altogether grander title 'Führer der U-boote'. At the same time the Flotilla took possession of the first of a new U-boat type – the 500-ton Type VII. A version of this boat would form the backbone of the U-boat force throughout the coming war. By autumn 1936 there were sufficient new boats to commission a second Flotilla; the right sort of volunteer would be needed to crew them.

In 1936 the twenty-two-year-old Erich Topp was serving on the light cruiser *Karlsruhe*. He was the sort of officer it was impossible not to notice; the 'perfect' German, tall, blond, with sharp blue eyes, he cut a dash in a naval uniform. As a boy he had read stories of the great U-boat heroes of World War I, but it was a personal encounter with Dönitz on the *Karlsruhe* that led him to request a transfer to the new arm: 'We were acting as a target-ship for the U-boats. They were carrying out combat training, firing torpedoes at us, and Dönitz was directing the whole thing. I gave up my cabin for him and it was this that drew us into conversation. He asked me if I was interested in joining the U-boat arm. I told him that I had always dreamt of doing just that, and he said, "Let's see what can be arranged."'

The following year Topp reported to the Neustadt U-boat School in the north of Germany: 'It was a dream come true.' He was altogether less misty-eyed after his first visit to a U-boat: 'It was a huge disappointment. I was taken into this confined space; of course I knew it would be confined, but I was now experiencing it for the first time, the smell and the humidity; it was so oppressive. That changed very quickly. The boat gradually became my home.'

Most of the officers whom Dönitz recruited were like Topp; young, ambitious, prepared to put up with the cramped conditions because the U-boat arm held out the promise of an early command. One such was Hanns-Ferdinand Maßmann, who in 1938, at the age of twenty-one, joined the U-boat arm straight from his officer training course: 'I was surprised and proud to have been immediately accepted for training. Unlike on a large ship, a battleship or a cruiser, you could reach a position of responsibility relatively quickly.'

It was the comradeship of a small boat that appealed to many of those, like Richard Amstein, who volunteered to serve as crew members. Amstein joined the navy in 1938 at the age of twenty and was trained as a Zentralegast or Control Room mechanic with responsibility for the U-boat's diving tanks: 'A friend of mine was in the navy and he said, "You might get to travel the world. Just make sure you get a small command – there isn't such a rigorous, barrack-like regime."'

These young men were drawn into Dönitz's U-boat family. Everyone knew each other intimately, and there were even family ties: Hans-Rudolf Rösing's brother-in-law, for instance, served as a commander alongside him. To a degree, this intimacy was imposed by the U-boat itself. After five weeks at sea it was difficult to distinguish officer from rating: no one shaved, no one wore an official uniform. This informality, absent from all other areas of German service life, was officially encouraged. It played its part in building the right sort of spirit, which was the first objective of Dönitz's training programme. He later wrote: 'I wanted to imbue my crews with enthusiasm and a complete faith in their arm and to instil in them a spirit of selfless readiness to serve. Only those possessed of such a spirit could hope to succeed in the grim realities of submarine warfare. Professional skills alone would not suffice.'[7]

Dönitz believed that 'this spirit of selfless readiness to serve' would set his men apart as members of an elite force. They were to become a service within a service; known to the rest of the navy as the Freikorps Dönitz, after the Free Corps volunteers who had banded together to 'protect' Germany from 'communist unrest' after World War I. For the men of the U-boat arm Dönitz was 'the Lion', a figure of cool, reflective authority, but also something of a father to them all. Topp remembers: 'He had enormous charisma, and the officers and men were captivated by this charisma. It wasn't just the build-up of the U-boat arm that was important to him; he also looked after his people. He was concerned with even the smallest details – when crew members went home on leave they were given a food parcel for the family. Dönitz had personal contact, not only with his officers, but also with all his men. He knew most of them by name.'

The image of the Kriegsmarine has always been one of professional sailors remote from the politics of the Reich, yet its ranks mirrored the views of the country at large and in the years after Hitler's rise to power in 1933 he and his National Socialist creed enjoyed the overwhelming support of most Germans. There were certainly many true believers in the Freikorps Dönitz. Membership of political parties was officially forbidden by the navy, but there were many who supported the Nazis and some like Erich Topp, who once carried a party card. He recalls: 'When Hitler came to power, he tried to gradually dismantle the burden of the Versailles Treaty and by doing so to free us. There were constantly fights in the streets between the socialists and National Socialists, and he wanted to put an end to this chaos.'

Hanns-Ferdinand Maßmann had also welcomed Hitler's nomination as Chancellor of Germany. His father had been one of the officers forced out of the navy when the Versailles axe had fallen on the country's fleet. After that, things had been difficult for the Maßmann family: 'At that time, for all the armed forces, the rise of Hitler was associated with the aim of gaining equality with the other powers and freeing us from the restrictions of the Versailles Treaty.'

Hitler was no sailor yet he was fascinated by the technical details of warship design – the thickness of armour plating, the calibre of a ship's guns. He was also totally committed to rebuilding a powerful navy. Naturally enough everyone from bridge to boiler room welcomed this message. Dönitz was introduced to Hitler for the first time in 1934; he was impressed. Here was a former soldier who shared his views about the need for 'a selfless readiness to serve' one's country – the kind of traditional, conservative values he believed should be at the heart of the new U-boat arm. Erich Topp remembers identifying the same values:

The stated idea of National Socialism – to serve the people and to do all you can to improve their lot – was also reflected in a small way aboard a submarine. The commander was single-handedly responsible for whatever happened on board and he had a close link with his men; we were 50 men strong and everyone knew each other very well; everyone knew precisely what he had to do. We were, as the English would say, a 'band of brothers'.

Not, of course, if you were a Jew. After 1933 the Nazis' persecution of the Jews reached into all corners of German life, including the navy. Those who did not actively support this were prepared to turn a blind eye to it. As Topp points out, this was often easier to do in the navy than elsewhere: 'We were at sea and only received news filtered by the Propaganda Ministry. If we had doubts about these activities we were quite prepared to rationalize them by suggesting, for example, that these were transitional problems, or that all revolutionary movements sometimes get out of hand.'[8]

With battleships of 30,000 tons once again rolling down German slipways, it was clearly more comfortable for the officers and men of the Kriegsmarine to take this view.

Not everyone, however, was swept along by the rising Nazi tide; some were quietly critical of where it might all lead. The son of a liberal Berlin artist, Jürgen Oesten surprised his family when in 1933, at the age of nineteen, he enlisted in the navy. He transferred to the U-boat arm in May 1937 and five months later became a watch officer on *U-20*. During a visit home to Berlin the following year, Oesten witnessed something of the state's increasingly vicious treatment of its Jewish citizens. In one night of carefully orchestrated violence thousands were beaten and humiliated, their homes and businesses looted and burnt. Reichskristallnacht, 'the night of glass', was the worst pogrom that had yet taken place in the Third Reich. Oesten was disgusted by what he had seen and visited a Jewish family friend in his best uniform to tell him so.[9] For all that, he believed it to be his duty to serve the interests of his country at sea.

The young Prussian aristocrat Hans-Jochen von Knebel Doeberitz was another sceptic. He joined the navy in 1936 at the age of eighteen, and transferred to the U-boat arm two years later. Life in Hitler's Reich had quickly become uncomfortable for the von Knebel family, he recalls.

Our father was put under observation by the party – it was well known that he wasn't a great supporter. We'd be sitting there in the evening quietly eating our dinner, and then the telephone would ring. You'd go over and then you'd hear a voice, '*Heil Hitler*'. It was a provocation to see whether you would answer in the same way.

You'd say, 'Oh, it's one of those again,' and you'd take the coffee-pot warmer which was standing by ready and you'd put it over the telephone.

For some the navy was a refuge from suspicion and harassment; a place where dissenting views were tolerated – at least if they were whispered.

Dönitz later wrote that, at the time of his appointment to the leadership of the U-boat arm, a future war with Great Britain had been unthinkable. Hitler's new Reich had just negotiated the Anglo-German Naval Agreement, which, whilst permitting a rapid expansion of the fleet, fixed its size at 35 per cent of British naval strength. By 1938 that had all changed; the German navy's plans were to be directed at what its Commander in Chief, Admiral Erich Raeder, called the solution to 'the England problem'. Austria had already become part of the greater Reich, and Hitler intended to annex Czechoslovakia; British neutrality could no longer be guaranteed. There was a certain grim inevitability about this; Britain was the world's greatest maritime power, and wanted to remain so. The Kaiser's attempt to challenge this supremacy had been seen off. His High Seas Fleet had spent most of World War I bottled up in the North Sea; it had all ended in mutiny and surrender. Only the U-boat force had emerged with its reputation untarnished. The ghosts of this humiliating capitulation were yet to be exorcised. Dönitz himself had finished the war as a prisoner of the British; a grudging admiration for the Royal Navy could not mask a lasting, deeper hostility – feelings he shared with many of his fellow officers.[10]

With a day of reckoning in mind, Raeder instructed his staff to examine the task Germany would face in the event of a war with Britain. A total economic blockade, the staff concluded, offered the best chance of success: 'the sea war is the battle over economic and military sea communications.'[11] It would mean an all-out attack on merchant shipping in an effort to strangle Britain's trade and force it into submission. For this Germany would need to build a navy capable of challenging Britain's powerful battle fleets. The question was, what sort of navy? Raeder was sure it should be made up of very big ships with very big guns: super-battleships of 50,000 tons, aircraft carriers, heavy cruisers. It was the sort of grand military vision that excited Hitler; in January 1939 the so-called Z Plan received the Führer's official blessing. Work was to begin at once.

For Dönitz this represented a sharp disappointment. He was convinced that U-boats operating in groups or packs could sink ships more quickly than the enemy could build them. If his boats could account for a million tons of shipping a month, cut Britain's lifeline across the Atlantic, the war would be won. In the first weeks of 1939 Dönitz staged an elaborate war game at U-boat headquarters; amongst the participants was the watch officer of *U-20*, Jürgen Oesten. Oesten remembers:

> The task was to find out how many submarines one would need in order to cut the supplies across the Atlantic. We found out that we needed at least a hundred in the Atlantic at any one time, which meant a total of three hundred: a hundred on operations, a hundred on the way to and from the operations area, and a hundred boats in the shipyards for refitting and repairs. If we had three hundred, it might take a year and a half to have a serious effect on the outcome of the war.

Dönitz concluded that immediate priority must be given to the development of the U-boat arm. A large U-boat fleet would be quicker, cheaper to build and easier to disguise from Germany's enemies than giant battleships. But Dönitz's attempt to convince the staff of this need was rebuffed. In Raeder's estimation, the war at sea would be won on the surface, not beneath it. Although the first object would be the attack on the enemy's merchant fleet, the Reich's battle groups would also need to be powerful enough to beat off its warships. The staff had always emphasized the importance of big ships, but their lack of faith in Dönitz's strategy sprang also from a belief that the British would prove more than a match for the U-boat. It was well known in Berlin that the Royal Navy was confident that its new underwater detection device, ASDIC (or sonar as it later became), would prevent U-boats finding refuge beneath the waves. Dönitz's protestations that the British had placed too much faith in ASDIC fell on deaf ears. The Führer der U-Boote was a well-regarded officer, but he was just a commodore and his views carried no more weight than his rank suggested they should.

For Dönitz, the rejection of his plans was all the more frustrating because he shared none of the staff's confidence that time was on their side. By 1939 it was clear that Hitler's ambitions in Poland risked plunging the country into war. Yet the timetable for Raeder's new navy did not envisage the last ship coming off the slipway until 1948, and even that was optimistic.

Dönitz did nothing to hide his concern from his men. Hanns-Ferdinand Maßmann first met him in spring 1939:

It was on a U-boat, during our training as U-boat gunnery officers. He came aboard in Kiel Bay. He had the trainees gather around him and he gave us an insight into his views on the building-up of the U-boat service, particularly in view of the foreign policy situation. At that time one could not really say for certain what would happen. England had offered Poland its guarantee and the first tensions between Poland and Germany were already visible. He said that, although he had been assured that it would not come to a war with England, given the circumstances he could not believe it and as a commander he had to be prepared. All he could do was demand a U-boat arm of three hundred submarines – only this number would be able to enforce a blockade of England.

The Commander in Chief of the navy demonstrated a touching faith in Hitler's political judgement when he addressed the officers of the U-boat arm in July 1939. The Führer, Raeder said, had promised him that under no circumstances would there be a war with Britain, for that would mean 'Finis Germaniae'. Within six weeks the unthinkable had happened; German troops had marched into Poland, and in response Britain and France had declared war on the Reich. Although Dönitz had made no secret of his forebodings, it was still a shock for him and his officers.

By 1939 Hans-Rudolf Rösing was commander of the Emsmann U-Flotilla; he remembers feeling a sense of burning anger: 'We felt that we had been pushed into this war by the other side – that was how the propaganda presented things to us. We really didn't believe, or didn't want to believe, that we were the ones who had started the war. We really did not think we could win a war at sea, we saw the situation as quite a desperate one.'

The Kriegsmarine was not prepared for war. The British and French had more than ten times as many warships. The three thousand men of the 'Freikorps Dönitz' were well motivated and trained and supremely confident in the effectiveness of their weapon; but they had just fifty-seven boats and most of these were small 250-ton 'ducks'. There were only twenty-seven boats large enough to carry out Atlantic operations. Hanns-Ferdinand Maßmann recalls : 'We weren't depressed but concerned. And at the same time there was also the challenge, because we now had a job to do. We would be seeing action, and we would have to prove ourselves. We simply hoped that we would play a part in this war – that we would be able to achieve our goal of forcing England to its knees.'

Seaman Richard Amstein was not keen to play a part. 'To be honest, I said, "Shit. Now the rubbish is starting." Well, I thought, at least the U-boat is quite safe – I didn't think anything could ever happen to it. We learned better.' On day two of the war Dönitz wrote to Raeder pressing once more for a rapid expansion of the U-boat arm; the magic figure of three hundred was raised again. This time his arguments carried the day. It was clear to the Commander in Chief that time and events had caught up with his extravagant plans for a large surface fleet. The first hurdle was passed, but the Führer too would need to be convinced.

The first wave of U-boat attacks had achieved some notable successes: the Atlantic boats alone had managed to sink thirty-nine ships in a little over a fortnight. Yet these had been overshadowed by the embarrassment caused by the sinking of the *Athenia*. It was also clear to Dönitz and his staff that, until the tight restrictions on U-boat operations were lifted, more decisive results would be impossible. Hitler's thoughts needed to be deflected from the forthcoming land battle back to the war already being fought at sea.

From the outset Dönitz had begun planning 'the boldest of bold enterprises';[12] an operation that would impress the leadership of the Reich and shake the confidence of the enemy. It was to be one of the great naval actions of the war, meticulously planned and brilliantly executed.

At the heart of the Orkney Islands off Britain's north coast lies the great open stretch of sea known as Scapa Flow. This vast basin, 10 miles across at its widest point, forms a natural harbour between the North Sea to the east and the Atlantic Ocean to the west. The broken concrete that still litters these islands bears witness to the Flow's importance as the main naval base for the British Home Fleet in two world wars.

While Hitler was rebuilding the new Germany, divers in Scapa Flow were busy raising relics of the old. In 1918 the German High Seas Fleet had steamed slowly into the Flow; four undistinguished years of war had ended in humiliating captivity. In June the following year, the remaining officers and men scuttled their ships and sent them to the bottom of the Flow. One by one, over the next twenty years, the pride of the Imperial navy was brought back to the surface and scrapped. The salvage companies paid well and, in difficult times, Orcadians had good reason to thank the Germans. 'For us, the First War seemed very close, personal,' Sandy Robertson recalls.

In the summer of 1939 the thirty-one-year-old Robertson helped float the battle cruiser *Derfflinger*, the last of the ships to be raised: 'there was nowhere to put her – the navy had taken the space.' By then the Home Fleet had returned to the Flow. On the eve of war the Royal Navy came knocking for Robertson; he would be needed for the duration. Urgent repairs had to be carried out on the Flow's defences. Robertson had spent the last ten years raising ships; in his new job he was expected to sink them. The three main entrances to the anchorage were protected by anti-submarine booms that could be opened to allow access to the Flow. Between the islands at the eastern end there were four smaller channels. During World War I the Admiralty had sealed these with block ships – rusty steel hulks filled with concrete that were sunk and then anchored in place with heavy chains. The tidal flow of twenty years had lifted some of these out of position, but the channels were narrow and shallow and the currents strong; protection enough, it was thought, against penetration by a U-boat.

Experience suggested as much; twice during World War I U-boats had attempted to breach the anti-submarine defences and failed. Nevertheless, within days of the outbreak of war Dönitz had ordered his staff to gather the intelligence necessary for just such an attack. By the end of September the Luftwaffe had presented him with a series of detailed aerial photographs of the Flow's defences. It was clear that any attempt would have to be made through the defences at the eastern end. Dönitz noted in the U-Boat Command Diary what appeared to be a route between the block ships in the Kirk Sound; 'there is a narrow channel about 50 feet wide, and 23 feet deep. To the north of the block ships is another smaller gap. The shore on both sides is practically uninhabited. I think it would certainly be possible to penetrate here – at night, on the surface and at slack water. The main difficulties will be navigational.'[13] The best opportunity seemed to be on the night of Friday, 13 October; then both periods of slack water would occur in a darkness broken by only a new moon.

The man Dönitz deemed to possess the 'personal qualities' necessary for such a daring mission was Günther Prien, the commander of *U-47*. Short, with a round, plump face, there was a deceptively boyish quality about him; Prien had spent nearly half of his thirty-one years at sea. 'He had served in the merchant navy and was an outstanding seaman, he had already demonstrated this in our peacetime exercises,' Prien's Flotilla Commander, Hans-Rudolf Rösing, recalls. 'He was also very committed, very decisive.' A man cast from the same mould as Dönitz himself.

On its first war patrol *U-47* had sunk three British freighters. Then Prien was approached by Dönitz and offered this special operation. He was given forty-eight hours to consider his decision, but his answer could never have been in doubt. On Sunday, 8 October *U-47* sailed discreetly out of Kiel Harbour bound for the Orkneys. The journey across the North Sea would be a slow one: the boat could use its diesel engines to make good speed on the surface at night, but during the day it had to remain submerged to avoid the risk of detection. At sea, safely bedded on the bottom, Prien told his crew the nature of the operation; no one expected them to survive, he said, but he was confident they would succeed. Prien's front might have cracked if he had known how many important targets would leave Scapa Flow during his journey. By 13 October, the day designated for the attack, most of the big ships had gone. The day before, a German plane had flown low over the Flow on a reconnaissance mission. Fearing that this was the prelude to a bombing raid, the battle cruiser *Repulse* had been ordered to make way at once. A procession of ships, including the aircraft carrier *Furious*, steamed out in her wake. The battleships *Nelson* and *Rodney* and the battle cruiser *Hood*, which had left some days before, remained in Loch Ewe on the west coast of Scotland.[14]

A veteran of World War I was still at anchor in the Flow: the battleship *Royal Oak*. Her great 15-inch guns had been in action at the Battle of Jutland; now her 20 knots was too little for her to be of lasting use to the Fleet. Yet she remained in service – a smart fighting ship with a frighteningly heavy punch. The young crew had joined the ship just four months before. Amongst the 1200 officers and men on board were 175 boy seamen. Leading Seaman Joe Instance, only twenty-two, was one of the ship's more experienced hands with six years' service under his belt, nearly half aboard the *Royal Oak*'s sister ship, HMS *Resolution*. He recalls: 'At first there was talk of the ship being posted to the Mediterranean for two and a half years. That hope disappeared when the order was given to paint her dark grey. I was disappointed. My wife and I were going to save up whilst I was away so we could buy a bungalow when I got back.' On the 13th the *Royal Oak* was in her customary position in the northeast corner of the Flow, from where her anti-aircraft guns could be brought to bear on the skies above the anchorage. The remaining ships of the Home Fleet were concentrated on the other side of the Flow close to the navy's main base at Lyness on the island of Hoy.

Prien had arrived off the eastern entrance to the Flow in the early hours of the 13th and spent the day on the bottom waiting for night and slack water. During the day those crew members who were able to sleep did so. After a meal at five, the torpedoes were checked and scuttling charges were carefully laid – if all else failed, at least *U-47* would not fall into the hands of the enemy. Finally at 19.15 Prien gave the order to surface for the approach.

From the conning tower the view was not what he had expected; the horizon was 'disgustingly bright', lit by the shimmering glow of the Northern Lights. Prien decided to press on regardless. The flood tide swept the U-boat westwards at what its log describes as an 'unbelievable speed'. Once in Kirk Sound Prien aimed for a gap between the rusty hulks blocking the passage to the anchorage. For a few nerve-jangling moments the boat was caught by one of the cables holding the block ships in place; 'Port engine stopped, starboard engine slow ahead and rudder hard to port, the U-boat turns very slowly at first and touches the bottom,' Prien wrote in the log. 'The stern touches the cable, but the boat is free, it's pulled to port and is only brought back on course with difficult rapid manoeuvring.'[15] Just metres away, the lights of a car on the nearby shore skimmed across the surface of the water. 'We're in,' Prien told the crew below. The time was half past midnight on 14 October.

As *U-47* ran silently westwards into the Flow the mood on her conning tower changed from quiet euphoria to bitter disappointment. Had they crept across the Royal Navy's threshold to find no one at home? After casting desperately about for a target, the lookouts managed to pick out of the shadows what they took to be two great battleships, anchored close to the shore. Prien identified these 'fat fellows' as the *Royal Oak* and the *Repulse*. In fact he had stumbled across the *Royal Oak* and the much smaller seaplane carrier *Pegasus*. The U-boat crept forward, and when the distance stood at 3000 metres tubes one to four were flooded. There was a sharp jolt as the torpedoes shot from the bow and ran silently towards the targets. On the conning tower the watch counted; three and a half minutes to impact.

Most of the 1200 men crammed between the decks of the *Royal Oak* were asleep. Joe Instance was on the main deck, just beneath the forecastle.

I was off watch so I had what they called 'all night in', and I was in my hammock when suddenly there was an enormous explosion, right up for'ard somewhere. It shook the ship from end to end. I hopped out of my hammock and went to the next bulkhead and looked at the clock, because the day previously a young seaman in my mess had said, 'Oh, we're for it today, Hookie. It's Friday the 13th.' And that was my first reaction. What's the time? Four minutes past one.

I went back and I said, 'Come on, lads, it's Saturday the 14th. Now get out of your hammocks and we'll find out what's going on.' They just sort of leaned over and said, 'No, don't worry about it', and not one of them got out. I thought, I'm the leading hand in this mess and I think I should try and find out what's going on. I got dressed, trousers and a service jersey, and I thought the best place to go was aft where the officers were – they would know more than we would.

A torpedo had blown a hole in the starboard bow. On the flag deck the men on watch had seen a plume of water rain back on to the forecastle, but below Captain William Benn was told that the likely cause was an internal explosion in the ship's inflammable store. In his judgement, there seemed little cause for immediate concern. Joe Instance recalls: 'One rumour was that one of the refrigerators had blown up. Nobody considered a submarine. In fact I, along with others, thought it was a high-flying bomber that had dropped a bomb somewhere near our bow.'

Most of the crew remained in their hammocks. It was not considered necessary to rouse them; no special precautions were taken.

In the darkness of the Flow *U-47* was preparing to fire another salvo. From the conning tower it had just been possible to register that one of the three torpedoes had reached its target. Prien thought he had hit the ship he had incorrectly identified as the *Repulse* but that the *Royal Oak* had been missed altogether. While the torpedo mechanics worked to reload the bow tubes he swung the U-boat round and fired his stern torpedo at the *Royal Oak*. The time to impact was carefully counted again: another miss. The boat edged into a new firing position, a little closer to the *Royal Oak*; '...at 01.25 three torpedoes from the bow. After just three minutes comes the detonation on the nearer ship. There is a terrible roaring, cracking and rumbling. Then columns of water and fire, fragments fly through the air.' This time all three had found their target.

Just ten minutes had passed since the first explosion had shaken Joe Instance from sleep.

I was aft waiting, trying to find out what was going on. And there was a small heads [toilet], and I thought, well, I'll go in here. And it was while I was inside there that the next three torpedoes hit, within ten seconds of each other. I remember saying to the chap next to me, 'If we go on like this we shall be back in Portsmouth for a refit.' But last torpedo set off the cordite magazine. We were just going out and this hot orange blast came up through the decks, knocked me right back into the toilet. How long it lasted I don't know, but all I could do was hide in a corner, cover my face, try and save my eyes and hope for the best.

The chap standing alongside me, all he had on was a singlet and a pair of pants and when this flame struck he went up like a match. Fortunately I had my woolly trousers on and my service jersey, and it saved my body. I was burnt on the hands, the face, the back of the neck and all my hair had gone – but not my body. I must have fallen unconscious, I think, for about five minutes at least, and when I came to I had no idea that the ship was sinking, but I knew I had to get out.

The explosion in the magazine plunged the ship into darkness. Water flooded in through three great holes torn in the starboard side; almost at once she began to list. Most of the ship's company were trapped in the groaning darkness between the decks. It was the time that Joe Instance had spent on *Royal Oak*'s sister ship, *Resolution*, that saved his life.

Even in the darkness I knew where to crawl. I had to cross to the starboard side of the ship and down the starboard passage to the screen door leading to the quarterdeck, which had just a blackout curtain across it. It wasn't until I got to the door that I suddenly realized I wasn't crawling on the deck, I was crawling on the bulk-head – she was over about 60 degrees. I pulled myself out of the doorway and looked out and the quarterdeck was like a long slide. I went straight up on my backside, slid down and got caught by the guardrails, one under my throat and one under my stomach. There was only one other person I saw. That was the midshipman of the watch, and he was leaning against the guardrails with his telescope still under his arm. I remember him saying to me, 'Do you think we should abandon ship, sir?' I don't know who he thought I was in the dark. Before I could reply everything went from under me and we both floated off.

It was clear to those watching from the conning tower of *U-47* that the old battleship was finished. They had seen the shuddering impact of the torpedoes; she was rolling and soon she would be gone. Fearing that his presence had been detected, Prien gave the order to make way at half speed for Kirk Sound. The tide was running strongly against the boat but Prien was again able to weave his way through the block ships; by 02.15 he had reached the open sea. With characteristic zeal, he wrote in the log; 'A pity that only one [ship] was destroyed.'

The Royal Navy gave no thought to the escaping U-boat; hundreds of men were waiting to be pulled from the water. No lifejackets had been issued, no lifeboats launched. From the water, Joe Instance had watched the *Royal Oak* die: 'She was over and all I could see was the great bulk of her bottom. Great spurts of water were coming up – the noise was terrific. I could hear the 15-inch shells – they weigh about a ton and a half each – I could hear them coming out of their racks in the shell room and going boom, boom, boom, as she was going over. And then she was gone, just like that.' With her went 833 officers and men. It had all happened in just thirteen minutes. Joe Instance was one of the very few to escape from below decks. Now, in the water, it felt as if he was swimming in treacle; thick black oil had haemorrhaged from the *Royal Oak*'s tanks.

In the back of my mind was, I've got to keep my head above water. I remember, funnily enough, my Divisional Officer coming over with a great lump of wood he was hanging on too. He said, 'Who's that?' And I said, 'Leading Seaman Instance and I'm burnt to buggery.' So he said, 'Oh, bad luck, old man.' I must have been floating around for at least half an hour. Then along came this little raft out of nowhere and I heard somebody say, 'Oh, there's one over here', and they tried to get hold of my hands to drag me on and of course my hands had been badly burnt so I screamed out, 'No, no no.' And the officer on the raft said, 'Pull him in by his hair.' Well, I didn't have any hair either – that had gone. And finally they got me under the armpits and they slid me on to this raft like a wet seal. And I went out.

Across the Flow on Hoy, Sandy Robertson was woken by a thumping at the door of his croft; the time was a little after three o'clock. Shivering in the dark was a messenger from the base; Robertson was needed at once. At Lyness he and two of his colleagues were bundled on to a dive tug and taken out into the anchorage. Halfway across the Flow the purpose of the dive became clear; they were to explore the wreck of a ship they had seen at anchor just hours before.

The news of the *Royal Oak*'s fate had caused universal consternation. The first confused reports to arrive at the Admiralty indicated only that she had been sunk by a series of explosions. The loss of the ship and most of its crew was bad enough; that a U-boat had penetrated the defences of the Flow was unthinkable. Senior figures in Naval Intelligence at first ruled this out.[16] Yet amongst the survivors was the ship's commanding officer; Captain Benn was quite sure his ship had been torpedoed. It was decided that divers should be sent down to put the matter beyond doubt.

By the light of day Robertson could clearly see the giant hull of the *Royal Oak* lying in less than 100 feet of water; the boat boom that had been attached to her side was sticking out above the surface. The first attempt to dive was hurriedly aborted when a nearby destroyer began a depth charge attack on what she believed to be a submerged U-boat. It was the first of many false contacts. Prien was long gone, but it was a week before the search for him was called off. When the divers did finally reach the ship, Robertson recalls, that they were confronted by a shocking sight: 'God, there were bodies everywhere – there were about a hundred just lying on the bottom. They told me to bang on the bottom of the ship and see if anyone rapped back. What was the point? She was in seventeen fathoms, and no one could have survived at that depth. Everything was shiny bright. The guns and decks were all right, but there were three big holes in her low down near the rolling chalk, the fin.'

Robertson found what he was looking for directly beneath the dive tug. 'The navy had been so confident that nothing could possibly get through the defences. There was no more argument when we got the propeller of the torpedo up. They shut up then.'[17]

The shattering news was broken to the public on the same day.

It seemed impossible – a British battleship had been sunk in the navy's most important anchorage. Winston Churchill, the new First Lord of the Admiralty, reassured his colleagues in the War Cabinet that, although a 'regrettable disaster', the sinking of the *Royal Oak* would not affect the overall naval situation. Privately Churchill felt the loss very keenly; the thought of the men trapped in the 'black depths' of the ship had brought tears to his eyes.[18] A board of inquiry began work on apportioning blame; but for now it was clear that, until improvements were made to the anti-submarine defences at the Flow, the Home Fleet would have to seek refuge elsewhere.

Leading Seaman Joe Instance was the only survivor from his mess. The days following his rescue passed in a blur of pain. His head and hands had been badly burnt; it took three weeks to remove the oil from his wounds. 'We were all bandaged up – just a couple of holes for your eyes and a hole for your mouth. I turned round to the chap next to me and said, "Do I look like you?" He said, "Yes." I thought, oh crikey. I was on the danger list for about a fortnight and they decided to send for my wife. She came into the hospital and just walked past me, she didn't know me. I had to shout and say, "I'm Joe."'

Yet within a year Instance was back in the Atlantic, this time on board a destroyer. 'On that ship and all the ships I had after the *Royal Oak*, during the night watches I used to walk around with my eyes shut until I got to know the inside of the ship, so that if the same thing happened again and there was complete and utter darkness I would know exactly where to go.'

The first news of Prien's success to reach Germany came via the BBC; the details were sketchy, but it was clear to Dönitz and his staff that *U-47* had crept into Scapa Flow, sunk a battleship, and successfully crept out again. Their faith in operation and commander had been completely vindicated. Dönitz had struck a humiliating blow to the prestige of the Royal Navy; he had also made an impact on the leaders of the Reich. Hitler was ecstatic. Propaganda Minister Joseph Goebbels was instructed to launch a public campaign extolling the Nazi virtues of the U-boat – the daring 'lone wolf'.

By the time *U-47* entered Wilhelmshaven its remarkable exploit was known throughout the Germany. As the U-boat swept past the *Scharnhorst* the sailors cheering from the battlecruiser's deck would have noticed the rough outline of a charging bull painted in white on its conning tower. The image had suggested itself to the U-boat's First Officer as he had watched his commander directing the attack on the *Royal Oak*; it had been added later to mark the kill.

Prien had been ordered to delay his return just long enough to ensure that the Commander in Chief of the German navy could be there to greet him. Raeder decorated him with the Iron Cross (First Class), but this seemed insufficient. The Führer himself was anxious to thank the Reich's new hero. The entire crew of *U-47* was flown to Berlin on his personal plane, then driven in stately convoy through streets lined with cheering crowds; it was all captured on film for those beyond the capital. At the Reichs Chancellery Hitler presented Prien with a new, more prestigious decoration – the Ritterkreuz or Knight's Cross of the Iron Cross. Worn prominently at the throat, it instantly marked the holder out as a true German hero. All U-boat commanders would covet the Knight's Cross; Prien – 'the bull of Scapa' – was the first of their number to earn it.

It was 'a unique triumph', the Führer told his audience, a deed of great daring achieved in the very place where a weak Germany had surrendered its entire fleet in 1918.[19] Only the month before Hitler had demonstrated open scepticism about the value of the U-boat arm; now it seemed the very image of military ingenuity, courage and skill. This was just the image Dönitz had sought to project.

Hanns-Ferdinand Maßmann, who at the time was training new crews, remembers the impact that Prien's exploit had on the popular support for the service: 'My cousin was with Prien as his second officer. I met him later in a hotel, totally by chance. He had a suitcase full of presents that had come for Prien's crew from industry and the public.

He was responsible for distributing them. This [exploit] had an effect everywhere in Germany – there was an overwhelming expression of popular support.'

The German navy's war diary recorded the sinking as a 'glorious success' that had 'awakened affection' for the men of the U-boat arm. Under the leadership of Dönitz it had demonstrated 'outstanding operational efficiency'.[20] The ghosts of the German navy's failure in World War I, so closely associated with Scapa Flow, had at last been banished.

Almost at once Hitler authorized an easing of restrictions on U-boat operations; all enemy ships, including liners travelling in convoy, would now be torpedoed on sight. The idea planted in the Reichs Chancellery that victory at sea might indeed be possible – that the Royal Navy could be defeated – began to take root in the country as a whole. If a single U-boat could sink a British battleship in the safety of its anchorage, what might a large fleet of boats achieve in the wide Atlantic?

CHAPTER TWO

PINGERS

IT WAS FAMOUSLY OBSERVED by Admiral Sir Andrew Cunningham during World War II that, whilst it took three years to build a ship, it took three hundred to build a tradition. The first losses at sea, especially that of the *Royal Oak*, delivered a serious jolt to a public still coming to terms with the prospect of a second world war in twenty years. Nevertheless, belief in a final victory remained unshaken. The country looked above all to its steadfast shield: the Royal Navy. Ships would be lost, but for three hundred years the navy had 'fought and conquered again and again'. 'One thought it was going to be bloody,' John Adams recalls, 'but one had the feeling that we'd been pretty good on the sea for many, many years, and somehow we'd get through.' On 3 September 1939 the destroyer HMS *Walker* was carrying out a routine patrol in St George's Channel off the southwest of England; twenty-year-old Sub-Lieutenant Adams was of her company: 'I can remember the signal coming in just after eleven o'clock on the 3rd, "Commence hostilities at once with Germany." There was a feeling of relief all round, because the fleet had mobilized the year before, we'd mobilized that year, and the public in general had kept on worrying about what Hitler was up to next.'

Relief was followed by stomach-tightening uncertainty: what now? The *Walker* had been called out of retirement only a fortnight before. A scratch crew had been hastily assembled; Adams had been educated for the sea, first in the training cruiser HMS *Frobisher* and then as a midshipman aboard the *Royal Oak*, but most of the ship's company were reservists – fishermen, bank clerks, shop-keepers.

Within half an hour of the declaration of war *Walker*'s patrolling companion, HMS *Walpole*, carried out her first depth-charge attack.

'An imaginary submarine,' Adams wrote in his diary. 'The splashes made a good sight anyway!' The same air of tense expectation was evident the following morning. The *Walker* was escorting the merchant ship *Corinthic* up St George's Channel; 'We thought we saw something in the water,' Adams confided to his diary. 'We turned to attack and gave the order "stand by" to the depth charges aft. One reserve rating in his excitement took the pin out of the hand release gear and fired a depth charge.'

The terrified crew of the *Corinthic* took the explosion to be a torpedo attack on their ship. Adams remembers watching in amazement: 'The *Corinthic* stopped engines, blew off steam, lowered the lifeboats and all the crew jumped in, and it took us a couple of hours to persuade them to climb back and hoist their boats up and get going.' Evidently not everyone had confidence in His Majesty's maritime shield. The master of the *Corinthic* had hoisted the Red Ensign – the flag of the British merchant marine – upside down, a recognized distress signal. Adams recalls: 'It was noticeable that on the lifebelts of this ship they had painted, "This is the wreck of SS *Corinthic*", a very pessimistic message, which we didn't think really quite the right thing to do.'

The *Walker* carried out two further depth charge attacks that day but managed to bag only a huge Basking shark. The following day there were two more; Adams sceptically logged in his diary that several members of the crew swore that they heard a submarine scraping along the hull and the whine of its engines. An imaginary sub-surface fleet accounted for countless depth charges in the first days of the war. This was perhaps to be expected; it was impossible to forget the terrible cost in lives and ships exacted by the U-boat only twenty years before.

The object of British maritime strategy was to deny Germany vital imports of food and raw materials, whilst securing its own. During World War I the former had proved much easier to accomplish than the latter. For most of the war, the Royal Navy had imposed a punishing economic blockade which had played no small part in the final victory. Yet British ships had been less successful in securing the country's own sea communications. The Admiralty had been unconscionably slow to recognize the threat posed by the U-boat and make the preparations necessary for war against it. By the spring of 1917 Britain appeared to be on the brink of defeat; the Secretary of State for War was obliged to admit to the country's soldiers that its sailors had 'lost command of the sea'. It was an unthinkable admission for the government of the world's greatest maritime power to make. In April 1917 a quarter of the ships that left the country's ports never returned. Almost 900,000 tons of Allied and neutral shipping was sunk in a month, and by September the U-boat had claimed 8 million tons in three years of war.[1]

Only the belated introduction of the convoy system put an end to these disastrous losses. It is hard to understand why it took so long to introduce, since the principles were the same as they had been in Nelson's day: merchant ships were required to sail in fleets with a close naval escort for protection. By concentrating ships in a convoy it was possible to reduce the number of targets; fifty ships scattered across the open sea presented the U-boat with fifty possibilities. In convoy these ships could be defended and there was just as much chance of a U-boat missing fifty in close order, as one ship in the middle of the Atlantic. At least that bitter lesson had been learnt; twenty years later, no one doubted the importance of the convoy system.

Amongst the flood of signals sent to HMS *Walker* on the first day of this new war was one from the Admiralty baldly stating: 'Winston is back.' At six o'clock on the evening of 3 September Churchill had stepped across the threshold of the Admiralty's handsome Georgian brick home in Whitehall to resume the post of First Lord which he had occupied during the turbulent early months of the last world war. Little had changed: his chair, chart case, even his charts were still as he had left them twenty-five years before. The task was also the same; as Churchill later flamboyantly put it, 'once again we must fight for life and honour against all the might and fury of the valiant, disciplined, and ruthless German race'.[2] It was clear, the new First Lord told his officials the following morning, that Germany's 'prime attack' would again be in the

Western Approaches to Britain.[3] This had long been the view of Naval Intelligence, which as early as 1935 had warned that: 'if Germany used all her surface ships to attack shipping, she might, along with air attacks on London and shipping there and ruthless submarine operations... hope to defeat us mainly by economic pressure. She will remember the narrow margin between failure and success she was able to reach in the last war.'[4]

The country's great strategic strength was, as in times past, its geographical isolation, as an island, from the rest of Europe. Nevertheless Britain's dependence on the sea made it acutely vulnerable once again to just such a campaign. Before the war Britain imported some 59 million tons of food and raw materials a year and every drop of oil, most of which came from the west across the North Atlantic.[5] This vital lifeline was maintained by the largest merchant fleet in the world: some three thousand ships totalling 17.5 million tons.[6] The country could also count on the resources of its Empire allies, although this worldwide interest had to be defended too.

In 1939 the Royal Navy was but a shadow of the force that had emerged victorious from the last world war. Its hardest battles in the inter-war years had been fought against successive governments determined to reduce spending on defence; most of these had been lost. Of the navy's twelve battleships, ten had been built during World War I; likewise two of its three battle cruisers. Only one of its six aircraft carriers was purpose-built; the other five were conversions from the 1920s.[7] There was also an acute shortage of the smaller ships that would be needed for convoy escort duty.

In spite of this, government and country were optimistic. The threat to Britain's maritime supremacy appeared altogether less formidable than it had twenty-five years before. This time confidence in ultimate victory at sea rested on twin pillars: the convoy system and underwater detection. The convoy system had taken three years to implement in the last war, just three days for the new First Lord to introduce into this one. The chief problem was the shortage of escorts. At first ships were only offered protection close to the British Isles. Outbound convoys from Liverpool or London were escorted to between 12 and 15 degrees west, then they were on their own.[8] The escorts waited at this point for a homebound convoy to shepherd into the Western Approaches. Making this vital rendezvous often proved difficult. Whilst the seamanship was good, the conditions were often appalling and there was no radar to fall back on; convoy and escorts wrestled with the same navigational problems Nelson had faced 150 years before. John Adams recalls: 'It depended upon DR, dead reckoning. If the convoy hadn't had a good sun sight crossing the Atlantic because of the foul weather, they could be 50 miles out of place. There was no other method than sun sights and star sights in those days. I can remember looking for a convoy for four days once.'

Only ships with between 9 and 15 knots were to sail in ocean convoy; the rest were left to fend for themselves. That at least was the hope, but convoys travelled at the speed of their slowest ships which was often much less than 9 knots. Even in close formation a convoy of forty to fifty ships could cover 20 square-miles of sea. Station keeping was essential and required a lot of organization. John Adams remembers:

We had a convoy conference ashore before we sailed, where ships were given their station in a box. You had a commodore of the convoy, who was a retired senior naval officer. You would steam out in succession from Liverpool and beyond the Bar Light Vessel there was open water where you formed up in your rectangle, slowly and then gradually getting underway, starting at 6 knots and then perhaps working up to 9 knots, depending on what sort of speed you had. The commodore then decided whether there was going to be any zigzagging or not. We, in the escort, went round at speed, looking at all the ships, checking them by name, checking they'd got their right positions in the convoy and so on.

Maintaining convoy discipline was especially difficult in the first months of the war when independently minded merchant captains, used to an empty horizon, were obliged to adjust to days spent in a nautical box. Some rejected the protection of the convoy, although most recognized it as the best chance of survival. It may not have seemed like that in the beginning; sailing in a phalanx of darkened ships as it zigzagged through an Atlantic night appeared to pose more of a threat than the U-boat.

This was certainly the case with a small convoy that the *Walker* was ordered to escort. It left Liverpool on 9 September with just the *Walker* and *Vanquisher* in support; 'How can two destroyers provide an adequate escort?' Sub-Lieutenant Adams asked in his diary. There were the usual false alarms, but the convoy's chief problem was with station keeping. On the 11th Adams noted: 'Column 1 and *Vanquisher* rushed off during the night owing to bad station keeping and had to return at dawn.' His diary entry for that day continues: 'I went to bed at 21.00 to get some sleep for the Middle Watch and was flung out of my bunk at 22.00 with a terrific lurch and thud. "Christ!", I thought. "Now I know what it's like to be hit by a torpedo." Luckily I was sleeping in my trousers and shirt with shoes on and got up on deck in about five seconds. Then I saw we had collided with *Vanquisher*.'

The captain of *Walker* had called *Vanquisher* over from the far side of the convoy and ordered her to form astern for the journey back to Liverpool. On *Walker*'s bridge the officer on watch could just make out a wishbone of white water travelling through the darkness, which he took to be *Vanquisher*'s stern wave. It was the bow wave; *Vanquisher* was crossing the front of the convoy. Too late the mistake was discovered: 'We went right through her, killing fourteen men,' Adams remembers. 'We were jammed in her for about eight hours.' There were appalling scenes; because of the lack of emergency medical staff and equipment the First Lieutenant of *Walker* was obliged to shoot some of the injured caught in the wreckage. 'There had been one signalman down in the wreckage, and he'd been holding on to a chum of his, but both his friend's legs were torn off as the ships came apart.' Mercifully the weather was good and both ships were saved, but it had been a grisly, shocking experience for *Walker*'s crew.

Despite the difficulties, the convoy system worked; the Admiralty's first defensive pillar was proven. Its second, the new science of under-water detection, was not. Since the end of World War I British scientists had been working on the development of ASDIC, or sonar as it was later called, for the detection of submarines beneath the waves.[9] Pulses of sound were sent out from a dome beneath a ship, and if they struck an obstacle they were reflected back. This ASDIC echo gave the bearing and range of a possible target. It was a revolutionary step forward, yet the claims made for it were extravagant. Once the submarine's 'cloak of invisibility' had been removed, one government committee suggested, attacks on merchant convoys would prove 'unprofitable'. The Admiralty boasted that 'the submarine should never again be able to present us with the problem we faced in 1917'. It was just a matter of detecting, attack-ing and sinking; if a depth charge salvo did not finish the submarine off, it would at least be in no position to threaten shipping.

It has been argued that these very public claims for ASDIC were part of a clever intelligence bluff; an attempt to convince Germany that money spent on building a submarine fleet would be money wasted. If so, it was to a degree successful; despite Dönitz's assurances to the contrary, the German naval staff clearly believed that ASDIC would seriously impair the fighting capability of its U-boats. Yet this campaign was a two-edged sword, for even the doughtiest critics of British naval policy were convinced. One such had been Churchill himself; he had spent the years before the war on the backbenches in parliament – the political 'wilderness' – but in June 1938 he had been invited to the new anti-submarine school at Portland on the south coast to see ASDIC in operation for himself. The new ASDIC specialist on the training ship HMS *Walpole*, Maurice Usherwood, remembers:

Churchill and the First Sea Lord were both on the bridge. I was explaining to them the various control instruments. Any success with the ASDIC depended not only on the skill and experience of the ASDIC operators, but also on a number of other factors, including such things as the temperature gradients of the sea. But on this occasion the weather was fine, the sea was calm, so it wasn't very long before we got an echo contact which the ASDIC operators and I were immediately able to classify as a submarine.

We held contact without any difficulty and carried out one or two simulated depth charge attacks. Now, in order to convince our guests that the submarine really was where we said it was, we made it indicate its position by releasing a smoke candle. I told Churchill and the First Sea Lord in which direction to look for the smoke candle, and glancing at the range recorder I told them how far away it would be. Every time, the candle popped up absolutely spot on. They were visibly impressed.

The captain of *Walpole* and I tried to explain that truly our ASDIC operators had done a splendid job, but operating conditions were by no means always as good as on this occasion. You could get echoes from all sorts of sources other than submarines – a shoal of fish, a wreck on the seabed – and one had to try and distinguish which was which. Judging by some of Churchill's subsequent utterances, it has always seemed to me that he remembered best what he'd seen with his own eyes, namely the smoke candle coming up exactly where we said it would.

Churchill wrote to the First Sea Lord, Admiral Sir Ernle Chatfield, 'I never imagined that I should hear one of those creatures asking to be destroyed'; the new submarine detector had 'relieved us of our great danger'. This view was clearly shared by Chatfield: 'our anti submarine methods[10] are now so efficient not of course 100% efficiency, but I do not think that 80% is too high an efficiency…that the number of destroyers and such vessels that we shall require in a future war…against submarine attack is greatly reduced.'[11]

Yet for all this confidence, not enough ships were equipped with the new device and too few operators were trained to use it well. The Admiralty also had great difficulty persuading young officers to take an interest in Anti-Submarine Warfare (ASW). One bright young who had was Maurice Usherwood, the officer instructed to guide Churchill in its mysteries. After his initial training the twenty-seven-year-old had elected to join the staff at Portland: 'It was only small ships, destroyers and the like, which were fitted with the ASDIC, and I liked the idea of being in small ships – you're a more compact company, it's congenial. The anti-submarine branch was a new branch in the navy, and I thought, "Well, that might have openings for me."

When Usherwood joined the ASW school in 1937 it was little more than a collection of wooden huts; the staff was small and the facilities limited. 'It was seen as a bit of a Cinderella service. It was really built up around the ASDIC and in the longer-established branches, like the signals branch, the gunnery branch, the torpedo branch, and so on, I think people were a bit inclined to look down on it at first.' Those who worked with the new detection device were known rather derisively as 'pingers', after the pinging echo made by the ASDIC as it sent out its pulse. Gunnery and navigation were popular and an established path to promotion; anti-submarine warfare was not. It was quite clear to young officers that the Admiralty expected Germany's small surface fleet to pose the chief threat to Allied shipping. It was not that 1917 had been entirely forgotten; but confidence could now be placed in the navy's 'underwater eye'.

It was also well known that the Kriegsmarine's first priority was the construction of bigger and better battleships and cruisers. A great deal of time was spent training for an attack on an imaginary fleet. Destroyers were to act as outriders, deploying their torpedoes against the enemy before a Jutland-style engagement between the big ships and big guns. The navy's own official historian later revealed that in the twenty years of peace between the wars there was not one exercise in the protection of a slow-moving convoy of merchant ships from submarine or air attack;[12] yet this became one of the navy's chief tasks within weeks of the outbreak of war. Many of His Majesty's ships were, not surprisingly, ill prepared. The guns on the veteran destroyer HMS *Walker* could be elevated to just 30 degrees, which rendered them almost useless when the ship was later attacked from the air. No one on board had any real experience of convoy protection work. 'I don't think I ever saw a depth charge fired until after the beginning of the war, not live ones,' John Adams recalls. 'As a sub-lieutenant in a destroyer, I practised operating the ASDIC but I had not done any anti-submarine courses.'

The story was much the same on some of the new fleet destroyers. At the outbreak of war Maurice Usherwood was serving as the anti-sub-marine specialist with a flotilla of destroyers in the Mediterranean. He saw his first action with one of its ships, HMS *Garland*, on day 13 of the war:

I was on the bridge and we got an ASDIC contact. I wasn't at all happy about that contact, but the captain decided he was going to drop depth charges. Now, there was a lever on the bridge that was held in the 'safe' position by a pin. If you removed the pin and pulled the lever towards you, a buzzer sounded aft in the ship and the depth charges were released. The captain having made his decision known, the man on the lever took the pin out and inadvertently moved it enough to sound the buzzer at the stern of the ship. The depth charge crew, hearing the buzzer, released the charges. They hadn't realized that the ship was only going at a very slow speed. You wanted the ship to be well clear by the time any explosions took place. The depth charges went in the water, exploded, and created havoc with the aft end of the ship. Fortunately there were no casualties, but it was a most unfortunate event. I remember leaving the bridge and going down to see what sort of state my cabin was in – it was a pretty awful shambles. Everything was covered in oil.

This sort of costly mistake would have been unthinkable for an experienced crew. The *Garland* spent the first months of the war in dry dock, at a time when the navy was acutely short of ships capable of carrying out escort duties.

To meet this shortage, plans were drawn up at Churchill's instigation for a special 'anti-submarine and anti-air vessel' capable of being mass-produced quickly. 'They will be deemed', Churchill wrote, '"Cheap and Nasties" (cheap to us, nasty to the U-boat).' The 'off the shelf' design chosen for the new escorts was that of the whalers built in Middlesbrough for the Norwegians. Displacing only 925 tons and just 205 feet long, the first ships were named rather incongruously after flowers; and yet these 'corvettes' would become the workhorse of the convoy escort force. It would be another year before corvettes would be available to the navy in significant numbers; in the meantime trawlers and whalers were fitted with an ASDIC set and depth charges, and pressed into service as escorts.

Officers and men were needed for His Majesty's fishing fleet; for some, it meant rapid promotion to the command of their own ships. One such was Ian Jamieson: 'I'd hoped to go to a destroyer as a sub-lieutenant, but I was told to report to the naval officer in charge in West Hartlepool. The Norwegians had ordered six whale-catchers but we had commandeered them and they were being converted into anti-submarine whalers. For instance, a 4-inch naval gun supplanted the harpoon gun on the front end of the ship. They were oil-fired, which most of the trawlers weren't, they did 16 knots and had quite a large re-fuelling range.' The nineteen-year-old Jamieson was a 'straight stripe', a regular who had joined the navy at the age of thirteen. He had just returned from the Mediterranean, where he had been serving as a midshipman on the battleship HMS *Warspite*. This new commission was not an entirely welcome one; 'Anti-submarine Warfare was nearly bottom of the list of things I wanted to do,' he recalls.

It was not just junior 'straight stripes' who found themselves in command of anti-submarine ships; 'wavy navy' reservists (so called because of the looping gold ring on their sleeves) in particular were called up for this duty. There were two types of reservists: the gentleman sailors of the RNVR, the Royal Naval Volunteer Reserve, dubbed by some unkind regulars as 'Really Not Very Reliable', and the merchant service veterans of the RNR or Royal Naval Reserve, who some were foolish enough to suggest were 'Really Not Required'. Both sorts were very much required, although some of those who did possess the necessary experience faced a battle to be taken seriously as volunteers. Reserve officer Colin Warwick had served for a time in the merchant service and held a commission in the RNR. In 1939 the twenty-seven-year-old Warwick wrote to the Admiralty with details of his experience. He remembers:

I got a reply back that said they would put my name on the Merchant Navy reserve list. The next thing I saw was my brother-in-law, who was a student at Edinburgh University, in naval uniform. So I said, 'You don't know one end of a ship from another. What are you doing?'

'Well,' he said, 'they gave out commissions to the students at the universities and I took one.'

So I wrote again to the Admiralty, and said I thought that my services were bloody badly needed right now, having seen my brother-in-law.

This time he found himself in a smoke-filled waiting room in London with a dozen other volunteers, all dressed in the blue Burberry raincoat of the merchant service.

You know, you could smell 'em. They were old sailors, all about my age too. I went in to see the admiral and he said, 'Sorry about your brother-in-law. How did he get in?'

I told him.

'Oh,' he said, 'that's right, we gave a lot of commissions to universities and now we're getting comments from commanding officers of destroyers about "What is this horsemeat that you're sending us as watch-keeping officers?" At the same time,' he said, 'there are a lot of fellas like you writing, well, rather rude letters to us. We didn't realize how many people there were who'd been to sea and then gone ashore...Well,' he said, 'right now we need people who can take ships to sea and fight them. If I were you, I'd go for an anti-submarine ship.'

So I said, 'All right, but I'd like to have my commission back – RNR.'

He said, 'Yes, we can give you a commission – Sub-Lieutenant RNR.'

So that was that. I was in the navy.

A few days later Warwick reported to the anti-submarine school at Portland, where he was welcomed by a convivial commander. 'I said I understood the course was going to last one or two months. He said, "We got the last lot through here in fourteen days. We're going to get you through in seven days, because we're going to work over the weekend."'

Within days of leaving Portland Warwick was commanding *St Loman*, one of the four trawlers of the 15th Anti-Submarine Group; her task was to hunt and destroy U-boats off the north coast of Scotland. 'She was a coal burner,' Warwick recalls. 'She carried about 250 tons of coal in bunkers and could spend about a month at sea with no problem at all.' The seamen's mess and sleeping quarters was in the old fish hold, whilst the 'skipper' was more comfortably accommodated in his own large cabin beneath the wheelhouse.

The first task of the new commanding officer was to win over his hard-bitten crew of deep-sea trawler men; this sometimes required less conventional methods than those usually employed on His Majesty's ships. Warwick remembers:

The commander of our group, Captain Turner – we called him 'Flash Alf' – told me that he had been sent to a ship that had a merchant crew on it. The mate had said to him, 'You're going to find things a little different to where you've been, sir, on the destroyer.'

He said, 'Why is that?'

'Well,' the mate said, 'there's only one thing we understand,' and he lifted up his fist.

Flash Alf went on an inspection of the ship. Whilst he was down in the engine room he asked one of the crew what he was. The man said, 'I'm a fucking greaser.'

Flash Alf said, 'I'll give you a tip. When you reply to your captain, say "sir".'

'Oh,' the man said, 'there's none of that bloody silly nonsense about me.'

So Flash Alf thought about what the mate had said, and he knocked the man down on the engine room bedplates and carried on with his inspection.

'After that,' Flash Alf said, 'there were some new fellows joining the ship. I could hear them outside my cabin. Someone asked the quartermaster, "What's the old man like?" "Oh," he said, "he's all right. He'll knock you down soon as look at you."'

So he said, 'I had found out something about handling men in the Merchant Navy.'

The captain of His Majesty's whaler *Windermere*, Ian Jamieson, approached the task of commanding his first ship in a very different way: 'There was me, a nineteen-year-old sub-lieutenant, the captain. We had a crew of between twenty-five and thirty men. My First Lieutenant and second-in-command had been in the Mercantile Marine, but he had retired twelve years ago and become the manager of a hotel in Margate. All the sailors were people from trawlers, not from the navy proper. We ran the ship as a sort of committee, and it seemed to go all right.' Like the *St Loman*, the *Windermere* joined an anti-submarine group operating off the north coast of Scotland.

From the first Churchill's instincts had been for robust action; 'the search for a naval offensive', he wrote to Admiralty officials, 'must be incessant'.[13] In this spirit he urged the formation of 'units of search' to 'catch and kill' enemy warships and U-boats. These hunting groups would rely on the new science of 'underwater detection' to harry the U-boat 'in the depths'. They were to include not just destroyers and specialist anti-submarine vessels but large 'capital' ships such as aircraft carriers. The reckless use of these ships on anti-submarine duties ended almost as soon as it had begun, when on 17 September *U-29* sank the carrier *Courageous* with the loss of 518 lives. Yet this event did nothing to dampen Churchill's enthusiasm for hunter-killer groups: 'The British attack upon the U-boats', he told the House of Commons, 'is being waged with the utmost vigour and intensity.' 'A tenth of the enemy submarine fleet', seven U-boats, were sunk in the first fortnight of the war, Churchill claimed, the country's trust could rest in the 'science and seamanship' of the navy's 'hunting force'.[14] The reality was less impressive; the fleet of small ships patrolling Britain's shores sank just two U-boats in September.

The futility of these tactics was obvious to many of those whose duty it was to carry them out. It was in luck rather than 'science and seamanship' that most placed their trust. The destroyer *Walker* was sent on more than one wild goose chase in those first months; John Adams remembers hours spent on ASDIC sweeps of empty sea:

I think the staff ashore were very fidgety. Where I drew the line was one particular report from the lighthouse on the south corner of the Isle of Man that a periscope had been sighted 6 miles away. Well, you're jolly lucky to see a periscope at 1000 yards, let alone 6 miles, and yet we were sent out from Liverpool to go and chase that particular contact which was obviously hopeless before we started. At 25 knots you'd be there in two hours, and if the U-boat kept submerged its radius of action at 7 knots underwater would only have been about a 10-mile circle, but that's an awful lot of sea to search as one ship and an ASDIC set that only on the whole goes out to 2000 yards.

The new anti-submarine groups fared little better, as *Windermere*'s commanding officer, Ian Jamieson recalls: 'The German U-boats were going in and out of the Atlantic between the Shetlands and the Orkneys, and our job was to try and sink them as they were going through. I don't think we ever really got very close to doing so.'

Just as it had in World War I, the navy found it difficult to accept that it was the timely delivery of ships and cargoes that was of primary importance.

Yet whilst September was a bad month with 41 ships (some 153,879 tons) sunk by U-boats, the next three months saw a sharp decline in losses. By the end of the year the principal menace to shipping was not the U-boat but the magnetic mine, of which hundreds had been sown round the British coast. It appeared that the Admiralty's trust in the twin pillars of convoy and ASDIC had not been misplaced. Of the 114 ships sunk in 1939 only 12 were lost within the umbrella of a convoy.[15] There had been many wildly optimistic reports of U-boats sunk or damaged, but nine at least were correct. In a typically colourful radio broadcast on 20 January 1940 Churchill spoke of his firm conviction that the U-boat was well on the way to being conquered. The convoy system was 'keeping the seas open', the 'faithful ASDIC detector' 'smelt' the U-boats out in the depths and with its help their strength would be broken.[16]

Just five days before the First Lord's broadcast, *U-23* had wheezed its way towards its berth at Wilhelmshaven. Those waiting on the quay could see two pennants fluttering from her periscope, indicating two ships sunk. This was an unremarkable tally; what was significant was the way it had been achieved.

It had been *U-23*'s third war patrol under the command of Otto Kretschmer. It was a 'duck', a Type II boat of 250 tons, just a third the size of an 'Atlantic' boat. Hunting was restricted to the North Sea where targets were harder to find than in the crowded waters of the Western Approaches. The twenty-seven-year-old Kretschmer had impressed U-boat staff before the war with his cool professionalism, yet the boat's first patrols were disappointing. As *U-23*'s First Officer, Hans-Jochen von Knebel Doeberitz, recalls, the third patrol also began badly:

> There was intelligence that, after Prien's successful sinking of the *Royal Oak*, the British fleet was no longer in Scapa Flow but had gone somewhat further north. Our task was to search the sea lochs to the north of Scapa Flow. *U-23* was a small boat so we had just four torpedoes, two of which were actually inside the boat. We found and shot at a steamer off the Orkneys, but the first torpedo exploded before it hit its target. We were going to have to shoot a second torpedo to blow this steamer out of the water and that's what we did, but this torpedo went under the steamer and exploded on the other side. That was the second torpedo gone. In the end we were obliged to use a third to sink her.

It was von Knebel's first experience of a problem much talked about in the U-boat messes. The complaints had been growing since day one of the war; 'torpedo failures have had serious effect on the morale of commanding officers and crews', Dönitz logged in his War Diary. It was the U-boat's main weapon but in Dönitz's estimation it was proving to be almost 'useless'.[17] Efforts were underway to correct the defects, but that was scant consolation to commanders and crews obliged to risk all on a faulty weapon. Such was the situation *U-23* now found itself in. It had taken three torpedoes to finish off the steamer *Fredville*. That left just the one, yet the boat was under orders to search the sea lochs around the Orkney Islands. Von Knebel remembers:

> On a small boat there were only two watch officers. We gave each other a questioning look. 'Is the old man going to go on with only one torpedo?'

'What course?' we asked him.

'Yes, yes, course 320,' he said, and, well, that was Otto Kretschmer, you know, going in with only one torpedo left.

The outbreak of war had found von Knebel reluctantly serving on the staff. 'A staff post was contemptible,' he recalls. For months he had fought for a combat posting. His luck had changed with his appointment to a new desk job, this time as adjutant to the Flag Officer Commanding U-boats (BdU), Karl Dönitz. Von Knebel remembers:

Dönitz approached me and said, 'So you want to come to work for me?'

I said, 'There's no question of my wanting to, Admiral.'

'Why is that, then?'

'Well, first of all I have no experience. I really have to learn to sail a U-boat. We might have had our training, but...'

Dönitz turned to Admiral von Friedeburg and asked, 'When does the other fellow, his predecessor, have to be relieved?'

'Well, in three months at the latest,' von Friedeburg said.

'Right, then. Get Knebel on to a submarine.'

And so I was given permission to sail on a U-boat.

The boat was Kretschmer's *U-23*. On the evening of 11 January 'the old man' set a course for Inganess Bay on the east side of the Orkney Isles, close to their principal town, Kirkwall.

The entrance to the bay was guarded by two ASW trawlers, equipped with ASDIC and depth charges. It was a clear, but moonless night; Kretschmer was able to edge the U-boat past the picket into the bay. A large tanker, the 10,500-ton Danish-registered *Danmark*, was anchored in the southwest corner, making very little effort to disguise her presence. Von Knebel recalls:

We could see the people on the bridge with their cigarettes.

We shot at it, and yes, it worked – that torpedo did explode at the right time. We were very proud and happy. The English didn't believe we could be so close by in the anchorage, and when the torpedo exploded they searched the sky with lights because they thought we were the Luftwaffe. They were even firing into the air. Of course for me, on this first voyage, it was quite an experience. Then we turned back and again we sailed very close to the lookouts but got out of there in one piece.

The shattered remains of the *Royal Oak* lay just 4 miles away from the tanker. Under the cloak of darkness *U-23* had approached, attacked and escaped on the surface. By dawn on the 12th she had gone. The ASW trawlers guarding the entrance to the bay had carried out repeated ASDIC sweeps but detected nothing.

The sinking of the *Danmark* marked a new phase in the war at sea. She had flown the flag of a neutral country. By January 1940, von Knebel recalls, the Prize Regulations that governed the conduct of the war at sea were being 'deliberately ignored'. To disguise this new position U-boats were instructed to choose targets with care. It was hoped that this would confuse the enemy, and perhaps create the illusion of a series of lucky strikes by mines.[18]

As Churchill was broadcasting his warm words of assurance, predicting an end to the U-boat threat, his officials were studying a series of baffling reports on losses off the northeast coast of Scotland. By the end of the month more than a dozen unescorted neutrals had been lost in the winter darkness. The Admiralty assumed mines to have been chiefly responsible, and many fruitless hours were spent sweeping the sea.[19] Amongst the ships registered as lost to mines was Kretschmer's first victim, the *Fredville*; his second, the *Danmark*, was thought initially to have been sunk by an internal explosion. The Admiralty only grasped the grim truth when U-boats were sighted on the surface by aircraft.[20]

In March the Admiralty's ASW Division reported that in the first six months of war the number of ships sunk by U-boats at night had risen from 3 to 58 per cent of total losses. His Majesty's ships, it concluded, could now expect the enemy on the surface at night. This should have come as no surprise to the Admiralty, for U-boats had used the same tactic during World War I. What in particular had been forgotten was how closely the U-boat was tied to the surface. This was where it was most effective, and where it spent more than 90 per cent of its time.

The main attack boat favoured by Dönitz, the Type VII, differed little from its World War I counterpart. It was powered by two large diesel engines capable of 17 knots. Air for the engines was channelled through an intake pipe within the conning tower to ensure the maximum possible distance from the sea's surface. Once the order was given to dive, these engines were shut down immediately and power was drawn from the boat's batteries. Beneath the waves the U-boat was capable of little more than 7 knots, and this for only an hour. At 2 knots it could only remain submerged for a maximum of 36 hours. It was then obliged to surface to recharge its batteries and replenish the air supply. On the surface a U-boat usually had the necessary speed to overhaul an enemy convoy; beneath it that was all but impossible. Here, too, it was almost blind.

In the spring of 1940 Jürgen Oesten was the commander of *U-61*; he remembers: 'All the boats we had during the war were actually surface craft with just the capability to dive. Attacks normally took place on the surface at night. Out of the twenty ships I sank, I sank nineteen at night on the surface. This sort of attack was more or less similar to torpedo boat attacks. At night, if you are closer to your target than 3000–4000 metres, then from the bridge of a normal ship the conning tower does not appear against the horizon. You offer only a small silhouette to your target – then the boat is practically invisible.'

The Royal Navy had prepared for a war against the submarine, and yet the enemy was really nothing of the sort; it was a submersible. Too much faith had been placed in the new science of underwater detection; ASDIC was almost useless against a U-boat on the surface. 'I don't remember ever being taught the First World War U-boat tactics,' the ASW specialist Maurice Usherwood recalls. 'I was expecting them to remain at periscope depth and attack from that depth.'

This was not just a case of institutional amnesia; there was also a clear failure of intelligence. Technically there were no surprises. The British Secret Intelligence Service had managed to recruit a remarkable source within the U-boat construction programme. By 1935 a steady stream of detailed technical intelligence had allowed the Admiralty to conclude that Dönitz's U-boats showed only a small advance on those of World War I.[21] It knew a great deal about the nuts and bolts, and yet its assessment of future U-boat tactics was not impressive. Good information on this was available, for Dönitz made very little effort to disguise his views. Naval Intelligence need only have purchased a copy of his book *Die U-Bootswaffe*, which was published in January 1939. In it Dönitz emphasized the importance of night surface attack and the thoroughness with which his U-boats had been trained in this tactic. The Admiralty might also have consulted the British submarine service, which had carried out successful night surface attack exercises of its own.

It is hardly surprising, given this catalogue of failure, that little attempt was made to exploit the potential of the strike force most capable of tracking and attacking the U-boat on the surface. The importance of air power in sea warfare had been clearly demonstrated in the closing months of World War I when convoys with air cover suffered significantly fewer losses than those without. Yet in the years that followed, the Admiralty's faith in ASDIC was so strong that it deemed aircraft to be no longer essential in this role. Almost all the aircraft available to RAF Coastal Command on the eve of war were incapable of long-range sea patrols, whilst their crews had been given next to no training in anti-submarine operations. To make matters worse, they were equipped with a bomb that proved a greater threat to the safety of pilot and plane than to the U-boat. To cause serious damage it needed to fall within 6–8 feet of the U-boat, which obliged crews to attack from very low altitudes. They soon discovered that the bomb had a nasty tendency to bounce back off the water before exploding.[22] It was almost entirely useless, and yet it would be the summer of 1940 before progress was made on a replacement.

Coastal Command was hardly better prepared to meet the growing threat to shipping from the air. Amongst the ships to fall foul of the Luftwaffe's increasingly muscular presence was the ASW whaler *Windermere*. Without support from the air it was usually a one-sided contest. Ian Jamieson recalls:

> We had set forth from Aberdeen to rejoin the other five ships of our group when we were caught by four Heinkel bombers, which presumably thought we were an easy target because we only had a single Lewis gun. It was possible to avoid the bombs for a little while – you could tell when they were releasing them and then you would try and alter course. Then this particular bomb, its bearing was absolutely steady as I looked at it, and I knew it was going to hit us. We were thrown across the bridge deck. There were three of us up there – we all survived, although the bridge was completely wrecked. The ship came to a grinding halt, whereupon they started to machine gun us and I got everybody to take cover.

Miraculously, no one was killed in the blast, but there were wounded: Jamieson's hand and arm were badly injured. Eventually, he presumed, the bombers must have run out of ammunition because they flew off.

Although Jamieson was a 'pinger', the closest he had come to the enemy was his brush with the Luftwaffe. It was five long months before his hospital treatment was over. In September 1940 he was posted to the Admiralty's ASW Division; by then the war at sea had undergone a profound change. The twin pillars had begun to shake.

CHAPTER THREE

HAPPY TIMES

IN THE FIRST WEEKS of the war Karl Dönitz established a daily routine which he was to follow almost religiously for the next five years. The morning of 22 June 1940 began like every other. At nine o'clock sharp Dönitz joined his small band of staff officers in the operations room for the daily briefing. There was an update on the events of the previous night, on signals and intelligence received, and then the current U-boat dispositions were discussed at length. The walls of the operations room were draped in maps on which the positions of U-boats and British convoys were marked with small coloured flags. There were precious few black flags – in the first nine months of the war Dönitz's fleet had shrunk; 24 U-boats had been lost, the majority to British escort ships, and by June there were barely more than a dozen boats at sea at any one time. The discussion over, the orders for the day issued, Dönitz took lunch; this was followed by a brisk walk through the farmland around Wilhelmshaven in the company of his new Adjutant, Hans-Jochen von Knebel Doeberitz.

After three war patrols with Kretschmer's *U-23*, von Knebel had been obliged to take up his post on Dönitz's staff. His disappointment was tempered somewhat by the openness of his relationship with the leader of the U-boat arm. On the afternoon of the 22nd the two men walked to a nearby farm. Von Knebel remembers: 'We used to play with the children at the farm. I always had to bring a bar of chocolate so Dönitz could give it to them. On this day, the farmer's wife came running out to meet us shouting: "They've capitulated, they've capitulated." France had fallen.'

It had been sudden and entirely unexpected. German armoured

columns had begun their relentless advance just six weeks before, rumbling through the Low Countries and round the French armies camped on the heavily fortified Maginot Line. Resistance crumbled. The British were able to scoop the remnants of their Expeditionary Force from the Dunkirk beaches, but the collapse was complete. The Reich's armies had achieved a remarkable victory; for its navy this was the opportunity long hoped for. Von Knebel remembers the excitement with which Dönitz greeted the news: 'He said: "We've got the French coast, we ought to get there immediately." At headquarters I organized this fabulous car, a six-cylinder BMW. Apart from Dönitz and the driver, only the intelligence officer Hans Meckel, and myself were to make the journey. We didn't know what to expect in France – it was enemy territory.'

The car was to make all speed for the ports of the French Atlantic coast. With these in German hands the U-boats would no longer be forced to make the dangerous seven-day journey across the North Sea and round the coast of Britain before they reached the Atlantic war zone. The time saved could be spent attacking shipping in the Western Approaches. Dönitz hoped this would go some way to restoring the battered morale of his crews, who had managed to sink only seven ships in April. Repeated torpedo failures had forced him to withdraw them from the battle for Norway. It had been a humiliating affair. Adjustments were made to the torpedoes, however, and enough were to find their mark in June to suggest that the problem had been resolved. Amidst the chaos of the withdrawal from France the Allies had lost nearly 600,000 tons of shipping; U-boats had sunk 62 ships, some 284,113 tons – their highest monthly total to date.

Dönitz's journey through France was not without event. The roads were crammed with refugees swept up by the advance, and a German army officer persuaded Dönitz to find room in the car for two who were making their way south. Von Knebel remembers:

We immediately understood that they were German refugees, leaving Germany because of the political situation – a tall, distinguished-looking Jew and his no longer youthful daughter. They wanted to try and get a ship for England in Bordeaux. Dönitz said to them: 'Give the English my regards. They started the war, not us – tell them to stop it.' This was how he joked, in a friendly way, you know. I think they got out of the car in Le Mans. It was an episode which made a very great impression on me, in hindsight, the fact that we took these Jews along.

Dönitz's survey of the Biscay ports convinced him that the greater part of U-boat operations should be transferred to western France. He was particularly impressed by the facilities at Lorient where the French dock-yard superintendent also appeared welcoming. Von Knebel remembers: 'We lived in one of the hotels there and were treated very civilly. The population was friendly towards us; we didn't feel there was any hostility.'

Dönitz chose Lorient as the U-boats' main operational base, and just outside the town he found a new home and headquarters. The Château Kernével stands on the tip of a peninsula at the mouth of the natural har-bour formed by three rivers, Scorff, Blavet and Ter. Built at the end of the nineteenth century for a wealthy sardine merchant, Kernével is more gaudy seaside villa than château. Today the view from the terrace is dom-inated by a vast broken jaw of brutal grey concrete. This is Keroman III, the largest of 7 pens built for the U-boats. Behind Keroman III are Keroman I and II and the unfinished IV; beneath it a labyrinth of service tunnels still crammed with rusting pipework and machinery. Nothing of this vast infrastructure existed when on 7 July the first U-boat swept up the river on the Atlantic tide. It was *U-30*, the boat that had struck the first blow in the Atlantic war, and radio operator Georg Högel was among the crew:

Everyone was ordered on deck because we thought the French could have mined the bay. I still remember today that Lorient was entirely peaceful – I could just see a plume of smoke from a burn-ing oil dump close to the town.

I had an overnight watch on the boat, but my shipmates were taken into town to the Hôtel Beau Séjour just by the market square. They fetched me the next morning. I was amazed to find a room reserved for me. There was even post from home there. To get post in France at that moment was the greatest surprise.

Whilst the German navy was in no doubt that the defeat of Great Britain was of the first importance, the Führer's gaze had already begun to stray eastwards. In Hitler's judgement, Britain could not fight on: sooner rather than later it would sue for peace. Planning could therefore begin at once for a war against Germany's natural 'communist' enemy, the Soviet Union. An early end to the war in the west was, of course, desirable. The Luftwaffe and Kriegsmarine were to squeeze Britain into submission; if this failed, the army might attempt an amphibious assault on Britain's beaches, codenamed Operation Sea Lion. The Kriegsmarine had neither the necessary landing craft nor a large enough surface fleet to protect it; success would therefore depend above all on the Luftwaffe winning complete air superiority over land and sea.

Frantic preparations were already underway in Britain to counter an invasion. Winston Churchill, who had become Prime Minister in May, put it in his own inimitable way: 'The Battle of France is over,' he told the public, 'I expect the Battle of Britain is about to begin.' Some of those who had witnessed the collapse of the French army had concluded that the country was better off alone; amongst them, a twenty-six-year-old officer in Naval Intelligence, Peter Smithers: 'There was a feeling, "We're on our own – well, thank God for that! We can depend on ourselves; we couldn't depend on the French. There was nobody else except the Empire. It would help us. We're on our own – let's go." After that, when one began to think soberly about the realities, it was a grim outlook.'

Smithers had transferred to Naval Intelligence just a few months before; a girlfriend had put him in touch with the director's personal assistant, Lieutenant Commander Ian Fleming, the future author of the

James Bond novels. His first important task had been the evacuation of Special Intelligence Service (MI6) personnel and documents from Paris. By July he was back in London: 'It was desperately busy. In the operations basement of the Admiralty, there was a sign up which said "Cromwell". This was the codeword for "Invasion Imminent". I watched the aerial photographs day by day which showed all the barges assembled. Every security operation, all the naval operations, were concentrated on this threat.'

The country's survival in the long run would depend on war material from the United States. Top of the British government's shopping list were destroyers, and Churchill made a personal appeal to President Franklin D. Roosevelt: 'The Germans have the whole French coastline from which to launch U-boats and dive-bomber attacks upon our trade and food and in addition we must be constantly prepared to repel by sea action threatened invasion.... Mr President, with great respect I must tell you that in the long history of the world this is a thing to do now.'[1] Roosevelt responded with a promise of fifty vintage destroyers, a generous gesture from a country not at war. It would be months, however, before they were fully operational; the invasion threat would be met without them. Destroyers and corvettes were needed for the defence of the Channel coast; it meant stripping the country's Atlantic lifeline of its protection just as the U-boat was preparing to launch a concerted effort to cut it. By July 1940 Britain's merchant fleet could count on an average of just two Royal Navy escort ships per convoy.

This was the start of what the U-boat men were to call their 'happy time'. Operating from their new French bases, a handful of U-boat commanders began to run up extraordinary individual tallies. One of the first to leave Lorient on war patrol was Otto Kretschmer in *U-99*, his new, larger Type VII B Atlantic boat. Dönitz's orders were typically to the point: 'Attack and keep on attacking; do not let yourself be shaken off; if the boat is forced away try to get in touch again and once more attack!' Volkmar König joined *U-99* at the age of 20 and served as a midshipman: 'Kretschmer was a very intelligent man, very cold-blooded – he knew exactly what kind of risk he could take'.

From Lorient Kretschmer set a course across the Bay of Biscay northwards towards the Western Approaches. There was enough diesel in *U-99*'s tanks for four weeks at sea, but the length of its patrol would be determined by the number of torpedoes it carried. If the boat was lucky the hunting would be good and it could soon return to Lorient. Until then the 220-foot-long steel cigar would be home for 43 men.

The crew was young and fit; it needed to be. Most of the men were aged between twenty and twenty-three; the commander, 'the old man', was just twenty-eight.[2] Almost half the crew lived in the bow compartment, *U-99*'s main armoury.[3] There were four torpedo tubes here and some ten torpedoes; a further two torpedoes could be fired from a tube in the stern and two more were carried in pressure-proof containers in the upper deck – to be brought below when space permitted. No one looked forward to going into action more than these men; life in their black hole became more comfortable with every torpedo fired. König remembers: 'They shared their bunk with a comrade who did the same job aboard. Whilst one man was on watch for four hours another would have time to rest. When the watch changed the other man would take over this bunk, still warm.'

Beside each bunk was a small locker for a handful of personal possessions. A glance into one of these left no doubt about the spartan life of the U-boat crewman. There was no need for clean clothes or razors, and precious little for soap. Within days of leaving Lorient the appearance of the crew changed, marked by a life without sunlight and the punishing routine. Faces were pasty white and bearded, eyes black-rimmed. Clothes were soon thick with diesel oil and brine. Fresh water was for drinking only and, whilst it was possible to wash with sea-water soap, no one made much effort. There were two toilets aboard but one was used for storage; more than 40 men shared the other one. A boat like *U-99* had its own unique aroma. König recalls: 'It was a combination of all kinds of smells. The smell of diesel oil was prominent, but then you had the smell of the food and the men. Put all this in a pot and stir it a little bit and you have the smell of a submarine.' Some of the crew used eau de cologne to mask this heady cocktail, but most just took it for granted.

Beyond *U-99*'s bow room were the officers' and chief petty officers' quarters. Life was a little less bleak for the nine men who slept and ate here. Kretschmer had his own bunk and a little writing desk opposite the U-boat's radio room. He ate with his officers at a table in the middle of the passageway; meals were constantly interrupted by traffic to and from the bow torpedo room.

At the heart of *U-99* was the Zentrale or control room, packed with an array of machines, valves, gauges and dials. It was the battle head-quarters of the boat; the ballast tanks that enabled it to dive or surface, trimming of the rudder and the diving planes were all controlled from here. One of the U-boat's two periscopes was operated from the control room; a longer attack periscope was housed in the conning tower above.

The next compartment held the petty officers' quarters and the tiny galley. The cook had just a three-ring range, two small ovens and a 40 litre boiling pot, but meals were surprisingly good; their quality helped to take the edge off the hardship of life on board. The German soldier in the field would have been amazed by the variety of sausages, smoked meats, cheeses, vegetables and fruit stowed in every nook and cranny of a front-line U-boat. There were also special items: chocolate and good coffee. It did not last, of course; there was always something dripping on a U-boat – a leaky housing or valve; everything was damp, and in this close, fetid environment the food began to gather a film of green mould within days. By the second week the bread was cut from tins and so, by the third, was the meat.

Beyond the galley was the clattering, thumping diesel engine room and then last of all the electrical compartment with the two 375 horse-power electric motors, which were activated when the boat dived. The crew would sometimes pray for this moment – respite for an hour or two from the constant pitching and rolling they endured when the boat was travelling on the surface. Those moments of relief were rare; for most of the war patrol a four-man watch would keep a constant vigil atop the conning tower, searching the horizon for a sign of the enemy. Volkmar König remembers:

> When the sea isn't rough it's a nice job. You observe the horizon to see if you can see some smoke. Perhaps that's a ship – there might be a convoy. You have to be on the lookout for enemy airplanes or at night an enemy destroyer.
>
> It's different if the sea is rough. Then the big waves swish over your boat. You have a safety belt which you fasten to the column in the middle of the tower, and you really go with the boat through the waves. The waves go over your head and you're in it. The conning tower crew had special suits like a diver for this kind of weather. We called them Mickey Mouse suits.

The second watch officer on *U-99* was twenty-three-year-old Horst Elfe. There were times, he recalls, when the sea was so rough that an attack on the enemy was out of the question:

> We had to ride some pretty massive North Atlantic storms. It couldn't have been worse. Underwater we couldn't do anything; no U-boat could be controlled at periscope depth during a major storm – it either had to be above or well below sea level. So underwater attacks were inconceivable. Surface attacks were unthinkable because nobody could see, move, aim or do anything. There were those occasions when you suddenly saw a single ship, which you would usually have attacked, but you couldn't. You'd steer a parallel course and neither party could do the other any harm. People thought only of their own survival in these seas.

If the bridge watch detected a column of smoke on the horizon *U-99* would jump into action. Then the boat seemed to throb with excitement as every ounce of speed was wrung from its diesel engines in an effort to close with the enemy. Yet those moments were rare; König recalls: 'Action was the exception. Normally you would drive along the surface some-where, looking for prey, and it was just routine. The rule was boredom.'

This was the small world the crew of *U-99* inhabited: just six com-partments bow to stern and the conning tower bridge. To an outsider, service on a U-boat might have seemed like a prison sentence; yet for all the discomfort, life was made bearable on most boats by a strong sense of camaraderie. König remembers: 'When I came down into the control room of the submarine for the first time, there was the crew and they were laughing. There was music on the radio and the humming of machines. It was a familiar atmosphere. Somehow you felt engulfed by comradeship.'

This was Dönitz's 'U-boat spirit'. On *U-99* it depended chiefly on the officers not the commander. König remembers: 'Kretschmer would never sit at a bar and drink a beer with one of his crew. He was in author-ity and when he gave an order, that was an order. In a crew you have to have superiors you can talk to and make jokes with and Kretschmer was lucky that he had others who could take over this job, who gave the crew a feeling of being a family.'

Inside the U-boat arm Kretschmer was known as 'Silent Otto'. 'He wasn't someone who gave big encouraging speeches,' Elfe recalls. 'He was always very matter-of-fact, very unemotional, but he was not without a heart.' For all that, the crew were happy to serve under Kretschmer; his judgement was proven, as was his luck. He was to demonstrate both again just three days after leaving Lorient. At a little after dawn on 28 July *U-99* found the 13,200-ton liner *Auckland Star* off southwest Ireland and sent her to the bottom. The following day the freighter *Clan Menzies* met the same fate. The patrol had begun well.

At the same time, the destroyer HMS *Walker* was preparing to escort another outward-bound convoy from Liverpool. With her sailed the new corvette HMS *Periwinkle*; 'a glorified trawler' was Sub-Lieutenant Adams of the *Walker*'s first impression, 'and damn all use'; a judgement he was soon to revise. The escort screen was to consist of just these two ships; the Royal Navy was stretched very thinly. The convoy set out on the evening of 29 July. Its route would take it through the box of sea that *U-99* was cruising off the northwest coast of Ireland.

In the early hours of 31 July *U-99* claimed its third victim with a straightforward attack on the surface at night. 'Bow attack. Fired once from 900 metres and hit astern,' Kretschmer wrote in his war diary. She was the 5475-ton freighter *Jamaica Progress,* bound for Liverpool with a cargo of bananas. Watch officer Horst Elfe remembers being surprised by how many ships like *Jamaica Progress* were still travelling alone after almost a year of war: 'They were prepared to take a big risk.' Later that morning *U-99* dived to reload torpedoes. Whilst it was submerged the sound of distant propellers was detected on the boat's hydrophones. The pursuit began. At a little after midday *U-99* spotted a convoy: 'Fifteen steamers in a three-line formation, minor protection,' Kretschmer observed in his log: 'I am in an unfavourable position but because of the starboard station of the destroyer I am able to approach the convoy. It tacks, which suddenly puts me on a collision course and forces me to dive under the outer column. I can only aim for the last ship in the central column and not for the tanker that I was hoping for. Fire once from 800 metres; on target. It is a large, old freighter.'

'It was a calm, smooth day in summer, and suddenly the *Jersey City* went bang,' Adams remembers. 'It was so calm one should have seen the periscope, but one didn't.' *Walker* went in search of the U-boat. 'One relied quite a bit on a ship saying, if it could, "The torpedo came from over there,"' Adams recalls. 'Then you went tearing over there. You went out in an ever-widening circle trying to find the submarine by ASDIC.'[4]

'Pursued by the destroyer's ASDIC,' Kretschmer wrote in his log, 'twenty depth charges fired, but inaccurately targeted.' Inside *U-99* the crew could hear the groaning of the *Jersey City* as she slipped under. Great bubbles of air escaped from her, metal grinding against metal.

Kretschmer had taken a risk. Elfe recalls: 'It was better and much safer to shoot from outside the convoy, but what could happen was that the convoy would change direction and you found yourself in the middle of it. Once inside you could shoot in both directions if you wanted to, but it wasn't always planned. You would feel a lot safer on the outside because your escape route was clear.' For all that, the *Jersey City* had been an easy kill, the escort screen too weak to trouble *U-99*.

Walker and *Periwinkle* steamed on with the rest of the convoy. When *U-99* eventually surfaced it was to find just two empty lifeboats. Kretschmer was nevertheless determined on pursuit. His best guess as to the convoy's likely direction was a good one. Within a matter of hours the bridge watch had spotted smoke on the horizon, but before *U-99* could overhaul the convoy it was found by a Sunderland flying boat of Coastal Command and forced to dive. It was five hours before it resumed the chase, and the evening of the following day, 1 August, before it was once again in a position to attack. By then the two escorts were preparing to leave the convoy. Kretschmer described in his war diary the events that followed:

1 August 22.18 As darkness falls I set course for the south and the favourable horizon. The convoy now appears in front of the bright evening horizon. The two escorting destroyers are on either side at the front.

2 August 00.05 The two destroyers turn around, give a short light signal, go astern past the convoy, and then disappear into the darkness. Just as I expected. What follows now resembles the raging of a wolf in a flock of sheep. We still have four torpedoes.

02.51 Fire at the largest tanker. Hit aft, near the bulkhead between the machine room and the rear hold. The aft of the ship, the Dutch *Barendrecht*, 9385-tonner, goes down quickly, doesn't send a signal, the crew takes to the boats . . . the convoy ships begin to tack: each one individually. Everything is in terrible confusion.

03.40 Fired on the next tanker. Distance 450 metres. Hit amidships. Ship breaks out of line and stops with a heavy list, but still sends signal with name and position. *Lucerna* 6556 tons. Crew takes to the boats...I penetrate the convoy and go with it and am surrounded by tacking ships. To get to the next tanker a heavily laden freighter has to fall. However, as we fire it gives off a short signal with its steam-whistle and turns away. The torpedo misses and then actually hits the tanker, whose turn it was going to be next. It hits the rear hold. The steamer comes to a listing halt. *Alexia*, 8016 tons.

04.27 So far the extraordinarily strong phosphorescence of the sea has enabled us to follow the course of each of the torpedoes from firing to target. The convoy now breaks up completely. The ships run in different directions. The strongest group includes a tanker, this we shall now attack...fire from the stern but it overshoots the ship. I go back to the damaged steamers so that I can finish them off if necessary, by using artillery. The *Alexia* is still afloat.

06.24–06.30 Thirty shots at 2500 m with the gun, aiming at the ship that is now sending radio signals requesting the presence of destroyers. Approximately 15–20 shots on target, most of which are into the waterline of the ship and her engine room. The tanker's stern sinks further. Thick clouds of smoke belching out of the funnel indicate that the boiler room is flooded. Steamer is undoubtedly sinking. On the way to join the *Lucerna*, which has already gone down.

06.52 Soon a destroyer's superstructure comes into view as it heads for the *Alexia*. I retreat northwards on the surface.

The attack had lasted for more than three hours and was only interrupted by the arrival of HMS *Walker*. In that time *U-99* never left the surface, and when its torpedoes had gone it had attacked with its deck gun. The crew believed it could add three tankers to its tally, which made seven ships totalling 56,000 tons in just six days. It was a remarkable achievement, but not as remarkable as Kretschmer thought. In the confusion of the night battle he had lost track of the tankers and, although they had taken a battering, they were still afloat. Adam recalls: 'They were still able to steam at 10 knots, all three of them. We formed them up into a little convoy and took them back to England. Each one had a hole the size of a London double-decker bus in it. It was quite remarkable.' Nevertheless it had been a sobering few days at sea for the crew of the *Walker*. The ship returned to a country under siege from the air; no one appeared to know or care about the battle being fought at sea. Adams remembers: 'We were an unseen war, we were at sea and even when we came ashore, no one saw the sunken ships or the survivors who never made it. There was nothing there to show for what we'd really lost.'

Kretschmer's war patrol had lasted just twelve days; barely long enough for the crew to grow a U-boat beard. The reception committee at Lorient included the Commander in Chief of the Kriegsmarine, Großadmiral Raeder. A cameraman from the Propaganda Ministry was there to capture it all on film for the German public. To the strains of the U-boat arm's traditional anglophobic anthem, *Englandlied*, Raeder stepped forward to present Kretschmer with his Knight's Cross. There were the usual Iron Crosses for the officers and most of the crew. Elfe remembers: 'Admiral Raeder was astonished to see all of us in British battledress. We hadn't had any uniforms sent from home yet, so we only had our dirty overalls on board and, just for appearance's sake, we had to dress ourselves in this battledress, which was part of the booty taken from the British army at Dunkirk.'

The Kriegsmarine's radio intelligence service, *B-Dienst*, had told Dönitz of the three tankers HMS *Walker* had saved; it was an inconvenient fact, and one he chose to ignore. Kretschmer showed the right aggressive spirit, so he deserved his Knight's Cross. The U-boat arm needed its heroes. For all the Führer's warm admiration, the number of operational boats under Dönitz's command had shrunk by September 1940 to just twenty-four, twenty-two fewer than at the beginning of the war. Goebbels's Propaganda Ministry recognized the star quality of Kretschmer and his fellow commanders, the 'grey wolves' of the Atlantic; Dönitz was grateful for any extra leverage that a higher profile in the Reich might win for the U-boat.

In fact there was no need to exaggerate the successes. A steady procession of bunting-clad boats made its way up the river Scorff to Lorient to be welcomed by Dönitz with champagne and decorations. Amongst the growing number of commanders honoured with a Knight's Cross that summer was Fritz-Julius Lemp; by then *U-30*'s tally, including the *Athenia*, was some sixteen ships totalling 80,232 tons. It was, Georg Högel recalls, a moment for the whole crew to savour: 'One certainly shared in the joy, because one had gone through everything too, from the very start. You had witnessed the high points and the low points and the risks and dangers. When the *Ritterkreuz* was awarded to the commander, somehow we felt included in this.'

There was a spirit of competition amongst Dönitz's commanders: who could sink the most ships? Erich Topp remembers:

'The political environment was geared exclusively towards war and victory, and everyone wanted to contribute to the victorious ending of this war. We were convinced after the first successes which we enjoyed in the Atlantic that the U-boat could contribute decisively.' The twenty-six-year-old Topp had taken command of a small Type II C 'duck', *U-57*, that summer. Painted on the conning tower were two Red Devils: 'The two figures carried torches – the torch of life on the one hand and the torch of destruction on the other. That symbolized the fine line between life and death upon which we balanced.'

As a young commander anxious to make a name for his U-boat, he chose an especially fine line. On 14 August 1940 the 'Red Devil boat' sailed on its second patrol under Topp's command.

Not long after leaving Lorient we were surprised by a British bomber that appeared out of the clouds. Its bombs fell quite close to us; one of the two diesel engines was torn from its foundations. I called a meeting with the chief engineer and the watch officer.

The chief engineer said, 'We've only the one engine, and if this one breaks down – well, then it'll be over for us.' He was all for turning back and repairing the damage.

I asked my watch officer for his opinion.

He said, 'We still have five torpedoes on board. We haven't fired a single one. Its our duty to attack the enemy.'

I said, 'That's my view too.' Because the boat was 'handicapped', we decided to go as close to the British coast as we could.

On the night of 23 August *U-57* edged its way towards the North Channel. 'A convoy came out and I attacked it from the surface with three torpedoes. All of them found the target,' Topp recalls. Within hours of leaving port convoy OB 202 had lost two freighters and a third had been badly damaged. This was not, however, to be another easy kill; retribution was fast. Topp remembers:

We were pursued. I tried to escape, but our pursuers were faster, and with only 50 metres of water beneath us they forced us to dive. I can only say that we must have had luck with us, because we found a trough on the seabed. Then they depth-charged us continually. We lay there and took this for twenty-two hours. Everything broke down; it was a catastrophe.

Of course, the depth charges make quite a noise – the boat shuddered and then lots of things stopped working. The lights went out, then the valves started to loosen; there were over a hundred valves linked to the outside of the submarine, and when they loosened water began to seep in.

The air became quite bad; our carbon dioxide content was far too high. Only the men needed to stop the various water leakages were allowed to move; I sent the rest to their bunks. We had the escape apparatus, and there we lay until almost midnight of the next night.

Then, after twenty-two hours under, I said, 'Now we have to surface. It's our last chance. Compressed air to all tanks!' Nothing stirred. I tried something else. I had one electric motor, which was still functioning. I started it and tried to turn the boat's screws – perhaps the keel had become attached to the sea floor. It worked.

The boat freed itself and shot upwards.

It was dark, of course. There was a destroyer about 1000 metres away, but it didn't see us. It was difficult to know which course to take – our compass was amongst the things damaged. I told myself, 'The wind came yesterday from the northwest!', so we put to sea against the wind and tried to repair everything we could by early next morning.

As the battered boat made its way northwards it met another convoy; this one was homebound. Topp remembers: 'I decided to attack a tanker at the rear of it with my last two torpedoes. They hit; the tanker exploded, burst into flames. We were depth-charged again, but this time it didn't do us any damage because we could reach a depth of 100 metres. After this we had a restorative meal and then set off back.'

It was an impressive war patrol, accomplished on just one diesel engine; it was also, Topp admits, 'the typical action of a young commander' and one very much in keeping with the spirit of the times. In the last week of August U-boats sank 110,000 tons of shipping; almost a quarter of the total belonged to Topp. It would prove to be the single most successful week of the war. And although he had taken risks, Topp knew he had kept the support of his crew:

In the first place, it is of course important that one is successful. The men want to return home with successes and that is certainly a decisive factor. But it was also important for me to establish personal contact with each individual and know what is going on in the soul of each man. On one occasion we went to sea and my second Watch officer was very quiet, pale-faced. I asked him 'What's the matter with you?' and he said, 'Nothing, nothing.' After a time I asked him again, 'I can tell you now, you can't convince me that you are in a balanced frame of mind!' Then he said, 'Well, OK, I have left my lucky mascot behind.' His mascot was a wreath of myrtle from his wedding day. He'd always carried it with him on board and now he didn't have it, he'd forgotten it. So then I changed course and went back to fetch it. After that I had a second Watch Officer on board who was absolutely top notch, who carried out his duties very well.

Topp's boat was not the only one to take a pasting that summer; several U-boats were found and attacked. However, between July and October only two were sunk. It was not just the weakness of the Royal Navy escorts or the inexperience of Coastal Command; no one had appreciated quite what a pounding the U-boat's pressure hull could take. By August 1940 the twenty-six-year-old commander of *U-61*, Jürgen Oesten, had sunk five ships totalling 20,000 tons. 'It was like big game hunting,' he remembers. 'Of course, if you attack a convoy and there are escorts then you can become the hunted.' This happened to *U-61* after an attack on a freighter to the east of the Orkney Islands. Oesten recalls: 'The depth charges were so close the U-boat's pressure hull was dented. We were lucky these hulls were welded with high-alloy steel. If they were riveted they wouldn't have taken any serious detonations.' The boat managed to limp slowly back on one engine. Dönitz was waiting dockside when Oesten eventually tied up. 'He said, "Hello! What do you want? You've been reported sunk." I said, "If you prefer, I'll go back again."'

It was typical of the warm informality that Dönitz demonstrated with commanders and crews. They felt their leader was one of them; he spoke to them as one sailor to another. When they were at sea he sent news from home of important events such as births; 'Onkel Karl' seemed to care. He expected his men always to give of their best and he was blunt if he judged they had not.[5] Crews wanted to do well for Dönitz; loyalty to the U-boat arm was in great measure a personal loyalty to him. Oesten recalls:

When you came back with a worn-out crew, Dönitz was usually there waiting. If there was an old petty officer who was fed up and tired and wanted to report sick, Dönitz would just look at him and say, 'Well, Meier, how many years have we known each other?'

He would say with pride, 'Eight years,' or something like that.

And then Dönitz would say, 'Well, then, let's carry on a bit, shall we?', and then the man was good for another two trips.

It was not just a 'happy time' at sea; Dönitz ensured his crews were well looked after ashore. Richard Amstein of *U-123* recalls: 'We did have a good life, yes. And we would make the most of it too. As a seaman first class I was paid a salary – it wasn't very much. But then when you were on board the boat you got more money, and when the vessel was outside the three (nautical) mile limit there was more money again. There was also a supplement for every dive the U-boat made whether you were on active service or not. You always had enough money.' There was good French wine and food to be found in Lorient's hotels and squares; in its back-street cafés, a chance to meet some of the prettier locals. Amstein recalls: 'We would usually seek out some dive. There were a few establishments that were very nice – they had a small brass band. And then, of course, if there were girls present we would try to dance with them. Sometimes we even succeeded. Drink didn't cost anything in those days. What was the price of a bottle of champagne? I think it was 20 francs, which was no money at all to us.'

Lorient was an old French naval port, well prepared to cater for the seaman's needs even if he sailed under an enemy flag. Georg Högel of *U-30* remembers: 'I was young and naïve. There was still a curfew in Lorient when we first arrived – you weren't allowed to be about in the streets after ten o'clock in the evening. But as far as the crew was concerned it lasted until ten minutes past ten. Then the commander left, then the officers and the petty officers, and in the end the rest of my comrades went too. I did avoid certain tensions because I'd stayed in the hotel – it became clear the next day that the little stoker had pinched a brothel girl from the engineer. Well, that wasn't for me. In those days I didn't approve of it at all, especially when I saw a queue and knew where it was going.'

Commanders were happy for their men to 'run ashore' as long as they were ready for sea when the time came. Topp remembers saying to his crew: "'Comrades, do whatever you like. Have a good time, but don't pick up an infection from some sort of call-girl." A senior machinist came back with a disease and I resented that. He couldn't go out to sea with us; I then had to take a different man with me. That was contrary to regulations and contrary to the loyalty that he ought to have shown me.'

The quieter, officially approved rest and recuperation on offer included crew holidays in what became known as 'U-boat pastures'. This might be a hotel in the Austrian Alps or a smart villa by the sea in France. No matter where the 'pasture', the food and service were always of the best. For those with more than a few days' leave, there was the special U-boat train home to Germany.

Some U-boat officers chose to set up home in France. Erich Topp was provided with a villa near his base at St Nazaire, which he shared with his friend, the commander of *U-46*, Engelbert Endrass (the former first watch officer of *U-47*, Endrass had fired the torpedoes that sank the *Royal Oak*). 'The villa belonged to an actor from Paris. He'd deserted it, but everything remained inside: crockery, glasses. Of course, we invited our girl friends from Paris: Endrass had a Belgian girlfriend, a singer called Monique, and my girlfriend was Russian, Patti – she was a dancer.'

There was also Paris. A club run by Russian émigrés, the Scheherazade, acted as an unofficial meeting point for U-boat officers. Topp and Endrass were among the regulars who met their girlfriends there. 'We all went to the Scheherazade. We felt quite at home there, in a way,' Jürgen Oesten recalls. If for many it was to be a short life, it would at least be a happy one; the girls, champagne and late night revels all helped. Oesten remembers:

The first time I had this feeling was after the depth-charge attack on *U-61* when the pressure hull was dented. I went skiing in Austria after that and I met a young girl. She was studying medicine. I thought, 'Well, life may be short, maybe you should do something.' We became good friends and I married her. I was married for seven years, but if I add up all the time we had together, it's only four or five months. I was together with lots of other women for much longer periods than with my own wife during those seven years. So we agreed to disagree and we divorced.

For the most part, good times ashore lasted only as long as it took to prepare a U-boat for its next patrol. Dönitz was determined to exploit Britain's inability to protect its Atlantic lifeline adequately; he later wrote, 'I was anxious that not one single day should pass without the sinking somewhere or other of a ship by one of the boats at sea.' The staff at U-boat Command kept a day-to-day log of British shipping activities assembled from the reports made by the U-boats. If more than two days passed without convoys being sighted, Dönitz would order his commanders to search a new box of sea. Although the U-boats were operating close to the British Isles, identifying a change of route into the Western Approaches was often a matter of guesswork. The view from the conning tower of a U-boat was restricted to 20 miles on a clear day, considerably less in the conditions that frequently prevailed in the Atlantic. There were often only six or seven U-boats in the operational area, so making contact with a convoy was uncertain. Dönitz had identified the need for air reconnaissance in support of U-boat operations, but his repeated attempts to obtain it fell on deaf ears. The Luftwaffe chief, Hermann Göring, vigorously resisted any claim that threatened to restrict his direct authority over the Reich's aircraft, and it was easy to argue in the summer of 1940 that the decisive battle was being fought in the skies above Britain.

Nevertheless buoyed by a summer of successes, Dönitz was determined to implement the strategy he hoped would win the war at sea for Germany. He had outlined the essential points in his reports to Raeder and his staff before the war; they boiled down to 'concentration against concentration', an attack on a single convoy by a group of U-boats. Whilst his commanders had achieved remarkable successes alone, only by operating in groups or 'packs' could they hope to destroy whole convoys. Then, perhaps, the U-boat stranglehold would be tight enough to force Britain to sue for peace. The strategy was a simple one, its implementation was not; it was first necessary to find the convoy, then to assemble a pack in time to attack it before it outstripped the pursuing U-boats.

Dönitz's plan was to deploy his groups in search lines across the convoy routes. The first U-boat to locate the convoy became the 'contact boat'; it would radio a coded sighting report to headquarters, which would then summon the other members of the group. This could take many hours; later in the war it was not unusual for a group to be strung across more than 300 miles of ocean. The 'contact boat' would have to shadow the convoy and radio regular position reports to the pursuing boats. No attack was to be attempted until the pack assembled; then, when night fell, the U-boats could attack on the surface. The impact of simultaneous attacks on the convoy would, Dönitz hoped, completely break down its defences. There was a risk; the role played by U-boat Command in assembling the pack would be pivotal, but controlling attacks from the shore would generate a great deal of signals traffic, it was inevitable that the British would intercept some of it. This was a risk Dönitz was prepared to take. Early attempts to mount a pack attack had produced only limited results, but as the war entered its second year Dönitz judged the time right to try again. 'I confidently expected substantial results,' he would later write. Britain's survival rested upon its ability to defeat the challenge of the wolf pack.

CHAPTER FOUR

WOLF PACK

ON THE EVENING OF 7 September 1940 the drone of three hundred bombers in the skies over London signalled the start of the most devastating attack yet launched from the air on a city. The focal point was London's docklands and those areas identified as 'industrial'. It was Sub-Lieutenant Ian Jamieson's first day at the Admiralty after five months recovering from the injuries he had received when his ship had been bombed; he arrived at his desk to be greeted by the wail of air raid sirens. 'I felt rather as though every bomb had my name on it by that time,' he recalls.

On 15 September two attempts to launch a heavy daylight raid on the capital were beaten off by RAF fighters; fifty-six German planes were shot down. It was a decisive blow; the Luftwaffe had failed to win daylight mastery of the skies over Britain, and it was impossible to contemplate an invasion without overwhelming air superiority. The night-time Blitz of London that had begun on 7 September was, by this token, an admission of defeat. But for all that the Battle of Britain had been won, the decisive battle in the Atlantic was hanging in the balance.

Jamieson's arrival at the Admiralty coincided with an apparent marked increase in the severity of night attacks on convoys. It was his task as a member of the Admiralty's Anti-Submarine Warfare Division to work on the analysis of U-boat tactics. What was Dönitz doing, the Admiralty wanted to know; where would the U-boats strike next? Jamieson recalls: 'I went to have a chat with the survivors...there was some quite interesting information we could build up.' The ASW Division used this intelligence to produce and distribute a bulletin to all escort ships; 'to help', in Jamieson's words, 'in their future meetings in the Atlantic'. One attack in particular struck ASW staff as different and altogether alarming. On the night of 21 September fast convoy HX 72 consisting of forty-one merchant ships was attacked and eleven were sunk. The commodore of the convoy was sure that at least two submarines had operated against HX 72; the senior officer of the escorts agreed. There was a suggestion that U-boats were beginning to coordinate their attacks. It was altogether unexpected and some influential voices in Naval Intelligence were sceptical.[1] Slow convoy SC 7 was to put the matter beyond doubt.

The motley collection of ships that would form SC 7 began to assemble at the Canadian port of Sydney in the first week of October.[2] This unprepossessing little town on Cape Breton Island was really no more than a coaling station, a place where ships could load up with fuel for the journey home. It had been designated as the start point for homebound slow convoys only two months earlier. Slow convoy SC 7 was not expected to make more than 8 knots; many of its thirty-five ships would struggle to manage that. Half of them had been built during or before World War I; the oldest, the Norwegian tanker *Thoroy*, was a veteran of forty-seven years' service at sea. The convoy's ships had spent the previous fortnight in ports up and down the Canadian coast loading cargoes of timber, grain, steel, copper and iron ore. Some, like the Tempus Line ships *Beatus* and *Fiscus*, had made the journey up the St Lawrence river to the port of Three Rivers. The *Beatus* had picked up a mixed cargo of steel, timber and aircraft that had been crated for the journey home. The *Fiscus* was altogether unluckier; she was loaded with 5-ton steel ingots.

Frank Holding recalls how apprehensive *Fiscus*'s crew were about the two weeks they would spend at sea with this cargo: 'If you had that sort of cargo you had no chance. Once a ship like that got hit it went down like a stone.' Holding counted himself lucky to be aboard the *Beatus*: 'She was a dirty old tramp steamer – she had the smell of sugar and oil on her. The cooks were Chinese and the engine room crowd were Indians. So there was only me and one other Liverpool lad.'

As Assistant Steward, Holding had a slightly easier life: 'We had some privileges over the deck crowd and the engine crowd. They lived in the forecastle, maybe eight or ten bunks in one room, but I was in a room with just the galley boy'. Holding was just nineteen but three years in the merchant service had already taken him round the world. It was still something of an adventure; the U-boat threat had just given it an extra edge: 'We were always told that if we were sunk by a U-boat no one would be taken prisoner – only the captain or the engineer. The rest would be left to drown. We feared machine gunning, and people used to talk about how they'd known someone who'd been adrift for many days in a lifeboat, but we never dwelt on this. On the *Beatus* we joked with the second officer. We used to say, "We're gonna get it this trip, you know!" That was just young fellas talking, like.'

While *Beatus* was loading at Three Rivers, Holding was visited by two old friends: 'They came on the ship looking for me, the lad from next door, Billy Howard, and the lad from opposite, his brother Eddie. I said, "I'm skint, so I can't go ashore for a bevy – and besides, we're sailing in the morning."' Holding could at least look forward to a night 'on the ale' in Liverpool; the Howard brothers were with the *Creekirk*, loaded with iron ore for the crossing.

By 5 October SC 7 was assembled and ready for sea. That morning its skippers were summoned ashore for the customary convoy conference. They were introduced to retired Admiral Lachlan MacKinnon, the Commodore of the Convoy; a man, they were told, who was yet to lose a ship. There was also the usual list of 'do's and don'ts': strict attention was to be paid to station keeping; no lights were to be shown at night; ships were to be careful not to make too much smoke; and the convoy was not to leave a trail of rubbish in its wake. Slow convoys were developing a bad name. Royal Navy officers grumbled that some of the ships in these convoys were commanded by distinctly bloody-minded skippers. There were always a good number of 'stragglers' and 'rompers', who lagged behind or raced ahead; once a ship had left the convoy's shield it was on its own. There were some skippers who considered that a safer place to be; what sort of protection could the Royal Navy offer? For the first eleven days of its journey SC 7 would be escorted by just one small sloop; only as it approached home could it expect additional protection. A third of the merchant ships, the *Beatus* among them, had been fitted with a 4-inch gun aft, but no one expected it to be of much use.

At a little after midday the first ships began to steam out of Sydney harbour. It would take most of the afternoon for the convoy to form up; there were to be nine columns with three or four ships in each. The commodore's ship, the *Assyrian,* was at the head of the centre column so the rest of the convoy could see his signals. From time to time he would order the convoy to make a defensive zigzag to either starboard or port. The order would usually be given via signal flags or a morse lamp; wireless transmissions might attract unwanted attention. A change of course required this unwieldy mass of ships to act as one and to do so promptly; there was only 600 yards or so between the ships in each column. The commodore needed judgement and luck in equal measure.

For merchant seamen used to an empty horizon, travelling in convoy was a slow and frustrating business. 'Six knots – you could walk faster,' Frank Holding recalls. 'You just looked forward to getting through each night and getting into port.'

After four days' orderly sailing SC 7 ran into bad weather; almost at once ships began to drop out. For a time the largest of the British ships, the 6000-ton *Empire Miniver,* was among these stragglers. 'I experienced some trouble with the turbines,' Captain Robert Smith was to write in his report to the Admiralty.[3] 'It was about 17.25 and very dark and as we dropped astern we soon lost sight of the convoy.' But the *Empire Miniver* was faster than most of the other ships and within hours Smith was able to make contact once again. The job was made all the easier by one of the ships at the tail of the convoy, as Smith explained: 'The third mate and I were on the bridge, and we were peering into the darkness when to our amazement we saw a white light on our port bow. I remarked to the third mate that some fool was being very careless. When we drew up to it we found that it was a Greek steamer which had been responsible for the light; it had been visible to us at an approximate distance of 6 miles.'

So much for the warnings made at the convoy conference.

On the other side of the Atlantic His Majesty's ships *Bluebell* and *Fowey* were preparing to leave Liverpool for the ocean rendezvous with SC 7. The *Fowey* was a sloop with a crew of regulars and her companion was a corvette, one of the Royal Navy's 'off-the-shelf' escorts; her odds-and-sods crew of regulars and reservists had joined her just two months earlier, almost as the last rivets were being hammered into the ship. Amongst them was a 22-year-old regular, Don Kirton; he remembers the crew's shock when they saw *Bluebell* for the first time: 'Some of the old salts with about five or six years' experience thought, "Well, what are we going to do in that?" She seemed more like a rowing boat than a fighting ship. The funnel was the biggest part about her. She had a very old 4-inch gun. It was a 1914 weapon and I thought, Well, we won't go very far with that.'

There were some further unpleasant surprises. On her first journey the ship ran into rough weather. 'I would say 75 per cent of the crew were really seasick,' Kirton recalls. The constant pitch and roll made life extremely uncomfortable. Kirton ran a particular risk. The navy had refused to accept him because his teeth were bad; so keen was he to join that he had had the lot removed, and this was to cause him problems.

I was at action stations on my depth charge thrower with my two helpers and it was very rough – she was rolling like mad. I had developed a cough, and suddenly I coughed my top teeth out on to the deck where all the water was swilling backwards and for-wards. My two assistants were laughing their heads off. There were my teeth, the only thing I'd got to eat with, going backwards and forwards in the scuppers. I was frightened they would be lost into the sea. I was watching them but I couldn't leave my station – I was waiting for instructions from the bridge to either fire the damn thing or stand down. At last the order came from the bridge, 'Action eased', and I got my teeth back.

The awkward motion of the ship was compounded by the constant trickle of water that seeped into the main seamen's mess for'ard. Conditions here were only marginally better than those on a U-boat. Kirton recalls: 'There was one so-called watertight door, which was opened and shut all the time. If there was a heavy sea running it would come in over the top. But you could never be sure where it came from. It was always damp; your clothes had mildew on them.' As Leading Supply Assistant, Kirton enjoyed the comparative luxury of a bunk in the naval store; most of the 80-strong crew squeezed into hammocks in the mess.

Hot meals were not helped by the uncertain journey from the galley across the wet, rolling deck to the seamen's mess. The crew's diet was occasionally supplemented by a fishing expedition; a well-placed depth charge could land the ship a shoal. The crew stood by with nets, buckets, bins, anything that came to hand. There was also the daily rum ration; chief petty officers at eleven o'clock, the rest at midday. The seaman with the barrel on *Bluebell* was Kirton; the challenge was to ensure that the ration got through no matter the weather: 'You'd walk along the port side hanging on to the lines that had been rigged up, and then you'd get two people to hold down the rum barrel. It had "The King, God Bless Him" on the sides. You mixed it two water to one rum; then you'd issue that to the messes.'

The captain of *Bluebell*, Lieutenant Commander Robert Sherwood, was, like most of the crew, a 'hostilities only' naval man. Although only thirty-three he had already spent fifteen years at sea, rising through the ranks of the merchant marine to command his own ship. Sherwood impressed those who met him with his confidence and quick wit. On the journey out to meet SC 7 he had slung a hammock on *Bluebell*'s bridge; he was to be available to the watch at all times. Sherwood's three officers were less experienced. The first officer was an east coast yachtsman, both the sub-lieutenants young Canadian volunteers; James Keachie was one of them: 'We were both very green. I relied a great deal on the coxswain of the *Bluebell*, who fortunately took a shine to me.' Keachie was a square-jawed, determined young barrister-to-be, who within weeks of the outbreak of war had volunteered for the Royal Canadian Navy. His initial training had not equipped him well for the role he was asked to play on *Bluebell*: 'There was no training at all about how to counter submarines on the surface or in the convoys,' he recalls. 'It was all about tactics related to the ASDIC.'

Fowey and *Bluebell* were to rendezvous with SC 7 northwest of Rockall Bank, some 300 nautical miles from home. The convoy's ships were already on their mettle. In the early hours of 16 October a distress signal had been picked up from a straggler, the freighter *Trevisa*; 'SSS', a submarine attack. There was nothing the convoy's lone escort, HMS *Scarborough*, could do; cargo and crew were lost. Spirits were raised that afternoon when *Fowey* and *Bluebell* were spotted on the horizon. Don Kirton remembers steaming towards SC 7: 'When you looked out over the ships it was just like a floating city. They seemed to be one block moving all at once, as if they were joined together. It was a marvellous sight.'

No one was happier to see the newcomers than the captain of *Scarborough*; yet it was still a feeble escort for a convoy that stretched across almost 6 miles of sea. *Scarborough* took up a position at the head of the convoy, *Fowey* to starboard, *Bluebell* to port. There was no plan for co-ordinated action in the event of an attack.

Late that night the watch on the bridge of *U-48* spotted what appeared to be the moonlit silhouette of a ship. As the U-boat closed it became clear that the convoy was a large one, the escort weak. The good news was dispatched to Lorient: 'Homebound convoy travelling at 7 knots, currently at map reference AL3388.' This sighting was immediately forwarded to a group of five U-boats that Dönitz had placed east and north of Rockall Bank. Their orders were simple: find, close, attack.

Instead of waiting for the rest of the pack, *U-48*'s commander Heinrich Bleichrodt chose to attack on the port side; it put the convoy's largest target directly in his line of fire. The first of *U-48*'s torpedoes tore through the side of the 9500-ton tanker *Languedoc*, sending a column of fire and water into the night sky. Two minutes later a second struck the freighter *Scoresby*. James Keachie of *Bluebell* recalls: 'The first indication of the U-boat's presence was when the ship was hit.' Those below decks did not need to wait for the order to 'Action Stations'. Don Kirton remembers: 'You heard the clang of the torpedo striking the hull of the vessel and exploding. It woke the ship's company up – the sound carries very clearly underwater. You knew that your little war had started somewhere very close by.'

By the time *Bluebell* had steamed up from the stern of the convoy the *Scoresby* had gone; her grave was marked by the hundreds of heavy pit props that had been stacked high on her deck. Keachie recalls: 'The amount of debris was just unbelievable. This lumber was just everywhere, and you had to be careful you didn't get any in the propeller. The captain didn't like steaming through it but you had to, to get close enough to the survivors.'

The *Bluebell* joined the other two escorts in a long but fruitless ASDIC search; *U-48* had slipped back into the night. The *Languedoc* was still afloat, settling slowly on an even keel. She might have remained in that state for many hours, a hazard to other shipping. Kirton remembers: 'She was a most beautiful ship, spotless white painted decks, and there she was totally crippled. We ran alongside and five or six of the crew went aboard and got the code-books and brought them back and that was it. You thought to yourself, "Well, what an absolute waste. Surely she can be towed, or something like that." But who was going to tow her? It was just war, full stop. War and waste – and what a waste it was. Terrible.' The *Bluebell* sank her; it was the only depth charge attack she had been able to make.

A good deal of the morning of the 17th was spent rounding up the convoy. Whilst a number of ships had dropped out of formation and bolted, others were completely unaware that there had been an attack. Frank Holding of the *Beatus* remembers one of the escorts visiting the ship that day: 'They came over with a loud hailer: "Anyone heard any explosions in this column?" But the convoy was spread out over maybe 18 miles; we hadn't heard anything. We knew then of course that we were getting into the war zone, so everyone was alert.'

The convoy was to enjoy a brief respite. Bleichrodt followed SC7 as he was expected to do, but was forced to dive by a Sunderland flying boat and contact with the convoy was lost. Tempted by the Sunderland's report, HMS *Scarborough* decided to chase *U-48*. In choosing this course her captain broke one of the golden rules of anti-submarine warfare: never leave the convoy. The little sloop spent many empty hours sweeping the Atlantic for the U-boat; it need only have stayed with SC 7. In the early hours of the 18th the two remaining escorts were joined by the sloop HMS *Leith* and the corvette HMS *Heartsease*, but these welcome reinforcements were not the only vessels to find SC7. Within minutes of their arrival there was an explosion at the rear of the port column: the steamer *Carsbreck* had been hit. Contact with the convoy had been re-established by *U-38*. Dönitz could once again be sure of its position. He wasted no time in informing the waiting group of five; these boats were to form the 'wolf pack'. Among them were the three leading aces; Endraß (*U-46*), Schepke (*U-100*) and Kretschmer (*U-99*). Kretschmer's log captures something of the pursuit:

> *17.45 U-101* is 2 to 3 miles further north. Gives the morse signal by light: 'Enemy sighted to port'.
>
> *17.49* A warship comes into view at 030, steering east. Shortly after this smoke plumes appear to the left of her. Finally the convoy. While hauling ahead to attack we sight a steamship in the southeast.
>
> *19.28* Submerge for attack.
>
> *19.50* Surface, as the ship is making off slowly to the east. Haul further ahead: at 20.00 pass within a few hundred metres of a U-boat on the surface, apparently *U-101* again.[4]

The conditions were almost perfect for the pack. Frank Holding of the *Beatus* remembers: 'That night I went to look over the side. There was a big white patch going from the side of the ship right out to the horizon.

Moon on water. And you're thinking, "Someone's out there." You took your lifejacket round with you all the time, on deck or wherever you were going.'

The first to sink a ship that night was Endraß in *U-46*. A mighty explosion on the port bow of the convoy signalled the end of the Swedish *Convallaria*. The escort *Leith*, at the head of the convoy, chased back to the port side and began an ASDIC sweep of ocean that would take her 10 miles adrift. By the time she returned, Endraß had claimed two more ships.

The *Beatus*, too, was on the port side. Frank Holding heard the explosion that sank the *Convallaria*:

I went out on deck; there was a young fella there, he was about sixteen, and he says to me, 'I reported a torpedo across the bow to the bridge. I saw it going across.' I went back in my cabin and I said to my mates, 'We'd better keep ourselves handy here.' The next thing I heard was this explosion and a sound like breaking glass from down near the engine room. The ship stood still. When I went to the boat deck one of the lifeboats was already in the water, full of water. Some of the Indians had let it go – it was no good to us. That left us with one lifeboat. We knew we were sinking. While we were standing on the deck by the funnel, all this wet ash came up over us – the sea must have got into the engine room where the fires were. The skipper told us to get the boat down and get into it. One of the firemen wouldn't come up – he didn't want to leave the ship – and the captain and the gun layer went down to find him. He was an Indian. I don't know whether his religion had anything to do with it, but they had to force him up. In fact we were in the boat while those two were still aboard trying to fetch him. We wanted to get away because anything could have happened – we could have got another torpedo. We were lucky.

We pulled away, and I had a mouth organ and I started playing, you know. I was enjoying this. It's a funny thing, isn't it? It was something like 'Give me land, lots of land where the buffalo roams'. Didn't get plenty of land – I got plenty of water. But then the second engineer said, 'Knock that off, will you? There's a U-boat on the surface.' I was short-sighted, but I could hear the engines racing and I could hear them shouting out in German. They were excited. They were in the chase, these U-boat men.

The last moments of the *Beatus* had been witnessed by the next ship in the column, the Dutch freighter *Boekolo*. Her master decided to stop the ship and pick up survivors. It was a generous act but a costly one. The crew had just managed to lift the *Beatus*'s cabin boy from the lifeboat when a shudder ran down the ship. A great sheet of flame was thrown upwards; timber rained back down on to the deck. Water rushed in through a hole in the number 4 hold and *Boekolo* began to list to port.

The free-for-all had begun. The first to go on the starboard side of the convoy was the old British freighter *Creekirk*. She sank like a stone, pulled down by her cargo of iron ore. The crew went with her. The *Creekirk* was *U-99*'s first victim that night. The whole sad spectacle was watched by the nearby *Empire Miniver*, warning enough for Captain Robert Smith; his holds were packed with 10,000 tons of iron ore and steel. 'I thought it best to put on full speed and get out of the mess,' he later wrote in his report to the Admiralty.

Smith was pushing forward at 9 ½ knots and was almost clear: 'I was on the bridge with the chief officer, who casually strolled over to the port side and looked over. The next second he shouted, "Watch out for the bump!" There was a dull thud, a big flash and a cloud of bluish smoke. Then everything went black; all the lights went out, the engines stopped, the ship shuddered, lay still and lost her way.... It blew all the hatches off and the pig iron was blown into the air just like shrapnel.' The torpedo had found the Empire Miniver's engine room; it sealed her fate. There was time to take to the lifeboats; Smith watched her last moments from a safe distance: 'About twenty-five minutes after the attack there was a terrific explosion amidships. She broke her back and sank immediately.'

She was Kretschmer's second success; *U-99* had slipped between the columns and was now in the heart of the convoy. The next to go was the Greek freighter *Niritos* with her cargo of sulphur: then the *Fiscus* and the *Thalia*; their epitaphs were a sparsely worded entry in Kretschmer's War Diary:

23.55 Fire a bow torpedo at a large freighter of some 6000 tons [*Niritos*] at a range of 750 metres. Hit abreast foremast. Immediately after the torpedo explosion, there is another explosion with a high column of flame from the bow to the bridge. The smoke rises some 200 metres. Bow apparently shattered. Ship continues to burn with a green flame.

19 October: 00.15 Torpedoes from the other boats are constantly heard exploding. The destroyers do not know how to help and occupy themselves by constantly firing starshells, which are of little effect in the bright moonlight. I now start to attack the convoy from astern.

01.38 Fire bow torpedoes at large heavily laden freighter of about 6000 tons [*Fiscus*], range 945 metres. Hit abreast foremast. The explosion sinks the ship.

01.55 Fire bow torpedo at the next large vessel of some 7000 tons [*Thalia*]. Range 975 metres. Hit abreast foremast. Ship sinks within 40 seconds.

'We never had the desire to kill,' *U-99*'s Second Watch officer Horst Elfe remembers. 'We did not think of our task as being one of killing people, just of sinking ships.' 'Rescue no one and take no one with you,' Dönitz had told his crews. 'Care only for your own boat and strive to achieve the next success as soon as possible. We must be hard in this war.' Kretschmer had carried out his orders with the necessary ruthlessness.

On the commodore's ship, the *Assyrian*, concern for the safety of the convoy had been replaced by a more immediate danger. Her captain, Reginald Kearon, wrote in his report: 'At about 21.00 I noticed a submarine on my port bow, 200 yards distant. I altered course to intercept and ram him but the submarine took evasive action.... I chased the enemy for seven minutes. We could plainly see his periscope and the track it made...at the end of seven minutes we could see the conning tower rise out of the water and smelt the exhaust fumes when he started up his diesel engines. Once he had surfaced he rapidly drew away.'

Shortly after that the *Assyrian* managed to avoid a parting shot, the third torpedo that had been fired at her that night. The fourth struck the ship on the starboard side. 'The top sides of the ship were opened up right to the boat deck,' Captain Kearon reported later. As the crew struggled to launch *Assyrian*'s boats an explosion on a nearby freighter swept a hail of pit props across the ship, badly injuring a number of the crew. Amongst those able to take to a raft was Admiral MacKinnon, the commodore who had 'never lost a ship', but the captain and three crew men were still on board as *Assyrian* sank. 'She went end on, practically upright,' Kearon reported. 'I was sucked down and after coming to the surface several times I found myself beside a spar....I noticed my Chief Officer on the other end – he edged along to me.' According to Kearon, a group of survivors began to gather round the spar: 'We discussed the chances of being picked up. I thought there was not much chance but he [the chief officer] replied that he was an elderly man and might go at any time, whilst I, being younger, would last longer. Two other men swam to us. One lay over the end of the spar and the other one, Naval Signalman Hall, came paddling along on a buoy; he said, "If it were not so cold it would be like the Serpentine."' Kearon and his men spent an hour in the icy Atlantic before they were spotted by HMS *Leith*; 'One man left the spar, crying for help; he swam 300 yards to the escort, was pulled on board, but then collapsed and died almost immediately,' Kearon told the Admiralty. By the time *Leith* was ready to fish the remaining survivors out, the chief officer too was dead.

What of the escorts, the convoy's defensive screen? *Heartsease* had been sent to shepherd a ship that was trailing in the wake of the convoy. This had left just three escorts to patrol a front 5 miles wide.

The personal touch: Admiral Karl Dönitz, the leader of the U-boat Arm, welcomes a crew home in November 1939 with medals and a warm handshake.

Above: In 1939, half the
U-boat fleet was made up of
Type II 'ducks' like this one.
The 'duck' only had the
fuel capacity for a limited
combat role in the North Sea.

Right: 'The Bull of Scapa'. The
Commander of U-47, Günther
Prien was accorded a hero's
reception in Berlin after
sinking HMS *Royal Oak* in
October 1939.

Above: One of the survivors of the passenger liner *Athenia*, which was sunk just hours after the declaration of war on 3 September 1939.

Left: Hitler personally decorated Prien with the Knight's Cross of the Iron Cross, for sinking the battleship HMS *Royal Oak*; it was 'a unique triumph', he told the crew of U-47, that had strengthened the German people's faith in victory.

Above: The Royal Navy at its mightiest: the 2nd Battle Squadron seen from beneath the 15-inch guns of HMS *Royal Oak*.

Below: The families of those serving on HMS *Royal Oak* hunt for names on the list of survivors; 833 officers and men were lost with the ship.

Above: The crew of the torpedoed merchant ship *Jersey City* are transferred to the destroyer HMS *Walker*. The *Jersey City* was sunk in convoy on 31 July 1940 by U-99.

Left: The destroyers HMS *Jupiter* and HMS *Javelin* astern of the destroyer HMS *Kelvin*, on escort duty with a convoy in the Atlantic, September 1940.

Right: Mrs Sarah Manson and her four grandchildren in the wreckage of their Liverpool home; nearly 4,000 people lost their lives in the Merseyside blitz of May 1941.

Below: As first Lord of the Admiralty and then Prime Minister, Winston Churchill spoke to the country of his confidence that the 'U-boat peril' would be defeated, but he would later admit that nothing frightened him more during the war.

Above: On the eve of departure, the captains of merchant ships were required to attend a conference ashore, like this one in Liverpool where the Convoy Commodore briefed them on the importance of convoy discipline.

Left: A woman leaves a shop in London, in February 1941, clutching a precious egg. The ration book became the key to survival for nearly every household in the country.

Bottom left: A series of brilliant campaigns by the Ministry of Food urged housewives to fight the battle against the U-boats on the 'Kitchen Front'; nothing was to be wasted – food supplies took up room on ships.

British ships were not accorded a warm welcome in every port they stopped at, and seamen were constantly urged to be on their guard.

TITTLE TATTLE
LOST THE BATTLE

After the attack on the *Carsbreck* on the afternoon of the 18th a further attack had been anticipated; its ferocity had not. One of the hapless three was HMS *Bluebell*. Don Kirton, at his action station on Depth Charge Thrower 2, witnessed the whole terrible pantomime: 'I watched this ship burst into one mass of flame – I should think the flames were 100 feet high. A frightening sight. We moved up slowly towards where she was burning and we could hear the cries from the ship's company, which had jumped over the side. They were in an absolutely shocking state. They swam towards *Bluebell* blowing the whistles on their lifejackets.'

The escorts swept back and forth across the convoy that night in search of a target to attack. *Bluebell*'s' sub-lieutenant, James Keachie, admits: 'It was chaotic. I remember feeling so helpless when we saw these ships being sunk. What do we do? Ships were sunk from different places in the convoy and we would scurry around and try to find the submarine, but the ASDIC was useless.'

As the carnage rolled on into the small hours of a new day it became clear that the assault was being carried out by a number of U-boats operating on the surface. *Leith* surprised one and was able to gain an ASDIC contact as it dived; but the contact yielded nothing. In their hunt for targets the escorts made liberal use of starshells to illuminate the surrounding sea; which, as Kretschmer had observed, proved almost pointless. 'We didn't know what area to light up, and submarines were very difficult to see from any distance anyway, and so they had it all their own way,' Keachie remembers.

If *Bluebell* had been fortunate enough to meet the enemy, she might not have been able to do more than shout at him. The new corvettes were no faster than a U-boat on the surface; it would have required a lucky shot from an ancient 4-inch. Keachie was *Bluebell*'s gunnery officer: 'You couldn't get range on them at night and you couldn't lower the gun down far enough for it to be effective.'

The frustration of those on board the escorts was sharpened by the knowledge that they too were offering themselves as targets. 'You were very eager to get up the steps and out into the open' Kirton recalls.

'Yes, I guess I have to admit I was scared during the time that we were undergoing attacks,' says James Keachie. 'But you become fatalistic. I guess I never really thought I was going to die.'

As the night dragged on, *Bluebell* abandoned her hunt for targets and began to trawl the wake of the convoy for survivors. It was a hazardous business. The ship needed to slow almost to a stop to haul survivors on board; she presented a tempting target. It was impossible to be sure where ships had gone and from which there were survivors; for all that, *Bluebell* managed to find them. Don Kirton helped to fish the survivors out: 'You could see the red bulbs on their lifejackets showing in the water. We put scrambling nets over the side. Two of the lads would get over to help them up and over the gunwales, and there were eager hands to take them forward where there was shelter. Many of them were violently sick from the fuel oil that they'd swallowed. Some were completely naked.' *Bluebell* was soon heaving with wet, frozen seamen: Lascars from India, Jamaicans, Frenchmen, Norwegian and Swedes. Every square inch of deck was filled, every available blanket and piece of clothing used.

By dawn the wolf pack had gone, the last of its victims claimed by the gunfire of *U-123*. The action underscored the freedom with which the U-boats were able to operate on the surface. There were times during the night when the greatest threat to their safety was posed by fellow pack members. In the dark chaos of the convoy there was always the chance that a rogue torpedo would miss a ship but find another U-boat. Enough, though, had found their intended targets; some eighteen ships had been sunk and two more badly damaged – a total of almost 80,000 tons. The pack had inflicted a terrible blow.

In the *Beatus*'s lifeboat, Frank Holding had listened all night to the distant explosions; would there, he wondered, be anything left of slow convoy SC 7 come the dawn? His lifeboat was afloat and that was something. In all other respects the boat had proved a disappointment; it was not well equipped. 'There was supposed to be a certain amount of alcohol, a compass, a sea anchor, all these things, but this was a tramp and no one had bothered,' Holding recalls. When would rescue come? Holding remembers: 'It was daylight, but the sea had started to get rough, so the first we knew was when we heard someone shouting to us over a loud hailer. He said, "I can't stop – there's a U-boat in the area. I've got nets over the side. When I come alongside you'll have to jump for it and scramble aboard." That's what we did. It turned out that it was *Bluebell*. We were the last she picked up.'

The survivors on *Bluebell*'s decks now numbered more than two hundred; almost four times that of the ship's company. There was no convoy to rejoin, no ship that could share this human cargo. *Bluebell* was still an uncomfortable day and a half from home. As if to add insult to injury, the weather worsened; the survivors were unused to the restless motion of a corvette and suffered badly from seasickness. Their ordeal ended on the evening of the 20th when *Bluebell* tied up alongside Gourock pier on the Clyde. Frank Holding remembers:

They took us to some hall and started having a roll call of the ships sunk – any survivors from this ship or that ship? And then it came down to *Creekirk*. I went up to ask if anyone had come forward and they said, 'No, they've all gone with the ship.' So I knew that two of my friends and neighbours were dead, Eddie and Billy Howard; I knew that.

They put me on the train and I arrived at Exchange Station in the heart of Liverpool at about eleven o'clock. There was an air raid on and when I got to my parents house the windows were all out. Someone said, 'Are you looking for your mother? She's under the church.' They had a shelter there for the people from the area. I went there, put my arms round my mother and I broke down. I couldn't tell her about Eddie and Billy till the next day. I said to her, 'Whatever you do, mam, don't tell their people. Leave it till they get a telegram.' So my mother knew that they weren't coming back. Their mother didn't know where they were, but a fortnight or so later they got the telegram from the War Office saying they were lost at sea.

Within a week Holding had found a new ship. There were ships aplenty down at Liverpool docks ready to take on an experienced seaman prepared to go back into the Atlantic. He was nevertheless careful in his choice; she was a troopship, faster than *Beatus* with 16 knots or more; she was better armed and would be properly escorted. Merchant seamen belonged to a 'reserved occupation'; they were obliged to return to the sea, but Holding needed the money too. The moment *Beatus* slipped under, his wages had stopped. Time spent in the lifeboat was time unpaid. In his record of employment it stated simply that he had been 'Discharged at Sea'. It was no longer an adventure for Holding; on his new ship he made a point of practising the route he would take to the lifeboats if the ship was torpedoed at night.

After disgorging her survivors, *Bluebell* returned to the Albert Dock in Liverpool for a few days' leave; the chance to forget. The crew were hell-bent on a good time: a drink or two at the Roebuck, then dancing and girls at the Grafton Ball Rooms; there was no need to pay, the word *Bluebell* was a pass at the door. Her captain had urged Sub-Lieutenant Keachie to write to the Admiralty: 'I learned that if you pick up survivors you got something like five shillings a day for them. And so I put in a requisition for two hundred survivors and we got back a cheque, which we put into the wardroom fund; we never had to buy a drink in the wardroom from then on. It was such a windfall.'

The Admiralty had not got its money's worth from the escorts; the screen offered to slow convoy SC 7 was woefully inadequate. There were, of course, too few of His Majesty's ships, but that did not tell the full story. Before *Bluebell* had landed a single survivor, Dönitz's wolves had attacked again; this time the convoy was accompanied by a small fleet of escorts. The convoy was HX 79 from the Canadian port of Halifax; it was faster and bigger, with forty-nine merchant ships and twelve escorts. A Dutch submarine was stationed at its heart to provide additional protection.

It was the 'Bull of Scapa', Günther Prien in *U-47*, who found the convoy. He had left Lorient too late to join the free-for-all on SC 7; his boat still carried the full fourteen torpedoes. On receipt of Prien's sighting report, Dönitz directed four of the boats that had attacked SC 7 to join *U-47* in a new pack. Just seventeen hours after claiming their last victim from SC 7 'the wolves' attacked again sinking twelve ships. The night had once more been lit by a bright hunter's moon, but at no point did the escorts detect a U-boat on the surface. The convoy's 'formidable' escort screen proved to be nothing of the sort. It was the same story; no attempt was made to coordinate the defence of the convoy; no one expected U-boats to attack on the surface at night in such strength.

Even after the disastrous four-day assault on SC 7 and HX 79, the Admiralty did not understand the full extent of the challenge. The Anti-Submarine Warfare Division could find 'no conclusive evidence' of U-boats attacking from inside the convoy. It did recognize, however, that something needed to be done about the night surface threat; 'ships must be given some means, other than the human eye, of detecting the approach of the enemy and of locating him'.[6] The answer was radar. It was still under development, but some of the navy's destroyers had already been fitted with primitive sets and early results were promising. An Airborne Radar was being developed for Coastal Command planes, though it was yet to prove itself of any use in hunting a U-boat at night. Work was also taking place on a shipborne direction finder that would be capable of exploiting the large volume of radio transmissions which U-boats made to their headquarters. A network of shore-based D/F stations had already demonstrated its worth in pinpointing the enemy close to Britain's coast.

In the meantime, the Admiralty was obliged to count the terrible cost of its night blindness. The final tally for October was 442,985 tons sunk, 352,407 by U-boats; some 63 ships, of which almost a third had been sunk in the attack on SC 7. The loss of the hulls was bad enough, for they represented a substantial slice of the merchant fleet, but with them went thousands of tons of food, timber, steel and ore, essential supplies for Britain's war effort. There was also the human cost; hardship at home, lives lost at sea. A veil of secrecy was drawn over much of this misery. The survivors were warned not to speak of their ordeal, and reporters eager for the story were told, 'What's the point? It will only be killed by the censor.'[7]

There were places, however, where it was impossible to ignore the price paid. The ships sunk during this U-boat 'happy time' were concentrated off the northwest coast of Ireland; it was here the Atlantic tide brought the flotsam of the convoy war. In the autumn of 1940 Bill Coffey, a tough, wiry, 21 year-old medical orderly in the Irish army, lived just a stone's throw away from this rocky shoreline. He remembers:

> The first body we found was away out on the rocks. There was a shirt on it, and a wound on the forehead about the size of a penny. We had half a dozen soldiers with us. A big, hefty fellow went down about 200 feet and tied a rope to the body, and we pulled it up and took it down to the crossroads, to Dorothy's Hotel.

Until then the war had seemed a distant concern for Coffey; 'I was shocked. All of us were sad – it wasn't something that had happened before.' There were to be more bodies. Coffey remembers one in particular:

> It was badly decomposed. And it was under a very steep hill and we had to climb up it. In order to get him on to the stretcher we tried to make a handy parcel out of him. We tried to pull his legs up a wee bit, but as soon as we pulled the legs up the stomach collapsed, burst – there was a terrible smell. Oh, it made me throw up. The smell was in our noses for months after that.

In Germany there was rejoicing. 'A colossal success,' Dönitz wrote in his War Diary; 'the operations justify the principles on which U-boat tactics and training have been developed since 1935 i.e. that U-boats in packs should attack the convoys.'[8] The dockside band played louder than ever, the U-boats returned with more tonnage bunting than ever, and Dönitz distributed even more decorations. Thousands of feet of film were shot by cameramen from Berlin; there the combined success of SC 7 and HX 79 was talked of as the 'Night of the Long Knives'.

Dönitz's own analysis credited the boats with almost a third more ships than were actually sunk, but for all that it was a staggeringly successful month. For Dönitz, the most important measure of success was what he called the 'effective U-boat quotient'; the average tonnage sunk per U-boat per day for all the boats at sea. In June that figure had been 541 tons; it had risen inexorably. By October it stood at 920. It would never be as high again.

On average there were only six U-boats operating against Britain's lifeline at any one time – about three hundred men. 'The decisive factor', Dönitz wrote later, 'will always be the ability of the captains and their crews.'[9] This was the hey-day of the Freikorps Dönitz, the small band of men he had personally trained before the war. They were now among the Reich's most celebrated heroes and the German public was hungry for news of the 'grey wolves', especially of Prien, Schepke and the 'tonnage king', Kretschmer. In the six months from mid-May to 2 December 1940 U-boats sank nearly three hundred ships totalling more than 1.6 million tons. Just eighteen U-boat commanders were responsible for most of this; five alone accounted for a third of the total.[10]

'Out there in the Atlantic a handful of U-boats was being called upon to fight a battle that would decide the issue of the war,' Dönitz later wrote.[11] This remarkable effort was nevertheless a long way from the three hundred boats he had predicted would be necessary for victory at sea. Morale was high, but the burden on a small band of men was immense. The trickle of new boats, about six a month, was projected to increase rapidly in 1941; this was the time to capitalize on Britain's weakness. But Hitler's priorities were now fixed on the planned assault on the Soviet Union, and the help needed by his Italian ally needed shoring up in North Africa and Greece.

Just a week after returning from his assault on SC 7, Kretschmer was at sea again. The hunting was still good; *U-99* sank two large merchant cruisers, the 18,700-ton *Laurentic* and the 11,300-ton *Patroclus*.

It brought his tally to 32 ships sunk, some 182,032 tons, and confirmed his status as the U-boat arm's leading ace. The Führer wanted to meet Kretschmer and decorate him in person. Over lunch at the Reichs Chancellery Hitler asked his guest how he could help the U-boats. With typical directness Kretschmer told him; give us the air reconnaissance we need to find the convoys, and above all boats, more boats.[12]

CHAPTER FIVE

MORTAL DANGER

THE SHADOW OF THE LOSSES in the Atlantic was to hang over the Admiralty and those who shared its knowledge throughout the winter of 1940–1. 'One understands the diver deep below the surface of the sea, dependent from minute to minute upon his air-pipe,' Churchill was to write after the war. 'What would he feel if he could see a growing shoal of sharks biting at it? All the more when there was no possibility of his being hauled to the surface!'[1] By how much could 'the U-boat peril' reduce our imports and shipping, Churchill asked his advisers. 'Would it reach the point where our life would be destroyed?'[2]

A steady stream of questions flowed from Number 10, down Whitehall and on to the desk of Professor Frederick Lindemann. 'The Prof' was one of Churchill's most important wartime advisers. It was his responsibility, as head of the Prime Minister's Statistical Branch, to monitor key trends in the war economy.

Every Friday, a parcel of charts and minutes was prepared for the Prime Minister to take to his official country residence, Chequers, and Lindemann would often be among the weekend guests. The topics included ships sunk and ships built, manpower needs, armaments output, food production and, of course, the latest import figures.

One of the economists responsible for its compilation was a bright young academic called Donald MacDougall. 'Knowledge is power,' he was told on his first day; the Prime Minister was to be kept well informed. Churchill was to spend hours poring over the branch's weekly presentation; by the winter of 1940-1 it had become a sobering ritual.[3] MacDougall remembers: 'There was an index I compiled of stocks of imported food and raw materials measured in tons, and that was falling rapidly towards a really dangerous level at which we should have run short.'

The charts demonstrated that before the war total imports of food and raw materials, excluding oil, were close to 60 million tons. By the end of 1940 they had fallen to 45.4 million tons and in the following year to just 30.5 million tons.[4] 'How willingly', Churchill later wrote, 'would I have exchanged a full scale invasion for this shapeless, measureless peril, expressed in charts, curves and statistics!' This 'cold drawing of lines on charts' threatened 'potential strangulation'. MacDougall remembers: 'There was the risk that we would suffer such a dramatic fall in our imports, we would have to cut our eating to impossibly low levels and morale would be very badly affected. Further reductions would also threaten the country's ability to prosecute the war. We wouldn't be able to produce munitions of war or pursue our overseas military operations. It was frightening all the time.'

The 'cold line' charting imports had begun to plunge in the six months following the Fall of France. Fear of the enemy was almost as important as the losses he inflicted. Under the convoy system ships were obliged to spend longer at sea; convoys took time to assemble and moved at the pace of their slowest members. There was also congestion in the ports, with too many ships arriving at once. On 21 January 1941 Churchill received a minute from the Branch pointing out that these delays were making 'the average round voyage last about one and a half times as long as formerly'.[5] A saving of fifteen days in the turnaround times of ships could deliver the country an extra 5 million tons of imports.[6]

The chaos in the ports was exacerbated by the growing ferocity of the Blitz. The Port of London, which before the war had handled a quarter of all Britain's imports, was closed indefinitely. As traffic in the Mersey and the Clyde increased, so too did the Luftwaffe raids. A raid on Liverpool on the night of 28–29 November 1940 was followed by three in the week before Christmas and more in the New Year. From the deck of HMS *Walker* John Adams watched the German bombers roll in over the city: 'A shower of frozen mutton came down as the ship ahead of us in Gladstone Dock was hit with a bomb and blew up all this meat from New Zealand and up into the air. Some ratings even tried to take some away for home.' There were, Adams recalls, some bizarre scenes: 'I can remember the warehouse outside the docks being on fire. The bacon fat was running down the gutter, and several women were running out of the houses with their pots trying to save the fat.'

In the nearby Albert Dock the crew of *Bluebell* was kept busy putting out incendiary bombs that had landed on deck. Leading Supply Assistant Don Kirton was on shore leave in the city when one of these raids began: 'When I got back to *Bluebell* I couldn't get aboard because there were three bombs just by the gangway.' For Kirton the air raid siren was not an entirely unwelcome sound. He was courting his girlfriend under the watchful eye of her mother: 'As soon as the siren went she'd dash round the house, picking up stuff as she went, straight out the door, straight to the shelter, and that was it, full stop – she left the door open and everything. I had a good laugh about that, and it was very convenient for me to get to know my wife-to-be better.'

Sub-Lieutenant James Keachie of the *Bluebell* was sent ashore with members of the crew to help the Home Guard: 'We were given buckets of sand, and when an incendiary bomb fell we would try and extinguish it.' It seemed a pointless task, for uncontrollable fires raged dockside and in the city centre. The Luftwaffe attacked Liverpool on eight successive nights in May 1941, killing nearly four thousand people and seriously injuring another four thousand; ten thousand homes were destroyed and more than 184,000 damaged.[7] Survival and ultimate victory rested on more than just the struggle at sea; this battle was being waged in the country's docks, shipyards, factories and shops. In the same series of raids all but twelve of the 130 deep-sea berths in the port were damaged.

The grim figures pouring into the Statistical Branch's spartan offices suggested that nearly 4 million tons of shipping had been lost to the enemy in 1940. British and Canadian shipyards were quite incapable of keeping pace with this rate of loss; their task was made the harder by a huge backlog of ships awaiting repair. More than 15 per cent of the British merchant fleet, some 2.5 million tons of shipping, was laid up in February 1941.[8] The acquisition of ships from countries lost to the Germans, like Norway and the Netherlands, did something to alleviate this crisis; nevertheless, urgent action was called for.

In an effort to bring order to the western ports, the government appointed new regional port directors with sweeping powers to commandeer local resources and labour. Forty thousand servicemen were to be sent to the shipyards and docks to help clear the backlog. A propaganda campaign was launched to impress on dockers and shipyard workers the vital importance of their work. Great efforts were also made to use the shrinking British merchant fleet more efficiently. Professor Lindemann and his team pressed for large cuts in the amount of iron ore, animal feed, timber, paper and pulp brought across the Atlantic. MacDougall explains:

> We virtually stopped all house building during the war. That saved an awful lot of timber. We went in for substituting bulky imports like iron ore. Before the war we imported a lot of iron ore and out of that we made steel; the iron content of this ore was only about 50 per cent. So if you cut iron ore imports and substituted them with steel imports, you saved about 50 per cent of the shipping.

For all that, the country's long-term shipping needs could only be met by the United States. Churchill was delighted when, on 4 November 1940, the American people returned President Franklin D. Roosevelt to the White House for a third term. Roosevelt had already shown himself a friend to democracy; every week crate after crate was lifted on to the dockside at Liverpool stamped 'From the USA'.

Yet survival and the ability to strike back at Germany required more of everything; and by the end of 1940 Britain was no longer able to pay for it. Roosevelt was prepared to push at the boundaries of American 'neutrality' once again. 'If Britain should go down, all of us in all America would be living at the point of a gun,' he told the nation on 29 December. 'We must produce arms and ships with every energy and resource we can command. We must be the great Arsenal of Democracy.' Britain would be lent the necessary tools to finish the job. 'Lend-Lease' seemed to promise a brighter future. 'The President is determined that we shall win the war together,' Roosevelt's personal emissary told Churchill early in 1941. On this Britain's hopes rested.

Yet the prospect of American jam tomorrow was scant consolation to a public well into its second year of war. The country felt under siege; almost every aspect of day-to-day life was subject to new rules and restrictions. The ration book with its little coloured tokens had become the key to survival. With it was born the food queue, dreary hours spent outside the butcher's and the grocer's.

'I think we expected it. I remember my mother saying, "Now, don't let your soap stocks drop too far because I remember in the First World War soap was difficult,"' Marguerite Patten recalls. When war came the 23-year-old Patten was working for a large electrical company as a home economist; that experience was to be put to good use by the Ministry of Food.

We all realized we were going to get a fair share of the important things, but I think a lot of people had shocks at the amount. We all speedily learnt about the difficulties of trying to manage with one- and twopence worth of meat per person per week. If I had two lamb chops, that would be my meat for the week. My mother was living alone because my brother was at sea and I was in Lincolnshire, so it was harder for her. If you were a big family, somehow rationing seemed to work better. Some people took sugar in their tea and some people didn't, so there was that little bit more.

It began in January 1940 with bacon, butter and sugar; six months later tea and margarine were added to the list; by 1941 next to nothing had escaped rationing. The size of the ration was also steadily reduced; an egg became a rare and much-cherished commodity. Before the war Britain had imported some 22 million tons of food a year, comprising more than half its meat, 87 per cent of its cereals and 85 per cent of its sugar. By November 1940 total food imports were running at less than 12 million tons a year.[9] As imports fell, home-grown production rose to meet the shortfall. Trees were felled and pasture broken by the plough. By 1941 some 4 million more acres of land was under cultivation.[10]

Members of the public were asked to do their bit by growing vegetables: 'Dig for Victory' was to claim gardens, golf courses, parks, school playing fields; in the end nothing was sacred. 'I think that growing food was a very good morale boost: you felt you were playing your part," recalls Marguerite Patten. Growing vegetables did not, however, mean knowing how to cook them. She remembers: 'I was loaned one day to go out with a scientist to a school canteen. 'I shall never forget the cabbage that came up to be tested. There wasn't a shred of vitamin C there. It was the greyest, most dismal, wet cabbage you could imagine. So that, of course, was something we attacked with great fervour: learn to cook vegetables correctly.'

The Ministry of Food launched a series of advertising campaigns aimed at the housewife, the foot soldier of 'the Kitchen Front'. The messages were simple: 'Cut Down on Waste', 'Save Flour', 'Eat More Potatoes'. This was not just the healthy thing to do, but a patriotic duty: 'Remember, Save Flour and Save Ships'. The Ministry established Food Advice Centres around the country, staffed by keen, sensibly dressed and very well spoken home economists. Armed with a small table cooker, these advisers went out into the world to spread the Ministry's word. Marguerite Patten was a senior food adviser in Cambridge:

I reported for duty in Cambridge on a Friday and the organizer said, 'Now, Marguerite, you want to be here nice and early on Monday because you've got to get a good pitch for your stall.'

Being young and stupid, I said, 'Stall? What do you mean, stall?'

She said, 'Well, you're going to give a demonstration in the market.'

'Oh!' I said, 'I've never given a demonstration in a market before.'

She very wisely said, 'No? Well, now's your chance to begin.'

I had to have a big platter of shredded carrot, turnip and parsnip – things that would give you vitamin C to take the place of oranges, lemons and grapefruit. 'And remember to tell them about the orange juice and cod liver oil,' I was told. That was the first important thing to put over: 'Are you getting all those things to which you're entitled?'

Puddings were important. If you had a main course with a microscopic amount of meat and lots of vegetables, you still want more. So the Ministry encouraged puddings to be made. We were deluged with recipes.

A very important lesson I had to learn was, wherever possible in a recipe, to replace some of the flour with mashed or grated potatoes. Much of the wheat came across the Atlantic from Canada.

Potatoes were so important that a cartoon character was created, Potato Pete; a big potato with eyes, a nose and a mouth; a jolly little man with a hat on his head. The idea was that children would feel some affinity with Potato Pete, but it was a very, very serious message. The slogan was, 'Potatoes don't take up room in ships', and all the time we had to be aware to pass on to the public that message in the form of sensible recipes.

I generally said, 'Well, of course, as you know,' (they probably didn't know), 'in Austria where they make those lovely gateaux, they use potato flour.' So that was a good bridge to get it over to people. Then when people made it and tasted it, they found that it was good.

The Ministry of Food was able to suggest a hundred and one different ways to substitute scarce commodities, with something more ordinary. Patten remembers:

> Mock oyster soup; it always makes me laugh. It sounds as if the whole British population had dined on oyster soup before the war. Many people had never tasted an oyster, but Jerusalem artichokes, which are a root vegetable, when they're cut up look a little like oysters floating in the soup. If the general public hadn't been imaginative during those long, long years of rationing, we'd never have survived.

The imagination of food scientists ran wild. Donald MacDougall remembers on one occasion being asked to taste a 'mock' meat that had been sent to Churchill for his approval: 'One evening at dinner we were served this meat which had been made straight from grass; some chemical process had turned it into artificial meat. It would, I suppose, have saved an enormous amount of feeding stuff – you need an awful lot of feed to get a pound of meat. Unfortunately, it tasted absolutely ghastly.'

There was a black market trade in food, and the Ministry had its own team of special investigators. For all that, most people took the view that 'We're in this together', and it helped that there was a funny side to it all. The Ministry of Food brought a bit of colour and humour to the drab austerity of the Kitchen Front. A lecture from a food adviser was entertainment, something different to do in the evening. Patten remembers:

> There was I extolling the virtues of dried egg. A lot of things I was baking were liable to make people laugh. What is a mock goose? It's sausage meat wrapped around whatever sort of filling I had the ingredients to make. I remember in some rather tough areas giving cookery demonstrations under police protection, and luring rather riotous young people to the door with a plate of cakes; the policemen let them take a cake and then gave them a good push through the door.

The Prime Minister recognized that food supplies played a vital part in ensuring the will to fight on. Professor Lindemann and the branch were often asked to examine proposed cuts in the ration; the question was always, 'Is this absolutely necessary?' 'Churchill was extremely keen on this,' MacDougall recalls. 'He kept a plate in the hall of Number 10 to show to American visitors the weekly ration of butter and cheese, meat and so on.'

This Herculean effort on the Home Front was to make the enemy's task harder. The Germans could not have envisaged, in MacDougall's opinion, the success with which Britain was able to cut imports and increase its own production. Yet whilst the battle could be lost at home, it could only be won at sea. Shipping was, Churchill later wrote, 'at once the stranglehold and sole foundation of our strategy', and it was the crisis at sea that preoccupied him in the winter of 1940–1.

Over Christmas, Atlantic storms had brought a respite from the enemy's pursuit, but the assault on Britain's lifeline was launched with renewed vigour in the New Year, this time spearheaded by large surface ships. The battle cruisers *Scharnhorst* and *Gneisenau* sailed from Kiel on 23 January to join the pocket battleship *Admiral Scheer* and heavy cruiser *Admiral Hipper* in the Atlantic. Over the next two months *Scharnhorst* and *Gneisenau* were to sink twenty-two ships (some 115,000 tons), sixteen of them in just two days. This was to prove the most successful time of the war for the small German surface fleet, with 86,000 tons of Allied shipping sunk in February and 119,000 tons the following month. For all that, it represented less than half the tonnage sunk by U-boats in these two months. It was a brief but thunderous flash, never to be repeated.

The disruption caused to convoy traffic by these big ships was as critical as the losses actually incurred. Nearly every available capital ship that the Royal Navy possessed was deployed on convoy duty. Blows rarely fall singly. News reached the Admiralty on 10 February of a combined air and submarine attack on homebound Gibraltar convoy HG53. Homing signals from a 'contact' boat had brought five long-range Focke-Wulf Condors to the convoy, and they had accounted for five ships.

The following day a U-boat sank another and, to add insult to injury, guided the *Admiral Hipper* to the area; she claimed a further seven ships.

Could the outlook have appeared bleaker? The Prime Minister clearly thought not. In the early hours of 26 February Churchill's Private Secretary, John Colville, was told of 'another serious disaster' to a convoy. He decided to withhold the news until morning, but Churchill had a nose for trouble. 'At 3.00a.m. he asked me point-blank if there was any news from the Admiralty and I had to tell him,' Colville wrote in his diary. 'He became very pensive. "It is very distressing", I said weakly. "Distressing!" he replied, "it is terrifying. If it goes on it will be the end of us".'[11]

Bad news from the Atlantic followed the Prime Minister wherever he went; he was told at Chequers on 1 March of another combined air and submarine attack. The Australian Prime Minister, Robert Menzies, found him 'steeped in gloom'. Churchill was to write that at this time the 'mortal danger to our life-lines gnawed my bowels'.

'Action this Day' was called for. 'We have got to lift this business to the highest plane, over everything else,' Churchill told the First Sea Lord, Admiral Sir Dudley Pound. 'I am going to proclaim "the Battle of the Atlantic".' The decision to proclaim a battle that was already being fought was intended, Churchill explained, to concentrate all minds and all departments on the U-boat war. A 'Battle of the Atlantic Committee' was to meet on a weekly basis with Churchill in the chair; he laid out its brief in a personal directive on 6 March 1941: 'We must take the offensive against the U-boat and the Focke-Wulf wherever we can...the U-boat at sea must be hunted, the U-boat in the building yard or in dock must be bombed.'

His tone reflects the desperate need to improve on the British military effort in this regard; only three U-boats had been sunk in the six months between 1 September 1940 and 1 March 1941. It was a dismal and dangerous record; U-boat production was easily outstripping losses. Great stress was placed on the importance of air support from Coastal Command. A further nine squadrons would eventually be added to the existing twenty-three, all to be equipped with radar at the earliest opportunity.

The directive again identified the need for destroyers; it stressed the importance of heavier anti-aircraft protection for the ports and called for further measures to help clear the backlog of damaged shipping. These were familiar themes, but the Prime Minister's personal commitment ensured that they would now be addressed with the utmost urgency. 'It is the Battle of the Atlantic', Churchill told the country, 'which holds the first place in the thoughts of those upon whom rests the responsibility for procuring the victory.'

Britain had struggled against the tide of war for many months; as one distinguished escort commander would later have it, this was 'the very nadir' of its fortunes at sea.[12] Yet it is one of those perverse ironies thrown up by history that, even as the Prime Minister was proclaiming 'the Battle of the Atlantic', its tide had begun slowly to turn.

CHAPTER SIX

THE END OF THE WOLVES

THE NEW YEAR began badly for the U-boat arm. There were just four boats in the operational area on 1 January 1941, and two of these were on weather-reporting duties. The Atlantic seemed to rage without respite; front after storm-filled front rolled eastwards, churning the ocean as it passed. Crews were tossed around on the surface, blind beneath it. Convoys were difficult to find and even harder to attack. More than one boat was obliged to signal U-boat Command: 'Operations suspended due to weather.' The battle seemed to be on hold. Repairs had to be carried out on the boats, new crew members trained; some commanders had followed Dönitz's example and taken leave.

There were holiday offers aplenty; everyone wanted to meet and entertain Prien, Kretschmer and Schepke. 'They were, for us boys, the heroes,' Anton Plenk recalls. Plenk can still remember the warm pride he felt as a nine-year-old when one of these heroes came to stay with his family. 'What boy would not be proud to meet a famous U-boat man such as Lieutenant Commander Schepke, and to have him stay at your house, and to be around him daily from early morning till late in the evening?'

The pretty Bavarian village of Ruhpolding was to play host to Joachim Schepke, his wife, his crew and a propaganda cameraman for a week in February 1941. The crew of *U-100* had been invited by the local Nazi party to spend time relaxing on the ski slopes; weather that proved such a handicap to operations in the Atlantic ensured good snow in the mountains above Ruhpolding. The twenty-year-old Schepke was the darling of the party. The best known U-boat commander was Prien; Kretschmer the most successful; but Schepke was both handsome and approachable. Blond, clear-eyed and crisply elegant in his dark blue U-boat uniform, he was much in demand as a speaker at party rallies. Plenk remembers the photo opportunities on the piste: 'They were all absolute beginners. They had no technique, they tried to stay on their skis as long as they possibly could, and they fell over, got up and kept on skiing. They were utterly fearless fellows racing down that hill.' The villagers too wanted to make the crew's holiday memorable. 'There were folk evenings at the Kurhaus, as is the tradition here in Ruhpolding on special occasions, with *Schuhplattler* [clog dancing] and music. They had great fun.'

Photographs show the crew dancing with local girls, drinking beer and laughing; Schepke and his men made friends in Ruhpolding. At the end of the holiday Schepke invited Plenk's father to visit *U-100*: 'He was allowed to go on the first test run after the completion of the maintenance work on the boat. I can remember Father telling us that he was allowed to open the conning tower hatch after a test dive, and the pressure had built up so much inside that the first thing that went through the hatch was his hat.'

Schepke and his crew had spent ten weeks ashore, as had Prien and Kretschmer. In that time U-boat successes had dropped markedly; only two ships were sunk in the North Atlantic in the first two weeks of January. Whilst the weather had played its part, so too had the dwindling number of boats available. Volkmar König, the midshipman on Kretschmer's *U-99*, recalls:

I was asked to go to one of the U-boat Command buildings near Lorient, and there was a map of the Atlantic on the wall with one or two U-boats pinned on it.

I said, 'Where are the others?' and the petty officer in charge said, 'What do you mean?'

I said, 'All the other U-boats. There are only two up there.'

He said, 'Come off it!'

You see, I thought there were lots more submarines out there but there weren't.

The number of frontline U-boats fell in February 1941 to a record low of just twenty-two. Prospects were better for the spring; new boats were being worked up, and for the first time Dönitz could look forward to a significant increase in the size of his fleet. Until then U-boat Command would have to rely on the same handful of experienced crews. There was, however, cheering news; for a short time the Condors of Luftwaffe group KG40 were placed under Dönitz's operational control; 'a great step forward,' he wrote in his War Diary.

Günther Prien set out in *U-47* once more on 20 February; Kretschmer's *U-99* followed two days later. Dönitz had tried to persuade both commanders to accept appointments ashore; neither was prepared to leave his crew. There were new faces aboard both these boats. Experienced crew members had been lost to new boats and the officer training school.

'What do you know?' Kretschmer asked one of his new midshipmen. 'Nothing,' came the reply.

At least one of the new recruits was well known to the commander and crew of *U-99*. Hans-Jochen von Knebel Doeberitz was to serve under Kretschmer once more. After six months on the staff, von Knebel had engineered a transfer back to the front by finding someone prepared to take his place as Adjutant. Although Dönitz was reluctant to lose him, he was impressed by his determination and eventually gave his consent. There had been good times; von Knebel remembers the warm informality of his conversations with Dönitz and the freedom with which he was able to speak of his family's hostility to the Nazis. Dönitz was prepared to turn a blind eye to his Adjutant's views but nevertheless, von Knebel sensed the time was right to move on: 'When I was at home I heard my father's constant criticisms of National Socialism, and I intuitively felt that more of this would come Dönitz's way and that one would then be drawn into the political side of things. Sooner or later there would be a conflict over political matters. Of course, we all wanted to go to the front anyway; I always insisted to Dönitz that I wanted to go to sea.'

The usual jamboree was laid on for Kretschmer and his crew on the day of departure, as König recalls: 'We'd been adopted by an army regiment stationed near Lorient. The leader of the regimental band composed the "Kretschmer March", and this music was presented to Kretschmer. The crew was lined up on the deck and the music played and a cameraman was there to film it all. In return Kretschmer gave them a lifebelt from a ship sunk by *U-99*.'

Prien was first into action. On 25 February he located an outbound convoy in the northwest approaches and sank three ships; his signals guided the Condors of KG 40 to the convoy and they claimed another seven.[1] By 6 March five boats including *U-47* and *U-99* had formed a patrol line west of Rockall. It was again *U-47* that found the target; outbound convoy OB 293. That evening *U-99* and *U-47* passed each other in the Atlantic and spoke by megaphone. The plan was, as always, for all boats to attack at night on the surface.

The first to sink was Kretschmer in *U-99* claiming the 6568-ton tanker *Athelbeach*. It was soon clear to the pack, however, that OB 293 was not going to be a pushover; two of the four escorts, *Wolverine* and *Verity*, were equipped with a new electronic eye, capable of sight in the blackest of Atlantic nights – radar. The three U-boats closest to the convoy were repeatedly found, chased and forced under. The ASDIC pursuit was as relentless; *U-70* was depth-charged to the surface, where there was just time for its commander and twenty-four of the crew to escape before it plunged downwards again. At some point that night *U-47* was lost. No one is sure precisely what happened to Prien – credit for sinking Germany's most famous U-boat commander was at first given to *Wolverine*, but recent research has discounted this and *U-47* is now recorded as lost to an unknown cause.

The stout defence mounted by OB293's escorts succeeded in fending off a pack that had included Germany's two finest U-boat commanders, one of whom had been lost. Only two ships were sunk in the convoy. It was an impressive performance, marked by the teamwork of the escort screen; demonstrated even in the face of a determined pack attack.

The failure of *U-47* and *U-70* to respond to signals caused acute anxiety at U-boat Command. It was quite impossible to imagine that Prien might have gone; failure to respond to signals, staff officers told themselves, perhaps indicated damage to *U-47*'s radio. Dönitz was still trying to reach him on 11 March when Fritz-Julius Lemp's new, larger boat, *U-110*, set out from Germany. In its radio room Heinz Wilde listened to the stream of desperate signals from headquarters. 'Prien's boat was ordered to report several times a day for a few days – we deciphered the messages. It was clear he was lost,' he recalls. Lemp had brought a core of old *U-30* hands with him on to his new boat; but there were many, like the twenty-year-old Wilde, on their first war patrol. The loss of Prien was, Wilde remembers, a sobering introduction to the realities of the U-boat war: 'We all felt downcast. During our practices in the Baltic Sea, it had seemed more like a game. Now it was clear; it was about war and death, not about honour or anything like that.'

Hard on the heels of Lemp came Schepke in *U-100*; both were to join Kretschmer and the remnants of the pack south of Iceland. It was Lemp who found the next convoy. At a little after midnight on 16 March he sent a contact report to U-boat Command and then closed for an attack. His target was the fast inbound HX 112, guarded by the newly formed escort group 5 under Captain Donald Macintyre. Lemp attacked and hit a 6200-ton tanker; she burst into a blinding sheet of flame. Macintyre watched from his new ship. 'I had never seen this most appalling of all night disasters, and on the bridge of the *Walker* we were shocked into silence by the horror of it,' he wrote later.[2] The escorts found and pursued Lemp, who was forced to dive deep to avoid the depth charges. He was nevertheless able to shadow the convoy, and by the following evening his reports brought *U-37*, *U-99* and *U-100* into contact with HX 112.

It was soon clear to the pack that this convoy too would be stoutly defended. Escort group 5 consisted of two corvettes and five destroyers, one of which, HMS *Vanoc*, was equipped with radar. This was the group's maiden voyage, but its leader, was a regular who had already demonstrated a talent for convoy work. Before the pack could sink, *U-100* was sighted on the edge of the convoy and pursued. While the escorts hunted Schepke, Kretschmer was able to slip into the heart of the convoy. 'We dived in front and surfaced inside it,' von Knebel recalls: 'We shot at one steamer after another and hit five ships. They were all ablaze because they were full of fuel.'

Kretschmer's devastating salvo accounted for some 34,000 tons of shipping. 'I racked my brains to find some way to stop the holocaust,' Macintyre later wrote. 'Our one hope was to sight the U-boat's tell-tale white wake, give chase to force her to dive and so give the ASDIC a chance to bring our depth charges into action.' Volkmar König, a midshipman on *U-99*, remembers: 'I asked to come up to the conning tower to have a look at the burning tankers, because for a navy man who was asked to sink ships, this was a wonderful sight. Then we left the convoy, because all our torpedoes had gone, and we went out into the open Atlantic to go home to Lorient. Feelings were running high aboard the submarine because we were so successful, and coffee was made and, I think, scrambled eggs.'

Kretschmer was the only one to launch a successful attack that night; the other boats were unable to penetrate the screen. Schepke in *U-100* persisted, but was constantly driven under. At half past one on the morning of 17 March *Walker* picked up a firm ASDIC contact and began a long and relentless attack: *Vanoc* joined the hunt too. The depth charges wrecked *U-100*; all control was lost and the boat began what threatened to be a long dive to the bottom. Schepke was faced with no choice but to blow all tanks – the U-boat shot to the surface.

Its position was instantly detected on the radar aboard *Vanoc*, which closed at speed intent on ramming. Desperate attempts to start *U-100*'s diesels came to nothing and, forced to limp forward on its electric motors, it was hit squarely on the conning tower. The impact crushed Schepke against the periscope and sent his boat on a final downward plunge. Only six of *U-100*'s crew were rescued.

Meanwhile, Kretschmer had taken *U-99* clear of the convoy and was preparing for home. Before he could set a course south for France he would have to circle HX112. König remembers:

> We hit exactly the spot where the two destroyers were attacking *U-100*. Just imagine: this big Atlantic, it's like a needle in a haystack. The watch on the conning tower was not as careful as it should have been. Suddenly the watch officer saw a destroyer very close and he sounded 'alarm', which was against standing orders. We dived, and the watch officer got a bawling out in the control room from the commander.

'Petersen [*U-99*'s 2nd Officer] was on watch. Thank God I wasn't. Kretschmer always reproached him for it,' von Knebel recalls.

No one had seen *U-99* on the surface but beneath it she was 'pinged' by *Walker*'s ASDIC. Macintyre ran in on a bearing and dropped six well-placed depth charges. König remembers the thundering shake as they exploded:

> All the instruments were destroyed. There was no light any more – only small flashlights. There was only one depth gauge working in the bow room, and the first officer of the watch [von Knebel] was standing beside it and shouting out the depth. The boat went deeper and deeper; he announced the depth 10 metres by 10 metres. Everybody could hear it; it was absolutely quiet. We went down to this unbelievable depth, then I said to myself, 'Well, this is it. One second more and there's one big crack and we are pressed together like an empty tin can.' I remember in the control room, the chief petty officer in charge of all the valves that give air to the diving tanks, he turned round with a white face and said to the

commander, 'The boat doesn't come.' It was sinking deeper and deeper despite all the compressed air going in all these diving tanks. And then the commander said, 'Come on, give it air. Give it air.' He was completely cold-blooded, quiet.

The U-boat slipped to 700 feet before sufficient air could be blown into the tanks to stop the descent. Macintyre had turned and was preparing to run in for a second attack when he received a signal from *Vanoc*: 'U-boat surfaced astern of me.' The gun crews on *Walker* and *Vanoc* blazed away at *U-99*, though to little effect. Kretschmer was considering fighting it out, but his gun had been destroyed by the depth charges. König remembers: 'Our captain asked for the flash lamp, and there was an exchange of messages: "Please save my men. Boat is crippled."'

'The British captain sent a message back, "Don't scuttle the boat."'

'And there was another message, "What does 'scuttle' mean?" "Don't sink the boat." The British wanted to capture it.'

Before abandoning the boat, Kretschmer sent a desperate message to U-boat Command: 'Depth charges. Two destroyers. 53,000 tons. Boat scuttled. Heil Hitler. Kretschmer.' Then commander and crew jumped into the sea. König recalls: 'We were swimming, and I was soon tired – in this kind of temperature the first thing that happens is you get tired and fall asleep. This is the first step to your end. But then I woke up, because there was a searchlight in my face and I was next to the destroyer.'

The *Walker* fished all but three of *U-99*'s crew out of the sea, although the U-boat itself was lost. Kretschmer and his officers shared the destroyer's mess with the merchant seamen rescued from HX112; it was a frosty gathering. It had been *U-99*, of course, that had poached the *Jersey City* from *Walker*'s convoy the summer before. That *Walker* should now act as grim nemesis was some sort of poetic justice.

Escort group 5 steamed back into Liverpool to a rousing reception; Kretschmer and his men walked down the gangplank into six years of captivity. König remembers: 'The army had to protect us with fixed bayonets against the public because they tried to throw stones at us.

Liverpool was being heavily bombed at that time, and many of those there had lost relatives at sea. They were furious at these German submarine sailors.' At the time König was confident that his time in captivity would be short: 'We said, "Well, invasion is coming one of these days and it will only take a few weeks and then they'll get us out of here."' The British interrogators who spoke to the crew reported that both the U-boat's midshipmen appeared to be 'typical Nazis', but in Kretschmer he observed a distinct war-weariness and in von Knebel a clear sense of disenchantment with 'many of the Nazi methods and most of their leading personalities'.

In the radio room of *U-110* Wilde followed headquarters' increasingly desperate search: 'Schepke and Kretschmer were asked to give their positions but, like Prien, there was no answer. The commander and the older crew members knew that we would never hear from them again. The question was: sunk or captured? Chances were that they were most probably sunk.' The first news of the disaster to reach U-boat Command came from *U-37*, which had picked up Kretschmer's final message. It was a bitter blow; all the more so as all hope for Prien had now been lost.

Dönitz was in no hurry to break the news to the public. Volkmar König's mother sat in a German cinema bursting with pride as the audience watched a newsreel of her son's boat taken three weeks before in Lorient. She assumed that he and the rest of the crew were already home, but by then König was a prisoner.

It was the British who blew the whistle; Churchill considered the news momentous enough to merit a personal announcement to the House of Commons. Dönitz was obliged to confirm his report. The German public was told of Kretschmer and Schepke, but Hitler felt that the loss of Prien would be too great a blow to public morale, and news of this was withheld.

Dönitz would later write that the loss of his three most successful aces constituted 'particularly heavy blows to me and my staff'. Between them Prien, Kretschmer and Schepke had sunk more than 600,000 tons of Allied shipping. Kretschmer's score of 44 ships for 247,012 tons was not to be equalled in the war. These three commanders represented the core of Dönitz's pre-war elite. The loss of Prien in particular was a personal blow. 'I held him in great affection and esteem,' he later wrote. 'Prien was all that a man should be...full of zest and energy and the joy of life, wholly dedicated to his service.'[3] It was, of course, this dedication to the U-boat Waffe that was, in Dönitz's eyes, the measure of the man's greatness.

Nowhere in Germany was the loss of Schepke and his crew more keenly felt than in Ruhpolding, where they had spent their last holiday. Anton Plenk recalls: 'I can still remember very clearly the news that Schepke had been lost with the crew. People were of course very upset.' It was impossible for nine-year-old Anton to understand that the hero who had seemed so alive only weeks before was gone for good. Schepke had given Plenk's elder brother, Horst, a model of *U-100*: 'We did diving tests and re-enacted what Schepke did – it was a magnet for all the children around us. There often used to be fifteen to twenty children in the house, and we played with it for a long time. It reminded us of the great U-boat captain.'

At the end of March *U-110* returned to Lorient after a disappointing war patrol. There were no confirmed successes, and the boat's deck gun had been damaged because the crew had attempted to fire it without removing a protective waterproof plug. To add insult to Lemp's injured pride, U-boat Command cancelled all shore leave. The crew of *U-110* had monitored the desperate radio messages sent to the three lost aces; news of Prien was yet to be released. Wilde recalls: 'We were ordered to keep this information secret and not to talk about it to anybody – neither in our quarters, nor with the crew members of the other U-boats stationed in Lorient, nor in letters home. As a preventative measure, the holiday which was normally given to half the crew was cancelled. The need for secrecy had utmost priority.' The crew was packed off to a 'U-boat pasture' on the French Atlantic coast while their gun was repaired.

The attempts to stifle news of Prien's death fuelled wild stories. These were pushed by British propaganda broadcasts that asked, 'Where is

Prien?' The Admiralty had learnt from the *U-99* prisoners that Prien was missing, and had passed the information on. Although it was strictly against standing orders, the first watch officer of *U-107*, the twenty-six-year old Helmut Witte, monitored some of these British broadcasts: 'They tried to undermine German heroes by saying that they died in some unnatural way or for political reasons or something like that. It was said of Prien that he wasn't killed in action, but that he was taken to the concentration camp at Dachau near Munich because he'd made anti-Nazi remarks.'

Such was the concern felt in the U-boat arm that Witte visited Munich intent on proving the claim false. He explains:

I made an appointment with the camp commandant at Dachau, and he promised me that Prien had never been admitted to his camp, that he wasn't there and that he never would be. I was able to walk through the camp for two days and have a look at every-thing I wanted. I didn't find Prien.

The final explanation was offered to the German public on 23 May, when a press release issued by U-boat Command stated: 'The hero of Scapa Flow has made his last patrol. We of the U-boat service proudly mourn and salute him and his men…they have become for us a symbol of our hard and unshakeable will to victory against England.' In the weeks between the loss of Prien and the release of the news to the public, a further six U-boats had been sunk in the North Atlantic.

it was a thin time for the U-boat; it seemed harder to find convoys, the ones that were found were better defended, and it was impossible to ignore the growing number of British aircraft. Above all, too much was being asked of too few U-boats. It was harder for lone boats to penetrate the larger screens, and there were just not enough boats to mount large pack attacks. Dönitz was forced into his first strategic retreat; all U-boats were to be withdrawn from the busy northwestern approaches and pushed further out into the Atlantic. A new operations area was established west of Iceland, where, it was hoped, the enemy's defences would be weaker. Some historians have interpreted this withdrawal as the beginning of the slow, relentless squeeze that would eventually force the U-boat from the North Atlantic.

That the morale of the U-boat arm had been badly shaken by the events of February and March 1941 was obvious to a crewman who joined *U-110* at this time. Georg Högel had spent almost three years in the radio room of Lemp's *U-30* and had proved himself capable and trustworthy. It was Högel who had retyped the commander's war diary after the sinking of the *Athenia*. He missed the first patrol in the new boat, but was to rejoin Lemp on 9 April. Högel recalls:

He was an experienced submariner and commander and you always tried to sail with people you knew, whom you could trust. That was important.But when I boarded the boat I immediately felt that everything was wrong. I quickly learnt that Lemp was part of the patrol line that had seen the end of Kretschmer, Schepke and Prien – and we knew them all. The mood wasn't at all good.

By the middle of April, *U-110* was ready for sea again. On this patrol Lemp had agreed to make room for, a 'PK' or propaganda reporter, twenty-three-year-old Helmut Ecke. Lemp could be confident of a good write-up; it was Ecke's job to accentuate the positive. He had already impressed the Propaganda Ministry in Berlin with a series of features on spring in the English Channel in which the war was barely mentioned. Ecke recalls: 'Of course it was supposed to have a positive flavour. No one told me how I was supposed to write, but that was certainly the expectation. The report was to be about the atmosphere – nothing technical. I wouldn't have had a clue about that anyway – I hadn't had any U-boat training.'

Lemp set out from Lorient on 15 April bound for the new operations area, west of Iceland. First reports indicated that the hunting was good.

Slow convoy SC26 had been located in the first week of April and attacked by a pack of eight U-boats. Half of the convoy's twenty-two ships had been sunk. At sea, *U-110*'s crew put the gloom of the previous fortnight behind them. Ecke was struck by their spirit: 'The men on board were all quite sure of victory. What could happen to us? Nothing ever happens to me! They appeared to have no fear.' Everyone had confidence in 'Fritz'; Ecke too was impressed; the captain seemed to exude bonhomie. 'If I have to characterize Lemp, I would say that he believed "My country right or wrong." I might not like these Nazis, but we are at war and I can't do anything else.'

The propaganda man was obliged to wait several days before observing his first action; on 24 April *U-110* was cruising in the Atlantic some 300 nautical miles west of Ireland. Lemp attacked on the surface; what followed was to leave an indelible mark on Ecke:

I watched the torpedo explode into a 200-metre-high tongue of orange flame, and in these flames there were human bodies and parts of the ship whirling round and falling back into the Atlantic. And then it was dead quiet. Lemp sailed a little closer. The ship had sunk quickly, but we heard shouts: 'Hitler *help*! Hitler *help*!'

And then something happened that I found terrible. Standing next to me was the second officer of *U-110*. He yelled into the darkness: 'Why do you pigs sail for England?'

I was horrified, and I gave him a jab and said, 'These people are doing their duty, just as you are. What do you expect?"

Lemp found survivors among the wreckage – there were pieces of wood, a small lifeboat as well, and the people in it were still shouting: 'Hitler *help*!' Lemp was able to take one of the survivors on board.' I offered him a cigarette and the seaman was puffing away barefoot – he was shaking with cold, of course. He was questioned: "Where do you come from?" We found out his ship came from Freetown, Sierra Leone. I don't know what was on board. Lemp knew anyway what he had sunk, what the tonnage was.

Erich Topp's U-552 – the famous 'Red Devil' boat – leaves St Nazaire on a war patrol. Topp sank 34 ships totalling 185,434 tons, making him the fifth most successful commander of the war.

Above: The bow torpedo room of the Type IXB U-124. Although this was the main armoury of the U-boat, it was also crammed with food and equipment, and served as home for at least 20 men.

Right: Although crews practised escaping from a submerged U-boat, the chances of surviving an ordeal like that were slim.

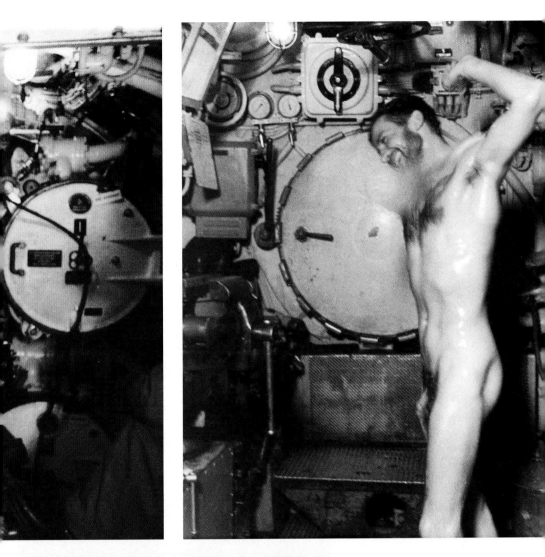

Above: U-boat men were obliged to leave concerns about personal hygiene ashore. No one shaved, but there was the occasional opportunity for a saltwater shower.

Left: Erich Topp at the periscope of U-552. This photograph was used as a template for a wartime postage stamp.

Right: Sports day on U-123. The crew compete for sausages during a quiet spell on a patrol to West African waters, in the summer of 1941.

Below: The crew of U-103 on their way to American waters in the spring of 1942. These men were obliged to live on top of each other like this for the full two months of the patrol.

Left: Erich Topp returns home to the customary fanfare and flowers.

Below: The commanders of U-46 and U-552, Engelbert Endraß (left) and Erich Topp, celebrate with their girlfriends at the 'Scheherazade', a favourite haunt for U-boat officers visiting Paris.

Right: Fritz-Julius Lemp's U-30 approaches the British freighter *Fannad Head*, on the morning of 14 September 1939. Aircraft from HMS *Ark Royal* attacked U-30 as she was preparing to sink the ship, but this was not enough to save her.

Below: The 'Tonnage King' Otto Kretschmer, seen here with papers and cigar in hand, in 1940. As Commander of U-23 and then U-99, Kretschmer sank 238,327 tons of shipping. Erich Topp is in the foreground on the right.

Above, left: The commander of U-30, Fritz-Julius Lemp, receives his Knight's Cross from Dönitz during the 'U-boat Happy Time' in the summer of 1940.

Below: Victory bunting is being marked by crewmen from U-132 with the tonnage of ships sunk on a war patrol to the Gulf of St Lawrence, in July 1942.

Above, right: Knight's Cross holder Jürgen Oesten on the bridge of his U-boat.

The Commander of U-123, Reinhard Hardegen, and his officers on the bridge of the U-boat as it approaches Lorient in 1941. In the summer of 1942 Horst von Schroeter (right) succeeded Hardegen as commander of U-123.

Then I went down into the boat; I had a little locker to myself where I had been able to store a big pack of cigarettes, and I gave it to the seaman. Lemp said, 'We can't take on any of the ship-wrecked men – we don't have any room on board.' The seaman went back into the boat. They got away with no more than a terrible shock. They were still alive, but how they survived that night and afterwards I don't know.

So much for the camaraderie of the sea, respect for the enemy; the boat's watch officer clearly shared none of those feelings. For the crew of *U-110* the sinking of the *Henri Mory* was a rare success – the only one in three weeks of hunting. While the bridge watch scoured the horizon for a tell-tale column of smoke, Wilde and Högel in the radio room waited for a signal from U-boat Command at Kernével; perhaps another boat had been luckier. Yet, although there were reports of convoys sighted, none was close enough to offer an opportunity to *U-110*.

It was at these times that the radio link to Kernével was essential; it formed the hub of U-boat operations, coordinating the search and then bringing the pack together if a convoy was sighted. All signals were, of course, sent in code; *U-110* carried its own Enigma machine. At first glance this device looked very much like a typewriter, but set into the body of the machine were three wheels or rotors, along which were engraved the letters of the alphabet. The rotors moved round as each key was depressed, and after every movement the enciphered letter would light up on a glass plate set into the top of the machine.

Before a message could be enciphered, however, the Enigma operator needed to know which three of the eight rotors available to him to select, and the order in which they should be placed in the machine; these 'inner settings' changed every two days. There were also 'outer settings' – the security of the Enigma machine depended above all on the plugboard at the front of the machine and the connections for this changed daily. The cipher tables listing these settings covered only a month at a time. Another list of settings enabled U-boat Command to send signals for the eyes of 'Officers only'. It was a complex, slow but ingenious system in which the Kriegsmarine placed complete confidence. Wilde recalls:

> How safe was the code? We came in touch with the machines for the first time in the Radio School in Flensburg where we were trained, and we were told that the chances of breaking in were one to one trillion. Today you would say that breaking in was as likely as winning the jackpot in the lottery. But the jackpot exists.

It was an enciphered message from U-boat Command that on 7 May 1941 ended *U-110*'s painful weeks of inactivity. Lemp was at last in a position to close a convoy, OB 318 en route to Canada. The westward march of the U-boat had been tracked by the Admiralty; three newly formed escort groups had been dispatched to Iceland to provide mid-ocean cover for the convoys. The nine warships of escort group 3 were on station around OB 318; it was a formidable screen. Lemp was first to make contact with the convoy on 8 May. Wilde remembers the discussion that followed:

> It was between the officers. I could follow the conversations because the radio room was opposite the commander's quarters and adjacent to the control room. These conversations were held openly, because the commander didn't have any secrets on board. The question was: attack from the surface – that was only possible by night, and it would mean travelling even further to the west; or approach the convoy – we were very near – and attack during the day. Commander Lemp decided to attack during the day because he didn't want to travel any further westwards and risk being stranded without fuel. The leading engineer disagreed.

Lemp's decision was communicated to the only other U-boat close to the convoy, *U-201*, commanded by Adi Schnee. A little before dawn on 9 May the two rendezvoused and the commanders discussed the attack on megaphones. It was agreed that Lemp would attack first, at noon, and Schnee half an hour later. Then both U-boats dived and began slowly cruising towards the approaching convoy. Lemp hoped that, by delaying the attack until daylight, he would catch the convoy without its screen. He was surprised to see escort group 3 very much on station. Wilde recalls: 'The risk was clear to all of us. An attack underwater with the periscope up is always a give-away for a careful watch on the bridge of a destroyer. But we couldn't hear any danger; we could hear the propeller noises of the convoy and of the escort ships, but no ASDIC signals.'

Lemp decided to press ahead. Four torpedoes were fired at four ships on the right flank of the convoy; two found their mark. Georg Högel, on duty in *U-110*'s radio room, remembers:

I followed the torpedoes with the hydrophones until they hit their target. We turned the boat round underwater so we could shoot with the stern tube, but at that point I noticed we were being hunted by ASDIC.

I said to my mate, 'Fritz, listen, they've got us. We're being echo-located.'

He said, 'No, no. When you sweep over 180 degrees with the hydrophones you go from one area to the next and you get strange sounds, and that's one of them.'

So I said, 'No, Fritz. I have been detecting in a fixed direction and I'm getting this pinging sound.'

Wilde too heard this ominous 'ping, ping' against the hull of the U-boat:

The commander gave the order for emergency diving. We could hear the propellers of the destroyer; it went at full speed and passed above us as it dropped the depth charges, and then slowed the engines again.

The commander changed the direction of the boat and we

went to a great depth. I think the depth charges exploded above us. They shook the boat violently, but didn't cause any damage.

We then tried to escape the ASDIC detection by constantly changing the direction and the depth of the boat. But again and again we heard the destroyers that were following us stop, take a bearing and then move to full speed again. We knew at that moment that there would be more depth charges. It was an unrelenting combination of stopping, accelerating, and then the detonation of the depth charges.

The last ones caused major damage to the boat. We had water and diesel oil coming in – the valves were damaged. The depth meter burst, the most precise one we had. None of the others worked. The chief engineer asked for damage reports from the bow and stern over the microphone. The report came back that the electric motors had failed.

Lemp gave the order to surface, and the chief engineer passed the order on to the control room seamen. But they said the surfacing valve was also damaged; coming up would be a problem. The chief engineer looked at it himself, and something must have worked because suddenly we were on the surface; the boat was being rocked by the sea.

The speed with which the U-boat finally surfaced took everyone by surprise. Lemp hurried up the ladder and flung open the conning tower hatch; daylight and fresh air flooded into the boat, and with it the hope that they were saved. Propaganda journalist Helmut Ecke recalls: 'I can still hear Lieutenant-Commander Lemp. As he opened the hatch he shouted down, "Uhlandstrasse, last stop, all change." This was the last stop for us.' The sight that greeted Lemp was terrifying: three warships were blazing away at the boat and two appeared to be closing to ram. Heinz Wilde remembers: 'The commander shouted: "We're surrounded! All hands abandon ship." At the very moment he shouted this, we heard shots above. We put on swim vests and *Tauchretter* [a lifejacket with a respirator] and stood in the tower hatch to get out. Lemp kept shouting: "Come, come, come!" The first one jumped overboard, then the second. There were more shots. Lemp shouted: "Wait until there is a pause in the firing." Then two or three men jumped every time there was a lull in the firing.'

Ecke was caught on the bridge by a barrage from the surrounding British warships: 'They opened fire on us with tracer shell. It was like a New Year's Eve party at two o'clock in the afternoon. A crew man in front of me took a dive, and during his flight from the tower into the water he lost half his head. There was just part of the ear left – he'd been hit right in the middle of the head. A shot went through the tower and suddenly there was this piece of metal lying at my feet. Then I jumped feet first.'

Lemp knew that it was now his duty to ensure *U-110* did not fall into the hands of the enemy. It was, above all, vital that the Enigma machine and all cipher material should either go down with the boat or over the side in a weighted bag. It seemed to Lemp that *U-110* was sinking by the stern, but to speed things along he ordered the chief engineer to flood the ballast tanks. Högel was still on board the U-boat:

Lemp was standing over the hatch, looking down into the control room. My comrade, who was the radio officer, and I were shouting upwards: 'What's to be done with the secret items?'

He shouted to us: 'Leave everything. Leave everything. Get out, get out, get out!'

In the end you have to trust what the commander says, and so we also set about leaving the U-boat. There was no question about it; the boat was going to sink very soon. I'd got up to the tower when I remembered a little book of poems that I had been given for my birthday by a lady friend. I'd devoted many hours to decorating this with calligraphy and I was very attached to it. I went back down into the boat and found it. I unbuttoned the top of my shirt and put it in there, so that I had it against my breast. Then it was important to get out of there again.

Another radio operator, Heinz Wilde, was the last to leave the boat:

> I was looking for my *Tauchretter*, scrambling around in the radio room; it was under the desk where we used to receive the wireless messages. I put it on and looked around. The boat was empty.
>
> The commander was above and shouted down: 'Is there anybody left?'
>
> I shouted: 'Yes, I'm still here. I'm coming.'
>
> The firing had stopped. I climbed through the tower and up to the bridge.
>
> The commander was still standing there. He said: 'Get off the boat quickly – it'll go down soon.'
>
> I said: 'Sir, we still have the secret things down there.' He said: 'Leave it, Wilde. The boat is sinking anyway.'
>
> So I jumped from the tower into the water. I had my eyes open and I saw beautifully clear Atlantic water. Like during diving training, I opened the oxygen container and the breathing sac filled.
>
> I looked around. Behind me was the U-boat. In front of me I saw a group of the crew and I swam towards them. Someone suddenly started singing a record that we radio operators had played many times in the boat over the tannoy, '*Im Leben geht alles vorüber*' ['In life, everything passes'], a hit from some operetta. It was a gesture of defiance, as I see it today; we were in the water, and we had enemy ships all around us.
>
> Actually, after a while we realized that our position was one more for despairing than for singing. Then we saw a destroyer leaving. Some of the crew tried to swim to it; most of my group stayed together so that we could be seen, because this was the only chance for survival.
>
> In the meantime, I thought: 'Well, that's it. What am I going to do in the North Atlantic? The water is freezing. The chance of survival is tiny. I can't go on swimming forever. I'll probably die of exposure, and because I have the *Tauchretter* on I will float as a

corpse in the Atlantic.' Then I thought: 'Well, you've got to hang on in there for as long as possible. Maybe there is a chance, maybe you will be rescued. You just have to stick it out. You can always let the air out of the *Tauchretter* in the end.' But I didn't want to give up quickly.

Georg Högel recalls: 'Then a corvette turned around and came towards us. They threw me a line over the bows and I heard someone near me snorting – he seemed to have swallowed quite a lot of water. It was the propaganda-company man who was supposed to be writing a nice article about our patrol.' The corvette was HMS *Aubrietia*; it was her depth charges that had forced *U-110* to the surface. Eager hands now helped the survivors up the scramble nets and on to the deck. They had spent an icy hour in the Atlantic, and not everyone made it: some died of wounds, others from hypothermia. Wilde recalls: 'They wanted to put me on my feet, but I couldn't stand up – I still didn't have any feeling in my legs. They stripped me naked on a cold May day south of Greenland, wrapped me in a blanket and massaged me warm. They obviously had some experience with survivors from the convoys that we'd attacked. Then I got a cup of tea. I can still remember the taste of the tea to this day.'

From the deck of the *Aubrietia* Wilde could see quite clearly that *U-110* was still afloat: 'The stern was slightly submerged and I had the impression that a rowing boat was lying next to the U-boat. I was then taken below into a mess room, where the rest of the crew, apart from the officers, were already assembled.' Lemp did not appear to be among the survivors. The last to see him alive was *U-110*'s first officer; he reported that for a time they had been together in the water. Lemp had seen that his U-boat was still very much afloat and had struck out towards it, no doubt with a view to boarding and sinking. Some have suggested that, when he realized this was impossible, he chose suicide. All that can be said for sure is that Lemp and fourteen of his crew were lost; two more were to die aboard *Aubrietia*. That left the thirty-two survivors.

Helmut Ecke recalls:

> I hadn't counted on the English saving us at all, because we had already torpedoed ships in the convoy. I had swallowed water and perhaps a bit of oil as well and was feeling sick. I crawled back up on deck so I wouldn't have to throw up in the room where we prisoners were all sitting down – and there was this very bizarre situation, with me stumbling up the last step and throwing up. The door of a nearby wash room opened up and an English lieutenant was standing there shaving – he started to whistle '*Deutschland, Deutschland über alles*' to me. He found it very, very funny.

The crewmen of *U-110* were beginning six long, dreary years of captivity that would take them first to Britain and then to Canada. British intelligence officers questioned them closely to judge how much they knew about the fate of their boat; it was soon obvious that none of the crew was sure quite what had happened. No one really wanted to consider the possibility that *U-110* had indeed been captured.

Ironically, as the crew of *U-110* were preparing to spend their first night in captivity aboard *Aubrietia*, Kriegsmarine officers and senior members of the Nazi party were attending a gala premiere in Berlin of a new film glorifying the selfless sacrifice of the U-boat arm.[5] *U-Boote Westwärts!* (*U-boats Westwards*) had been made aboard *U-123* with the blessing of Dönitz, who had also agreed to appear as himself. In the last scene Dönitz was called upon to address the actor crew of the film's imaginary U-boat; speaking in a strong but surprisingly high-pitched voice he urged them on to 'Struggle, sacrifice and victory. The fight goes on.' As the curtains swept together at the end, the audience burst into thunderous applause.

Lemp was to be remembered for his sacrifice and heroism, the third Knight's Cross holder to be lost at sea. Thirty years would pass before Dönitz was to learn of his part in the disaster that was now to be visited on the U-boat arm.

CHAPTER SEVEN

SPECIAL INTELLIGENCE

THE FIRST INSTINCT OF those who watched *U-110* break the surface was to finish the job. The destroyers *Bulldog* and *Broadway* closed on the U-boat with all guns blazing, bent on the kill. Yet as the *Bulldog* bore down on the boat her captain, Joe Baker-Cresswell, the leader of escort group 3, saw a more important opportunity. Turning to a young sub-lieutenant he barked: 'Take a boarding party and get what you can out of her.' The officer charged with this nerve-jangling task was twenty-year-old David Balme, who recalls: 'The team was organized, one man from every department: a signalman, a stoker who does the engineering, an electrician and so on. The chief gunner's mate gave us all a revolver – highly dangerous for any of us sailors to have a loaded revolver. Then it was "Away sea boats and crew."'

Balme had been educated for the sea; it was a family tradition. He had followed the classic path: Royal Naval College at Dartmouth, then service as a midshipman. In the first months of the war he had seen a good deal of the U-boat's work; unforgettably, he had watched the aircraft carrier *Courageous* roll and slip away. Balme's ship, *Ivanhoe*, had been one of her two escorts. It was hard to suppress the thought that she had shared some responsibility for the loss of five hundred men.

As the *Bulldog*'s whaler edged closer to *U-110* Balme began to wonder just how badly damaged the U-boat was – would it go down with his party on board? The U-boat's crew expected her to sink; most had chosen to take their chances in the Atlantic. As Balme recalls, the U-boat was wallowing in a heavy swell: 'Submarines have a round hull, and the water was splashing over the deck. She was obviously down a bit and damaged, and so it was very slippery. I had to walk along this wet deck with a loaded revolver in one hand. When I got to the bottom of the conning tower I holstered it and climbed up this vertical ladder on to the top of the tower. It was empty.' Balme found the hatch into the boat closed: 'I couldn't quite believe that they'd just left this U-boat. I opened up the first hatch. There were two ladders going down to the bowels of the submarine. There seemed to be no one about, so I went down the first one to the next hatch. The final one was the really frightening one, because I felt sure there must be somebody down below trying to sink the U-boat. I felt terribly vulnerable and very frightened.' Yet the U-boat appeared deserted. There was an alarming hissing noise, which sounded like compressed air escaping from a tank, and Balme remembers the splash of the Atlantic against the hull. 'The main lights had gone, and there was dim blue secondary lighting only. Very eerie. It looked fairly dry underfoot, so I went up to the bows. Still nobody about. Came round, went down to the stern. Nobody there. Then I shouted up to my boarding party to come down.'

They set about ransacking the boat. Balme remembers: 'I had a signalman in my boarding party and he immediately went to the wireless office. He came back to me and said, "Look, there's something very interesting here. You'd better come and see." So I went along and there was this typewriter thing. We both pressed a few buttons and it lit up in rather a strange way.' It was an Enigma machine. With it Balme found cipher tables, signal books, navigational charts and charts indicating the location of German minefields; a veritable treasure trove of intelligence materials.

The boarding party worked swiftly: the Enigma machine and documents were passed along a human chain up on to the deck of the U-boat, where the Broadway's whaler was standing by. Balme and his men were to spend six hours in the U-boat, long enough for Baker-Cresswell to deem sandwiches to be necessary. Balme ate his at the commander's desk, surrounded by Lemp's personal belongings: his Knight's Cross, white hat, letters and photographs.

There was one chilling moment when the U-boat was rocked by the shock of a nearby explosion. The escort group had detected and attacked what it took to be another U-boat. Balme recalls: 'What really worried me was that we were down below, our own ships were dropping depth charges about half a mile away and we were vibrating a lot. If the U-boat crew had set scuttling charges it could have set them off.'

The haul from *U-110* filled two packing cases; a working naval Enigma machine, a book used for the *Offizier* messages – the double encrypted messages intended for officer's eyes only, the U-boat short signal codebook and a score or so of valuable charts and technical manuals.[1] Efforts were made to tow the U-boat to Iceland, but on the morning of 10 May she sank. Ultimately her loss helped to ensure that Operation *Primrose*, as the boarding had been codenamed, remained a secret.

Within days of the capture the packing cases were sitting in a Victorian mansion in Buckinghamshire. This was the home of the Government Code and Cipher School; a place considered too secret and important to be called by its real name, Bletchley Park, officially it was known as 'Station X'. Here the government had assembled a collection of high-powered academics and charged them with the task of breaking into the enemy's codes. Of these, the German Enigma codes were the most important and to prove the stiffest test.

As the Bletchley operation grew, the code-breakers began to spill out into surrounding huts: Huts 8 and 4 for naval codes; Huts 6 and 3 for army and air force. By the summer of 1941, one thousand two hundred men and women were employed in code-breaking.[2] Early successes with army and air force ciphers had not been matched on the naval front. It was clear that something was needed to get the code-breakers started – a 'pinch'.

Valuable cipher material was captured from the armed trawler *Krebs* in February 1941; it was enough of a start to allow the cryptographers to read some naval traffic in February and April. The weather ship *München* yielded yet more, and the two crates of material from Operation *Primrose* all but completed the process. The 'pinches' gave sufficient insight into the naval Enigma to ensure that the U-boats' main operational cipher, Hydra, could usually be decrypted and read within 24 hours, even when the monthly tables changed.[3]

When the First Sea Lord, Dudley Pound, learned of the haul he sent *Bulldog* the signal: 'Hearty congratulations. The petals of your flower are of rare beauty.' Decorations were presented by King George VI to the men involved in the operation at a special ceremony in Buckingham Palace; a Distinguished Service Cross for Balme. 'Perhaps the most important single event in the whole war at sea,' the King muttered to one of those present.

By the middle of May a steady flow of decrypted material was clattering into the teleprinter room at the Admiralty. The fruit of Bletchley's labour was christened 'Ultra' or 'Special Intelligence'; access to its secrets was restricted to a small, charmed circle, many of whose members worked in the bowels of a bleak concrete block known as 'the Citadel'. This was the home of the Royal Navy's Operational Intelligence Centre (OIC), where information relating to the disposition and likely movements of enemy warships and U-boats was collected and assessed. At its heart was the Submarine Tracking Room, a dingy, windowless bunker which was usually thick with cigarette smoke.

The director of the Tracking Room was a thirty-eight-year-old reserve officer, Commander Rodger Winn. A barrister in civilian life, Winn cut a distinctive if unusual figure in the OIC; somewhat owlish in appearance, as a boy he had been disabled by poliomyelitis, which had left him with a twisted back and a marked limp. Winn was to demonstrate an almost uncanny ability to second-guess the intentions of U-boat Command. Amidst the charts and technical drawings pinned to the walls was a large framed photograph of Dönitz.[4] Winn had insisted on this; the Tracking Room was to shadow as closely as it could the movements and decisions made by Dönitz in his Situation Room at Kernével in Brittany.

It was the task of this small team to assemble all the available intelligence on U-boat operations and offer its best guess as to the convoy routes to be attacked. 'Special Intelligence' was a godsend; Winn was not only able to read signals from the U-boats at sea but he was also privy to the constant flow of instructions sent by Dönitz from his headquarters. It was now possible to plot U-boat positions in the Atlantic with considerable accuracy.

Whilst 'Special Intelligence' was Winn's most important source, it still offered only a partial insight into the enemy's plans. To help fill the gaps the Tracking Room could draw on some fifteen additional sources.[5] The network of shore-based Intercept Stations that logged enemy signals and dispatched them to Bletchley for decoding was also able to provide intelligence on the general position of the U-boats and ships that sent them. No delay was necessary for decrypting, so intelligence gleaned from Direction Finding or D/F was usually bang up-to-date and of operational value. Analysis of the traffic itself was another useful source; the strength of a signal, its length, the time and number of U-boats to which it was sent – all these helped form the overall intelligence picture. This was, in one shape or form, Sigint or Signal Intelligence; there were also, of course, the more traditional sources.

By the summer of 1941 the Royal Navy had pulled many U-boat men from the Atlantic; they all had a story to tell. Responsibility for ensuring that they told it rested with the interrogators of Naval Intelliegence Division 1; Lieutenant Commander Colin McFadyean was one of the senior officers who worked for this section of Naval Intelligence and recalls: 'On the whole the prisoners were reasonably willing. On no occasion did we do threaten them with execution or God knows what. The psychology was to treat them very reasonably and gently.'

McFadyean joined NID1 after two years' service at sea, talent-spotted by Ian Fleming. There was talk of sending him to Bletchley, but this was ruled out on security grounds because his wife was a refugee from Germany. Yet his excellent German, quick brain and genial disposition made him ideal for the gentle fishing in which NID1's interrogators were engaged. Most of this took place at the Combined Services Detailed Interrogation Centre, the Buckinghamshire holding camp shared by all three services. This is McFadyean's recollection of CSDIC and its work:

The prisoners were accommodated there in quite decent, small rooms. What they didn't know, and very few of them even thought of, was that in the light fitting on the ceiling there was a concealed microphone. This was in all the rooms.

We called them up into an interrogation room; this was just a plain room with a table and a few chairs and us with our bits of paper. Sometimes it was purely a formality – they weren't of any great interest; but if it looked promising it would go on. You might ask about wives and children and where were they and all that kind of thing, and did they come from a naval family – that's all just chit-chat in order to get going.

Really we knew more about U-boats than any one U-boat sur-vivor, officer or not, because we had a huge overview from intelli-gence which emanated from the Tracking Room. They knew one hell of a lot and it filtered through to us. We used to go and talk to Winn, and he would tell us what he might be looking out for.

When we'd finished in the interrogation room the prisoner went back to his room, and if he had someone there with him he might well be asked, 'Well, what are they asking you about?' and so forth, and the prisoner would say, 'What they really wanted to know was so-and-so, but I wasn't going to tell them.' And all this was coming through the microphone in the ceiling and was recorded. Quite often we got the information we wanted by just listening in after-wards. At the next interrogation you could take it up and get round to it – there was no need to reveal we'd been listening.

If prisoners proved especially tough to crack NID1 could call on the services of a 'stool pigeon', usually a German refugee but sometimes a disenchanted U-boat crew man. McFadyean remembers: 'We put the prisoner in with the stool pigeon, who was dressed up as a U-boat man, and maybe had a broken leg for effect – a false one – and he had been told what we wanted and there again it came through the mic in the ceiling.' There were also some less conventional interrogations. McFadyean took one prominent U-boat commander out to dinner in London's Soho and then on to visit the First Sea Lord. Some prisoners were interrogated in the countryside around CSDIC: 'I used to come back with a cap full of lovely mushrooms which I'd take home to my wife to cook – all chosen by the German prisoners.'

This relaxed style produced results. NID1 was able to winkle out information on the number of operational U-boats and the state of the construction programme; technical details such as the maximum diving depths of Type VII and IX boats; and later the first indications that new large U-tankers had been constructed to supply boats on long-range operations. Some subjects were taboo: prisoners were not to be questioned about the Enigma ciphers – nothing was to jeopardize the steady flow of 'Special Intelligence' already available to the OIC.

Sooner or later, anything of worth would end up on Winn's desk. In time he was able to piece together an extraordinarily detailed picture of the U-boat arm: current dispositions, the speed, size and endurance of the boats, the training and combat histories of their commanders. In the summer of 1941, however, the immediate concern was to find a way to use this intelligence, especially the new insight offered by Ultra, without alerting the enemy to its existence. This posed a serious challenge, as was soon apparent.

Almost all U-boat operations stopped at the end of May when the pride of Hitler's navy, the *Bismarck*, sallied forth into the Atlantic. This extraordinary battleship posed a unique threat to the convoy routes; there was little afloat that could outpunch her. When told of her imminent breakout Churchill had commanded: 'Sink the *Bismarck!*' This was accomplished, but not before her 15-inch guns had sent the battle cruiser *Hood* to the bottom. The *Bismarck* was caught and sunk by the guns and torpedoes of the British Home Fleet on 27 May 1941; she took more than two thousand men with her. The whole episode served to underscore the weakness of the challenge offered by the Kriegsmarine's small surface fleet; only the U-boat was capable of defeating Britain at sea. 'Special Intelligence' played only a small part in the *Bismarck* affair, but it was the key to the Royal Navy operation launched in its aftermath.

It was clear from Enigma decrypts that, with the *Bismarck* gone, the large network of supply ships that was to have supported her patrol would to be made available to U-boats. This would enable them to extend their range and time in the operations area. Attacking the Kriegsmarine's supply network would severely restrict Dönitz's options. This small fleet of tankers was scattered throughout the Atlantic, but its whereabouts was soon betrayed by the signals sent to customers arranging a rendezvous; 'Special Intelligence' was able to provide the Royal Navy with almost all the information it needed to act.

The first ship to go was the 10,000-ton tanker *Belchen*, caught on 3 June off Greenland by the cruisers *Aurora* and *Kenya*. Within a fortnight the Royal Navy had rolled up almost the entire network at sea; some nine tankers and supply ships sunk in the North and South Atlantic.[6] There was understandable euphoria at the OIC; this was real operational intelligence. But it was risky; it was inevitable that the Kriegsmarine would ask how it had been possible for the British to sink or capture almost every ship in the supply fleet in a matter of days. The Royal Navy officers involved were asking the same question.

The key to an effective but more cautious use of 'Special Intelligence' was the Tracking Room plot upon which Winn marked known and suspected U-boat positions. This information could be matched with the estimated position of all merchant ships in the Atlantic. Convoys that appeared to be in danger of running into a U-boat patrol line could, with the help of Ultra intelligence, be rerouted round it. There would be no significant increase in the number of U-boats sunk; the priority was the safe and timely arrival of the convoys. Soon no convoy set out from Britain without a route that had first been checked against the Tracking

Room Plot. The priceless information contained on this was sent to the Operations Room at the new combined headquarters established to direct the battle in the Atlantic. It was Churchill who had bullied the Admiralty into opening a Western Approaches Command centre. The site chosen was a nondescript white stone office block close to the Liverpool waterfront – Derby House. By February 1941 a huge concrete bunker had been constructed beneath it to house; a warren of corridors, switchboards and teleprinter rooms. At the heart of the bunker was the huge Operations Room with its main Atlantic plot, upon which the position of every convoy, escort group, air patrol and U-boat was mapped. A team of WRNS (members of the Women's Royal Naval Service) updated 'the Plot' day and night. It was an unsophisticated operation judged by the standards of the electronic age, with cardboard symbols and convoy routes mapped out in coloured elastic, but it worked well.

From his office above the Ops Room floor the new Commander in Chief Western Approaches, Admiral Sir Percy Noble, was able to take in the state of the battle in the Atlantic at a glance. The appointment of this clever, fastidious, popular officer greatly improved the morale and efficiency of the Royal Navy's escorts. It was Noble who had systematically set about organizing the escorts into groups and training them to operate together. On the floor of the Ops Room below, sky and navy blue uniforms worked alongside: Derby House was also the new home of No. 15 Group Coastal Command; its senior officer occupied the office next to Noble's.

The successful rerouting of convoys depended above all on the speed with which Western Approaches Command was able to react to 'the Admiralty guess' – the regular update on U-boat movements provided by the Tracking Room. A white U-boat symbol was used to indicate an estimated position on 'the Plot', black if it could be confirmed; in June 1941 most of the symbols were black.

The value of 'the Admiralty guess' was clearly demonstrated at the end of June when Western Approaches Command was warned of a pack preparing to attack homebound convoy HX 133. Noble was able to reinforce it with escorts from a nearby outbound convoy to provide a screen of ten ships. The convoy was to be protected for its entire journey.

The U-boats found HX 133 on the night of 26 June; over the next three days fourteen attacked, managing to sink six ships but at the cost of two of their own. For Dönitz, this was an entirely unacceptable exchange rate.

Remarkably, HX 133 was the only eastbound convoy attacked in the North Atlantic in June. Winn's 'guess' enabled Western Approaches Command to reroute convoys clear of the waiting packs; some 380 ships loaded with vital war supplies were able to cross unmolested, a 99 per cent success rate. The country had cause for celebration.

That there was a problem was obvious to U-boat Command; the successes tailed off dramatically. In spite of the shortage of operational U-boats, hunting in the first half of 1941 had been good with 363 ships sunk – some 1½ million tons of shipping. In June the U-boat fleet sank 310,143 tons of shipping in all theatres; the following month that figure fell to just 94,209. About four hundred loaded merchant ships were to cross the North Atlantic in July; not one was sunk by a U-boat.

What made it all the more baffling was that it coincided with a marked increase in the U-boat fleet. Dönitz had begun to doubt the security of radio transmissions in the spring, long before the flow of 'Special Intelligence' had turned to a flood. On 18 April 1941 he wrote in his War Diary of a distinct 'impression that British traffic had been diverted around our attacking formations because the enemy had learned of their location from an unknown source…every possibility of a security leak must be obviated at all costs.'

Dönitz was pacified by constant assurances from Kriegsmarine 'experts' in Berlin that all was well; most of his commanders accepted the security of the Enigma codes without question. Yet one eminent German scholar has claimed that, in the second half of 1941, 'Special Intelligence' saved as much as 2 million tons of Allied shipping. Whilst the U-boat staff learned nothing of this setback, by the summer of 1941 there were pressing problems that were all too obvious.

The long-awaited increase in the number of frontline boats was a cause for celebration at U-boat Command. Dönitz was able to deploy some thirty in April 1941; within three months that number had doubled. Yet this expansion was not without its price. Established officers and crewmen had been transferred to form a core of experience on the new boats, but they were very thinly spread. The new crews had been pushed through a crash training programme which had done little to prepare them for battle conditions. Hanns-Ferdinand Maßmann took command of the *U-137* in December 1940 after serving as a watch officer for six war patrols. He remembers: 'I became a commander without having had any kind of training or practice in how to go about an underwater attack. I had no option but to organize a steamer myself, which I managed one way or another. We then used that for one or two days as a target boat out in the Baltic. There is no doubt that the quality of training was no longer adequate.'

One incident in particular was to graphically demonstrate this failure. In August the young, seasick crew of *U-570* was found and depth-charged by a Hudson of Coastal Command. The pilot's log picks up the story:

> The U-boat fully surfaced in a slightly bow-heavy position and 10 or 12 of crew came out of the conning tower wearing yellow lifesaving jackets and stood on the deck. Made an attack on them with front turret and belly guns. The U-boat crew ran back inside the conning tower and aircraft continued attacks with guns firing about 2000 rounds. A white flag was then waved from the conning tower and on the deck they displayed a large white board.

It was surely impossible that the crew of a U-boat had surrendered to an aircraft? It had been the *U-570*'s first war patrol; only four of her crew had any previous combat experience. The Hudson's depth charges had exploded close to the U-boat, throwing the crew into a blind panic. Although the attack had caused only minor damage, its commander gave the order to abandon ship. No attempt was made to resist the aircraft or the Royal Navy trawler sent to capture the U-boat. The crew had enough presence of mind to throw their Enigma machine and ciphers overboard, but the Royal Navy had the U-boat. She was eventually recommissioned as His Majesty's submarine *Graph*.

When news of *U-570*'s capture reached the U-boat arm, senior petty officers sucked their teeth and asked: 'Why was its commander deemed fit to carry out a war patrol?' Experienced crew men knew success and survival depended on the ability of their commander. In the first half of 1941 a number of established commanders left their boats to take up posts ashore; it was an unsettling experience for the crews they left behind. The large Type IX-B *U-123* had enjoyed its fair share of success during the 'happy time', and also some celebrity as the U-boat featured in the film *U-Boote Westwärts*. The crew had been in some tough scrapes with British escorts but trusted its commander, Karl-Heinz Möhle, to get them home safely. Leading control room mechanic Richard Amstein had served alongside Möhle from the beginning: 'He was prudent. If there was a danger that threatened the crew or the boat he would go out of his way to avoid it without forgetting why he was there in the first place. He was not over-cautious. We sank ships with Möhle.'

This successful partnership came to an end in May 1941 when command passed to a twenty-eight-year-old unknown who had trained as a navy pilot. A reluctant recruit to the U-boat arm, Reinhard Hardegen had nevertheless demonstrated to its senior officers a crispness of thought and determination to succeed. Hardegen in some respects resembled his Commander in Chief: tall, thin and rather vulpine in appearance, restless and purposeful by disposition. He had served as first officer on *U-124* and as a commander for one patrol only with a small Type II boat before Dönitz chose him to take over *U-123*. Hardegen recalls: 'It wasn't all that simple taking over a successful boat whose commander had been awarded the *Ritterkreuz* [Knight's Cross]. For the crew I was a newcomer and, what's more, I came from the naval air service. And navy men didn't really take us pilots very seriously, because they didn't think we understood the navy properly. I had to impose myself.'

The U-boat's twenty-two-year-old watch officer, Horst von Schroeter, had been on just one war patrol with Möhle before the change in command. 'The crew was rather full of itself. It wanted to know what this new commander was capable of,' he recalls. Before joining *U-123* von Schroeter's only combat experience had been with the battle cruiser *Scharnhorst*; he too was an outsider, but the crew took to him. Adapting to the new commander proved altogether more difficult. Amstein recalls: 'You couldn't say Möhle was comradely, but it wasn't 100 per cent "I am the master, you are nothing". Hardegen had little consideration for his men. When he didn't like something and there was someone to blame, that person would be bawled at immediately. I even experienced it myself.'

Hardegen admits: 'I certainly wasn't very easy, but I never asked more of people than I asked of myself. I always tried to be correct – for example, there was absolutely no alcohol on board. You weren't supposed to have any, but there were commanders who took crates of beer along, which I still don't think was right, because when people have drunk a bottle of beer and there is an "alarm", sometimes it's only a question of a tenth of a second. If one person makes the wrong move this could cost the whole boat.'

Success alone would, in Hardegen's view, establish his position with the crew. He was lucky; his first patrol was to quieter waters. In May, while most of the U-boat fleet was struggling to make an impact in the North Atlantic, a handful of larger boats had found rich pickings to the south. Hardegen left Lorient on 15 June bound for Freetown on the West African coast; he found his first target after just five days. It took three torpedoes and several rounds of gunfire to finish the freighter off; only then did he discover she was a neutral Portuguese ship. But a few days later *U-123* attacked Sierra Leone convoy SL76, and sank three Allied freighters. At one point the U-boat was detected by the escorts and subjected to a lengthy depth charge attack. This incident was enough for some of the older hands to conclude that their new commander was prepared to push them to the edge. 'Hardegen had "throat trouble"', says Richard Amstein. 'He wanted to have the Knight's Cross. All the other decorations were put on the chest, but he wanted one round his throat. You only got one if you really went hell for leather.' Hardegen denies this; with a wife and two children in Germany, he was as anxious as any man to return home safely. 'There were just a few older petty officers who would perhaps have preferred it if I had skipped a ship every now and then,' he recalls.

For all that, British air patrols were infrequent and convoy protection less well organized than on the main routes to and from North America.

The atmosphere was sufficiently relaxed for the new commander to organize games on *U-123*'s decks. Amstein remembers:

> Hardegen said, 'Let's have a nice day.' A watch had to remain below, of course, but we had a temporary shower put up on the deck – the water was even hot. We took our clothes off – everyone was naked. I remember we caught a shark; we put a rancid piece of bacon fat on a big meat-hook and it wasn't long before there was a shark hanging on it. We had fun. At one point Hardegen came up with a chocolate pudding and two men sat facing each other around the pudding, blindfolded, and they each had to feed the other with chocolate pudding. That looked really funny.

That it was quiet enough for sack races on the U-boat's deck was no accident. It was unusually quiet. The hunting was bad, and yet these waters should have yielded a rich harvest of ships. Where were the convoys?

Once again the answer lay in the Submarine Tracking Room, where *U-123*'s progress had been closely marked; on Winn's advice, convoys that appeared in danger of crossing Hardegen's path were being rerouted. In fact the radio traffic between *U-123* and Kernével was being read with great interest by all those in the 'Ultra' circle. Amongst these was the Prime Minister, who loved secrets of any kind and this one in particular. In the daily bundle of decrypts sent to Downing Street on 28 June 1941 Churchill was able to read Hardegen's own report to Dönitz[8] of his successful attack on Sierra Leone convoy SL 76 the previous day. Another decrypted signal from *U-123* revealed that she had refuelled from a ship at a port in the Canaries on or around the 25th.

It is clear from the decrypts and the explanatory notes that sometimes accompanied them by the summer of 1941 Winn and his colleagues were piecing together an extraordinarily detailed picture of the U-boat arm and its leader. On 24 June a British listening station intercepted a message from Dönitz to his U-boats, which included this phrase: 'At them! Attack them! Sink them!' Why, Churchill inquired, had Dönitz used this forceful injunction at this time? The Naval Section at Bletchley Park offered an interpretation of Dönitz's words: 'His interest in the game is a very personal one. It engenders in him the enthusiasm of a crowd at a football match. Cries of encouragement are frequent, though it is not often he gets as excited as this. This particular mixture of sea-doggery and hysteria is due to the fact that for some time before he had been having a pretty lean time, which as several fault-finding signals show, had made him rather tetchy.' Naval Intelligence knew its enemy. This indeed was Dönitz the man.

Hardegen's war patrol was to fizzle out; by the time *U-123* reached the assembly point for Sierra Leone convoys at Freetown, almost all traffic had been rerouted away from the area. Just one more freighter was sunk, bringing the total to four in seventy-six days. Of course, no one on the boat thought to blame their Enigma machine. While Hardegen was here he encountered the other serious challenge that the U-boat faced that summer. 'Off Freetown we saw ships going in and we had them in our sights. We wanted to sink them. But then it got dark and suddenly they were brightly illuminated and they all had the American flag painted on the side. They were neutral and we couldn't do anything.'

'One already felt in those days that the Americans were doing quite a lot that could not truly be reconciled with neutrality,' von Schroeter recalls. Hardegen was not the first commander to be frustrated in this way. A U-boat had sunk an American freighter off the West African coast just the month before, in spite of explicit orders from Hitler to the contrary. A signal was sent by U-boat Command sternly reminding *U-123* and all the other boats in southern waters that contact with American ships was to be 'avoided at all cost'. The reason for this uncharacteristic caution soon became apparent.

All eyes in Berlin had been turned eastwards for months. On 22 June 1941 the armies of the Reich began the 'great crusade' against the Soviet Union. Operation Barbarossa would, Hitler told his generals, cement the foundations of a thousand-year Reich by creating the *Lebensraum*, the living space, that the German people needed. Nothing was to threaten this most important of tasks. The Battle of the Atlantic would continue, but America was not to be drawn into it.

Hitler's policy was defined on 21 June, the day before the launch of Barbarossa. Dönitz was obliged to send the following signal to his U-boat fleet: 'The Führer has ordered that during the next few weeks all incidents with the USA are to be avoided...only clearly identifiable enemy cruisers, battleships and aircraft carriers may be attacked. Should darkened warships be sighted, this is no proof that they are hostile.'[9] This was very unwelcome news indeed; it severely restricted the U-boat's ability to attack its chief enemies, the convoy escorts. At night it was almost impossible to tell whether a darkened destroyer or battleship was British or American. This situation was, Dönitz later wrote, unique in the history of war.

Of course, the British kept the United States well informed of German intentions. By the summer of 1941 London had begun to share with Washington some of the information it was gathering from 'Special Intelligence'. The objective of this policy can be characterized thus: 'Hitler is anxious to avoid war with America, so America is at liberty to do more.' It was a difficult and delicate message, for many in the United States were still opposed to the tightening of transatlantic bonds. Peter Smithers, was working for Naval Intelligence in the British Embassy in Washington at this time, he remembers: 'It would have been very dangerous if anybody in the Embassy had given the impression that that was why we were there. But we all knew it; the one thing we hoped for was that the Americans would come into the war. If they did, the war would be won.' Smithers had been sent to America to help coordinate the exchange of naval intelligence: 'We were giving them everything that we dared give them. There were certain risks we dared not run with our own code and cipher material, but, broadly speaking, we were giving them a great deal.' The British considered they were taking quite a risk. From the first, Smithers was struck by how woefully slack US navy security appeared to be:

When I went to the United States to take up my job in intelligence there I travelled with Captain Earl Mills, head of the US Bureau of Ships, and he had the plans of our newest British battleship, the *Prince of Wales*, which he was carrying in a little bag in the aeroplane. The plane was to land in Lisbon where we were to pick up the clipper.

We arrived late at night in Lisbon; all the hotels were full. Finally we found a friendly concierge, who said, 'Well, gentlemen, you must have a bed, and I think if you go to this address at least you'll be able to get some sleep.'

So we went to the address. It was opened by a nice-looking woman, who showed us up to a room which we could share and we were told that the bathroom was down the passage. The captain went down to have his bath, and when he came back he said, 'Say, Lieutenant, there sure are a lot of handsome dames walking about in this house with very few clothes on.'

We were in a naughty house with the plans of the latest British battleship. So Earl put this under his pillow and slept with his head on top of it. But this was the order of American naval intelligence at that time. It was pretty rough.

For all that the British were reluctant to share their secrets, this was an exchange. The US Navy Department was able to furnish Smithers with valuable intelligence from Japanese codes broken by American cryptographers. The links that would be needed if the Americans were coaxed into the war were already being forged.

The American occupation of Iceland in July 1941 signalled to friend and foe that their participation could not be long delayed. The British had established ships and aircraft in Iceland to extend the convoy shield across the Atlantic. The large American military presence was to relieve the British of the responsibility of securing these bases. This was welcome indeed, for British troops were desperately needed in the Mediterranean and North Africa.

With the arrival of US troops it was agreed that US air and naval forces would assume responsibility for the protection of convoys between Canada and Iceland – a move that threatened to bring the U-boat into even more direct confrontation with the United States. News of this further provocation was greeted with dismay by Raeder and Dönitz; this was surely tantamount to a declaration of war. The Führer disagreed. The position remained the same. It left the U-boat in an impossible straitjacket. By September 1941 the ships of an officially neutral country had begun escorting the supplies Britain needed to make war on Germany, and yet the U-boats were powerless to prevent it.

The American sabre was rattled in September when the destroyer *USS Greer* depth-charged *U-652*. Although the US navy was under orders to attack only when attacked itself, *Greer* chose to pursue the U-boat for at least six hours. Hard-pressed, *U-652* fired one torpedo before managing to escape. In one of his 'fireside chats' with the nation, President Roosevelt rather disingenuously accused the U-boat of unprovoked 'piracy'. His tone was harsh and uncompromising: 'When you see a rattlesnake poised, you don't wait until it has struck before you crush it. These Nazi submarines and raiders are the rattlesnakes of the Atlantic...American warships and planes will no longer wait until Axis submarines lurking under the water, or Axis raiders on the surface of the sea, strike their deadly first blow.'

This sounded very much like war in all but name. Raeder and Dönitz flew to the Wolf's Lair, the Führer's field headquarters in East Prussia, to argue again for the lifting of restrictions on U-boat operations against American ships. Once again Hitler was unmoved. Nothing could be allowed to impede the vigorous pursuit of victory in the east, he told his admirals. Dönitz had already been ordered to divert a number of U-boats into Arctic waters to attack convoys carrying war supplies from Britain to the Soviet Union. In a further dilution of the Atlantic fleet, boats were also ordered to the Mediterranean to support the German war effort in North Africa. The already difficult task of finding Atlantic convoys was now made harder, as the number of available U-boats that Dönitz was able to deploy in his search groups began to dwindle. It was a bitter pill for a man who believed that the war in the west could only be won in the Atlantic.

There were, however, some notable successes. On 11 September six boats of group *Markgraf* found slow convoy SC 42 east of Greenland; over the next five days the pack sank nineteen ships. Just three days later SC 44 was attacked by *U-74* and Erich Topp's *U-552*; the two U-boats claimed seven ships between them. Both attacks demonstrated that, if a convoy was found by a pack, ships could and usually would be sunk. Although the hunting was bad that summer, some experienced commanders still prospered; Topp managed to sink enough to secure the Knight's Cross. Overall figures were nevertheless disappointing. In August and September close to half the U-boats sent into the Atlantic returned without anything to show for weeks on patrol.

By the end of October 1941 the high hopes with which the U-boat force had begun that year were forgotten. That autumn Dönitz's packs were concentrated in the western North Atlantic where the convoys were screened by American warships. On the night of 16 October, during a fierce pack attack on slow convoy SC 48, the American destroyer USS *Kearney* was hit by a torpedo; although the ship was saved, eleven crew men lost their lives. 'We have tried to avoid shooting,' President Roosevelt told the American people, 'but the shooting has started.' The issue was put beyond doubt just days later. In the early hours of 31 October *U-552* sighted the fast eastbound convoy HX 156, escorted by five American destroyers. Through the periscope of a U-boat in dawn's half-light, it was impossible to tell which flag the escorts sailed under. Yet with the instinct of an aggressive, experienced hunter Topp decided to attack a destroyer on the edge of the convoy.

His target was the USS *Reuben James*; a torpedo hit her port side, cutting the ship in two. The forward section blew up, sending a plume of flame, twisted steel and bodies skywards. The stern remained afloat for a further five minutes, as fuel spilt into the sea from the ruptured tanks and covered the survivors in a black, choking coat of oil. From the water men could hear the screams of those trapped inside the ship as she sank. As the twisted remnants of the destroyer slipped under her depth charges exploded, killing many of those left struggling in the water. Only 45 of the 160-man crew were saved. She was the first US navy ship to be sunk in the war; her loss was a profound shock to American public and politicians.

Topp had witnessed the explosion and seen the ship sink, but knew nothing of the carnage he had caused until after the war: 'I only found out about all this afterwards, but for nights on end, I must confess, it really distressed me and I just couldn't get the catastrophe out of my mind.' Of course, by the time the *Reuben James* met her end Topp had already accounted for more than 100,000 tons of British-controlled shipping.

The Führer's orders had been broken again, but Topp found Dönitz remarkably relaxed about the whole thing. He recalls, 'I reported every detail and Dönitz said, "It's all right. You acted correctly."' Hitler's directive forbidding attacks on darkened warships was to remain in place just a few weeks longer.

The American historian Clay Blair estimated that in the last three months of 1941 some 3700 merchant ships passed back and forth along the Atlantic lifeline, and of these just 54 were lost to U-boats.[10] It was a feeble rate of return. Dönitz blamed it on the transfer of U-boats to the

Mediterranean and Arctic waters, decisions he vigorously opposed. This was certainly an important factor in the closing months of the year, but the rot had set in long before; inexperienced commanders, the continual lack of air support and the growing American presence had all played their part. Above all, it was 'Special Intelligence' and the skilful use made of it by the Admiralty's Submarine Tracking Room that was the chief cause of this dismal decline in fortunes. 'Coincidence always seems to favour the enemy,' Dönitz remarked in his War Diary. The staff at Kernéval had estimated in June that to strike a 'mortal blow' to Britain the U-boat would need to sink some 800,000 tons of shipping a month; the monthly average for the year was to be less than a quarter of this figure.

The final convoy battle of 1941 was to underscore the transformation in the U-boat's fortunes. Dönitz learned from German spies in Spain that a convoy was due to sail from Gibraltar in the last two weeks of the year, and there was time enough to deploy the group *Seeräuber* across its route. What the spies failed to discover, however, was that HG 76 was protected by seventeen warships including the new 'jeep' or escort carrier *Audacity*. This converted merchant ship would ensure an air screen for the convoy when it passed beyond the reach of Coastal Command aircraft. The escorts were under the command of a hard-bitten, determined anti-submarine specialist, Commander F. J. ('Johnny') Walker.

The journey began well for the British. A signal from Dönitz urging the boats of *Seeräuber* to find and attack HG 76 by 17 December was decrypted at Bletchley; the convoy was put on its mettle. Walker managed to steer the convoy through the Seeräuber patrol line undetected. On the night of 15 December one of the pack, *U-127*, was spotted on the surface. Contact was made as the U-boat dived; the Australian destroyer *Nestor* carried out a short, accurate attack and a deep, dull rumbling was heard below. First blood to the Royal Australian Navy. On the morning of the 17th a plane from *Audacity* found another of the pack, *U-131*, about 20 miles ahead of the convoy. With escorts to spare, Johnny Walker decided to take his sloop, the *Stork*, and four other ships out of the convoy screen and give chase. His reward was a second scalp in as many days. The following day Walker's group claimed another: *U-434* was forced to the surface and the crew jumped into the ocean after setting scuttling charges.

The loss of these three U-boats, each one commanded by a novice, presented Dönitz with a dilemma: abandon, or persist with the attack? Aircraft from the *Audacity* posed a constant threat to the shadowing pack, repeatedly forcing the boats to dive or withdraw. 'The sinking of the aircraft carrier is of particular importance not only in this case but also in every future convoy action,' Dönitz concluded. The attack called for older, wiser heads. Dönitz decided to send three of his most experienced commanders to intercept HG 76, including the Knight's Cross holder and reigning U-boat ace Engelbert Endraß.

The other pack members claimed their first success before these three reached the convoy. In the early hours of the 19th one of *U-574*'s torpedoes hit and sank the destroyer *Stanley*. Retribution was swift. The *Stork* pursued and forced *U-574* to the surface; Walker described what followed in his report to the Admiralty:

> The U-boat appeared to be turning continuously to port just inside *Stork*'s turning circle. I kept her illuminated with Snowflake flares and fired with the 4-inch guns until they could not be sufficiently depressed.... Bursts of machine gun fire were let off when they could be brought to bear, but the prettiest shooting was made by my first lieutenant with a stripped Lewis gun from over the top of the bridge screen. He quickly reduced the conning tower to a mortuary. Eventually I managed to ram her just before the conning tower and roll her over. She hung for a few seconds on the bow and then scraped aft where she was greeted by a pattern of ten depth charges. I was informed that a Boche in the water, who was holding up his arms and crying, '*Kamarad*', received the content of the depth charge thrower in his face instead.[11]

The remaining boats of *Seeräuber* continued the pursuit, but were constantly forced under by *Audacity*'s aircraft. This chasing group was joined by Dönitz's cavalry on the afternoon of 21 December, and that night one of the new boats found *Audacity* on the edge of the convoy and sank her. It was the success Dönitz was hoping for, but at a price; Walker's escorts tirelessly harried the pursuing pack, and at some point during the same night Endraß's *U-567* was lost.

It was a grimly fitting end to a disastrous year for the German navy. The loss of five boats. was the greatest loss inflicted on the U-boat arm in a single operation to date. The death of Endraß was a particular blow. The former first officer of *U-47*, Endraß had been at Prien's shoulder when the *Royal Oak* was sunk; as a commander he had accounted for twenty-five ships, totalling some 138,000 tons. Again, Dönitz chose to withhold news of this loss, but Erich Topp learnt of his friend's death at sea: 'We listened into the communications with other boats, and when Endraß didn't report back any more I deduced that his boat had gone.' Topp and Endraß had enjoyed a special friendship; comrades had referred to them as Castor and Pollux, the inseparable U-boat twins. They had trained together, shared a villa, celebrated each other's successes and survival. Topp remembers: 'As he was putting to sea on his last operation, I stood on the pier and I waved as I had always done. I had the impression then that he was full of misgivings.' The two men had always celebrated success and survival with their girlfriends at the Scheherazade Restaurant in Paris. It was there that Topp went to remember his friend: 'The staff knew that I had been very badly hit by his death. It was already very late at night, and the guests had already left. There was just the small circle of those who had been our friends. The people at Scheherazade laid out a remembrance meal for Endraß.'

The attack on HG76 seemed to mark the culmination of three months of failure; some on Dönitz's staff were now beginning to question the wisdom of persevering with the convoy war in the North Atlantic. Dönitz rejected this pessimistic assessment, but he was prepared to admit to his War Diary on 23 December 1941 that 'the chances of losses are greater than the prospects of success'. By Christmas Day the war at sea had all but ground to a halt, with not one U-boat on station and ready for combat anywhere in the North Atlantic.

At the Admiralty, there was a growing sense of optimism that the tide had turned. In the first two years and four months of the war U-boats had sunk 1124 ships, some 5.3 million tons of British and neutral shipping. Total losses to all causes totalled more than 9 million tons which represented a substantial slice of the British merchant fleet. As a result, imports had fallen from 60 million to 30.5 million tons, yet by the end of 1941 there was reason to hope that British forces had stopped the rot. In the Submarine Tracking Room Roger Winn logged: 'There is still no sign of any renewal of attacks in the North Atlantic on any scale comparable with that of the recent campaign and the primary objective seems, at least temporarily, to be no longer destruction of merchant shipping.'

As the New Year approached Britain knew it could count on the industrial and military might of a new ally. Final victory in the Atlantic seemed assured.

HMS *Starling*'s depth-charge crew carries out 'Operation Plaster' on a U-boat in the winter of 1944. The *Starling* was commanded by the Royal Navy's most successful U-boat killer, Captain 'Johnny' Walker.

Right: A signalman aboard HMS *Vanoc* signals an American destroyer on convoy duty in the Atlantic, November 1941. Although the United States was still offically 'neutral', its warships had already begun escorting British convoys.

Below: A terrified Indian seaman is among a group of survivors rescued from the Atlantic by a British destroyer in November 1940.

Above: Captain 'Johnny' Walker directing the ships of the 2nd Support Group from the bridge of the *Starling*.

Below: The Atlantic plot in the main operations room at Derby House in Liverpool, in the summer of 1941.

Opposite page: A message is taken in the radio room of a U-boat; it will be decoded on the four-rotor Enigma machine in the foreground. The radio link with headquarters was vital for intelligence on convoy movements.

Above: The boarding party from HMS *Bulldog*, led by Sub Lieutenant David Balme, makes its way towards the U-110 on 9 May 1941. Balme was able to recover vital Enigma intelligence from the U-boat before it sank.

Below: Churchill and Roosevelt first met in August 1941. Among the senior US officers present was Admiral Ernest King (2nd right), whose refusal in 1942 to implement coastal convoys in American waters, was to place Anglo-American relations under strain.

Above: A convoy ot ships assembles on the east coast of the United States for the journey back to Britain.

Right: An American destroyer in stormy seas off the coast of Iceland. In the summer of 1941 US warships were involved in escorting convoys across the Western Atlantic, to the waters south of Iceland; from there they were a British responsibilty.

Above: The 7,451-ton tanker
R.P. Resor burns off the
American coast after being
torpedoed by U-578 in the
early hours of 27 February
1942. Only three of her
50-man crew survived
the attack.

Horst von Schroeter (top, extreme left) directs U-123's fire on the British freighter *Culebra*, pictured here sinking by the stern (centre and right) on 25 January 1942; U-123 was returning from its 'Drumbeat' patrol to the American coast.

CHAPTER EIGHT

BEATING THE DRUM

ALTHOUGH THE U-BOAT took Germany to the brink of war with the United States, it was the dive bombers of a distant ally that pushed it over the precipice. On Sunday, 7 December 1941 the Japanese launched a devastating strike on the US Pacific fleet at Pearl Harbor. Waves of bombers attacked almost entirely unopposed, sinking four battleships and damaging most of the rest of the fleet. Hitler was taken completely by surprise; the Japanese had not seen fit to inform their principal ally. The timing could hardly have been worse: the German advance into the Soviet Union had stalled in front of Moscow, and news was reaching him of a counter-offensive. That the forces of the Reich were thinly spread was all too obvious, yet Hitler chose to honour his pledge to Japan. On 11 December Germany declared war on the United States.

Dönitz was delighted; in his view America had waged war on his U-boats for many months, and here was the opportunity to strike back. He had outlined his plans for an attack on shipping off the US coast to Hitler in person some three months before. It would take time to organize a convoy system along the eastern seaboard of America; in the meantime he expected hunting in these 'virgin waters' to be good. The U-boat, he told the Führer, could strike a sudden heavy blow; the war would begin with a *Paukenschlag*, a roll of drums. After the sharp failures of the autumn, here once again was a chance for success.

Donitz had hoped to muster a sizeable force, but by December the best part of his fleet was involved in supporting German and Italian forces in the Mediterranean. Of ninety-one operational U-boats just six of those that were available to him seemed suitable for this new theatre. One of these was the *U-123* of Reinhard Hardegen, who recalls: 'I was with my wife on a speaking tour in Italy when I found out that the Japanese had attacked Pearl Harbor. I said straightaway, "Oh, there's a chance for me," because I knew I had a big U-boat with the fuel capacity to sail to America and back.'

Some in the U-boat arm harboured strong misgivings about war with the United States, but Hardegen was not one of them; he was angry. On his patrol to African waters that summer he had watched ship after ship with the Stars and Stripes painted boldly on its sides run the blockade with war supplies for Britain. As far as he was concerned, the charade of American neutrality was over; there was a score to settle.

Hardegen returned at once to Lorient to supervise the preparation of *U-123*. On 19 December he was summoned to U-boat Command to meet Dönitz:[1] 'Before every patrol we would be called to Kernével, where we were given our last briefing.' Hardegen and his comrades were told very little about their mission: 'We were given an envelope that we were only supposed to open after receiving a specific radio message. We were just told to make the U-boat ready for a long trip, to take as much fuel and supplies as we could manage.'

By December 1941 the first of the great concrete sea bunkers built in Lorient was operational. It was in Keroman I that *U-123* was prepared; Second Watch Officer Horst von Schroeter knew only that supplies were needed for a long patrol: 'The week before we left, things were pretty frantic. We had to take on food and, as always, we had to use every free corner of the boat to store it. There was the ammunition for the guns; fuel was up to the maximum and we carried 15 torpedoes. There were also a few last checks, diving trials, to make sure everything was water-tight.' Additional space needed to be made for a reporter from the Propaganda Ministry.

Hardegen chose to set out on 23 December; 'I said to myself: I don't want to leave on Christmas Eve after the men have got drunk somewhere because they're homesick and so on. I wanted to leave the day before, so we'd be able to celebrate Christmas peacefully.' There was a good crowd to see the boat off; *U-123* was an old Lorient hand. Soldiers from a nearby army battalion were there to present the crew with a Christmas tree and a cake. After the usual cheers, tears and short speeches *U-123* slipped her mooring lines and to the strains of the unseasonably warlike, 'Sailing Against England', set off down the Scorff to the sea.

A modest Christmas celebration was held on board the following day. Hardegen recalls: 'I went to 50 metres' depth because it would be peaceful there, and we celebrated a Christmas like the ones I remembered from childhood at my parents' house, and as I celebrated it in my own home – a Christian celebration of Christmas. I read the Christmas story, we sang carols, I read from the prophets, and we celebrated appropriately.' Ironically, it is the framed face of Hitler that dominates one of the propaganda photographs taken of this Christian Christmas afloat. The season of goodwill was a short one on *U-123*; control room mechanic Richard Amstein played his accordion, there were presents from home and even a glass of weak punch, then the boat surfaced and resumed its westward journey. Beyond the Bay of Biscay radio contact was made with Kernével and the order given to open the envelope.

Dönitz had decided that this first wave of boats would operate between the St Lawrence river and Cape Hatteras on the North Carolina coast. The shallow waters here were not ideal, but they were busy and there was every reason to suppose the defences to be weak. Surprise was essential: the beat was to be sounded by the six boats at once; the commanders were to reach their stations and await Dönitz's final order to go into action. Hardegen recalls: 'My mission was to operate off New York. I was to carry out no attacks before I arrived there so that I wouldn't betray our position. The exception was if I came across a 10,000-ton ship – I was permitted to attack that.' To ensure the utmost secrecy, U-boat Command had decided not to issue charts of the American coast. Hardegen remembers: 'There were spies everywhere. They had infiltrated all sorts of places, and so this was very deliberate. We only had large nautical charts and I also had a Knaur pocket atlas, and on a page of the atlas, there was a map of New York. That was all I had.' New York was not entirely unfamiliar; Hardegen had visited the city as a naval cadet in 1933, and had gazed across its skyline at night from the top of the new Empire State Building.

The news that *U-123* was America-bound was broken to the crew over the loudspeaker. Richard Amstein recalls: 'A few of the crew wondered whether we would get back from there in one piece, but most of us were enthusiastic.'

To increase the weight of the blow, Dönitz had also decided to send twelve medium-sized Type VII boats into Canadian waters. These U-boats would have fuel for just ten days or so in the operational area, less if they were obliged to chase hard for targets. Erich Topp's *U-552* was bound for warm, southern waters when he received the order from U-boat Command to divert to Newfoundland.

In the Admiralty's 'Citadel' the Submarine Tracking Room was quick to pick up from Enigma decrypts the first signs of this westward movement of boats. By 12 January 1942 the matter was beyond doubt; Rodger Winn was able to report a heavy concentration off the North American seaboard from New York to Cape Race. 'Two groups have so far been formed. One, of six U-boats, is already in position off Cape Race and St John's, and a second, of five U-boats, is apparently approaching the American coast between New York and Portland. It is known that these five U-boats will reach their attacking areas by 13 January.'[2] That this warning was passed to the staff of the Commander in Chief of the US navy, Admiral Ernest J. King, is certain, but no serious action was taken. Admiral King had other problems to consider, most of them in the Pacific. The US navy was still reeling from Pearl Harbor; the Japanese were rolling like an unstoppable tide through Southeast Asia and their submarines had claimed their first successes. The United States also entered the war with an acute shortage of escort vessels. Fifty of its oldest destroyers had been transferred to Britain in 1940; of the 170 or so remaining, some 90 were involved in escort duties in the Atlantic.

Yet for all the difficulties, King cannot escape some blame for the shocking lack of preparedness on America's eastern seaboard. In December the admiral charged with this responsibility had warned King that 'should enemy submarines operate off this coast, this command has no forces available to take adequate action against them, either offensively or defensively'.[3] Above all, no serious attempt was made to corral shipping into coastal convoys. King stands accused by his critics of failing to learn from the British experience that a poorly escorted convoy is better than no convoy at all.

This hard-bitten navy veteran was, it has been suggested, stubbornly unprepared to learn anything from 'a bunch of Limeys'. Peter Smithers, who was working at the British Embassy in Washington, recalls:

Admiral King was a typical bluff old sailor. There were an awful lot of rough edges on him. He was a great professional and tremendously US navy-minded. I think at the back of his mind, though there was a feeling, 'Here are the British. Their navy has an awful lot of fighting experience and is pretty good, but the US navy should be indebted to nobody whatsoever.' I think in a way he had a bit of a chip on his shoulder. He needed handling with some care and some skill.

Whilst Dönitz hoped for favourable conditions on the American coast, he could never have imagined just how favourable they would be. The westward progress of the Drumbeat boats had been monitored carefully at U-boat Command. On 2 January Dönitz decided to break his own orders and authorized *U-123* to search for a Greek steamer drifting some 200 miles east of Newfoundland with a broken rudder. Hardegen remembers: 'There was a pea-souper of a fog when we arrived there. It was a sudden surprise to see the shadowy outline of the ship. I could see that there were two tugs in the process of taking on lines. I couldn't really shoot – I was too close. And then the fog lifted and suddenly I saw two destroyers. I turned around immediately and the fog closed in again. They couldn't see me.'

Dönitz's message to Hardegen had been intercepted by Bletchley, decrypted and passed to the Tracking Room. The two Canadian destroyers were lying in wait for him. 'I said to myself, "If I sink this freighter, and perhaps one destroyer, there's still the second one. It's shallow water and I can't escape, so there's a good chance of my boat being sunk." My mission was to get to New York, so I let the ship go, though I felt very bad about it.'

The U-boat trap did not close, but it took *U-123* 300 miles off course and wasted a great deal of fuel.

Hardegen was to have more luck on the 12th, when he came across the British freighter *Cyclops*. Although some distance from his operational area, this 9100-ton target was too tempting to leave. The two torpedoes that sank *Cyclops* were the first beats on Dönitz's drum. All but two of a company of 180 escaped, but 85 more would freeze to death in the lifeboats.

By the evening of 13 January the Drumbeat boats were all on station. Hardegen was cruising off the Long Island shore when he found his second victim: a 9600-ton German-built tanker, the *Norness*. The following night Hardegen edged *U-123* into the outer reaches of New York Bay. Von Schroeter remembers: 'It was really groping one's way into No Man's Land. Hardegen, perhaps more than the other commanders, went in very close. We could see the cars driving along the coast road, and I could even smell the woods.'

Hardegen recalls:

They simply weren't prepared at all. I assumed that I would find a coast that was blacked out – after all, there was a war on. I found a coast that was brightly lit. At Coney Island there was a huge ferris wheel and roundabouts – I could see it all. Ships were sailing with navigation lights. All the lightships, Sandy Hook and the Ambrose lights were shining brightly. To me this was incomprehensible.

Only our tower showed, and what fisherman would recognize a

German U-boat tower? I saw pilot boats and tugs and fishing smacks they must have thought we were some kind of motorboat. I had flooded the forward tanks because the water was shallow, so if we ran aground I could blow the tanks and be free again. We passed along the coast of Long Island, and in the background the sky was bright. You could see the glow of New York on the clouds.

A few days earlier, the whoop of air raid sirens in Manhattan had sent New Yorkers scurrying for shelter in the subway. This drill might have helped to raise public consciousness of the war; in all other respects it was entirely useless. Whilst there was no risk of a New York Blitz, the enemy was in residence some 50 kilometres offshore. No one had prepared the public for this threat. Hardegen was to spend a week there, picking his targets at leisure.

The hunting was especially good off the large barrier island on the North Carolina coast known as Cape Hatteras. Here the busy shipping lanes were in easy striking distance of deeper water, an ideal killing ground for the U-boat. The night of 19 January 1942 was, von Schroeter recalls, an especially memorable one for the crew of *U-123*:

We had up to twenty steamers in sight at one time. We could tell, because they were all sailing with lights burning. After a sinking the steamers would extinguish their navigation lights for a short while, but they felt so uncomfortable without them that they would light them up again after half an hour or so.

That night we could take our pick. We came across a tanker; we saw its small outline from astern, and we thought it was a smallish coastal tanker of about 2000 tons. Hardegen said, 'It's not worth a torpedo, we'll do it with the deck gun.' So we fired I don't know how many shots into the tanker, which then started to burn. As we got closer to it we realized that it was big, over 8000 tons. It was the last one that night, that and in the end we sank her with a torpedo. We sank three ships that night and it was really a question of choosing the easiest.

Below, in the hull of the U-boat, the crew could hear the muffled crunch of a torpedo impact and the desperate creaking of the ship as the bulkheads gave way. Richard Amstein recalls: 'Lots of the men would shout, "Hurrah, a hit!" I never did, because there were people on board the ship that was sunk, and they would be in the water. I always thought about that. The others would shout: "We've sunk another one!" Well, no, that was never something I enjoyed.' 'Of course we felt positive about the success we had achieved, this was our mission after all,' says Horst von Schroeter. 'There were cases when a large fire erupted on a tanker. That was a bitter feeling – the thought that people might be jumping into the water and straight into the flames.'

The desperate calls for help made by these merchant ships almost always went unanswered; they did, however, provide *U-123* with valuable intelligence. Von Schroeter recalls: 'They gave out an SOS with their name. Our radio operator would be sitting below, listening on the 600-metre band, the merchant-shipping wavelength, so we knew the names of the ships we'd sunk.'

The closest brush that *U-123* had was with a potential victim, a large Norwegian factory whaler, the *Kosmos II*. 'The whaler was about as fast as we were and took us on and wanted to ram us,' von Schroeter recalls. 'This was a captain with war experience who knew what he was doing. He came close, to about 500 metres. He had his gun on the stern and we had ours in front, so we couldn't do anything to each other. Slowly the distance increased. Using all the power we had we managed to get a little bit ahead of him. He was constantly radioing, "In pursuit of submarine." In the end he realized he couldn't catch us.'

Nearly two hours after *Kosmos II* sent her first signal a navy aircraft appeared; *U-123* dived and the plane gave up the chase. 'That was all the anti-submarine defence we met during the patrol,' von Schroeter recalls.

The American public was told an entirely different story. At least the US navy propaganda machine proved itself capable of vigorous action. Hardegen remembers: 'We listened to the American radio transmissions and we heard, "We have sunk a U-boat." We were supposed to have been sunk three times. Every time we sank a ship we were sunk again. The Americans obviously needed this as a consolation – the idea that they had done something. But it wasn't true.'

By the end of January 1942 five of the six Drumbeat boats had sunk twenty-three ships, a total of 150,000 tons. Hardegen's share of that total was nine ships, 50,766 tons. His last two victims were claimed on the journey home; one of the ships, the 3000-ton British freighter *Culebra*, was prepared to make a battle of it. Von Schroeter recalls: 'We were east of Bermuda. Hardegen took a careful look at her through the periscope. The sea was relatively calm, so it was possible to consider a gun attack. She sailed past us and then we emerged. We got the gun crew down on the deck at once, ammunition was handed down and we started to fire.'

Hardegen remembers: 'She started to fire back at us from the stern. We were hit a few times, but nothing penetrated the hull. I felt a little bit queasy when they started to shoot, of course. At first they were short, and then there was a long one over the boat, but we were lucky. Von Schroeter had to fire his gun at theirs to put it out of action, which we did. The crew took to the lifeboats. Then we were able to finish off the ship.'

Hardegen approached the lifeboats and gave the survivors food, fresh water and a course to the Bermudas before resuming his homeward journey. Dönitz was delighted: *U-123*'s war patrol had been a complete success. He sent a typically pithy but warm signal to the boat: 'To the Drumbeater Hardegen. Bravo. You beat the drum well.'

The smaller Type VII boats had also notched up successes in Canadian waters, but it had been much tougher. The commander of *U-552*, Erich Topp, recalls: 'We entered these icy waters and a number of the crew ended up with frozen feet, limbs; we weren't dressed warmly enough. People were standing on the bridge with icicles hanging off their caps; everything was under ice. The water that came on deck froze immediately; the temperature was minus 10 degrees; the balance of the boat was threatened, and every two hours we had to dive to melt away the ice. That was a bad time.'

To make matters worse, all the U-boats in these frozen waters were plagued by torpedo failures. Topp managed to bag just three ships, 'a derisory number'; overall, the twelve Type VIIs sank 18 vessels.

For all that, Dönitz was well satisfied with these first attacks on the American coast. The Propaganda Ministry was grateful for a chance to report U-boat successes after so many disappointing months. The German public learned of Hardegen's sight-seeing visit to New York and a photograph of Manhattan, reportedly taken from *U-123*'s conning tower, appeared in the press long before the boat had returned to port.

When *U-123* did reach Lorient, von Schroeter was embarrassed by the size of the reception committee: 'A boat with propaganda men came out to film us. I didn't like this circus much, because for us it was really almost like target practice – there was no defence, the steamers weren't even zigzagging.' Hardegen recalls: 'The U-boat commanders who happened to be in port were there. There were the so-called "Blitz maidens", the radio assistants, with bunches of flowers. And then there was Dönitz, who came on board and pinned the Knight's Cross on me on the deck of my boat. That was, of course, the special thing about the whole business.'

After hearing Hardegen's report, Dönitz concluded that 'peacetime conditions' would ensure successes for some time to come. The maximum possible effort must be put into attacking the Atlantic coast of America; boats would be sent as far south as the Caribbean and the Gulf of Mexico. Dönitz's objective, as outlined in his War Diary at this time, was simply to sink more than the Allies could build: 'The enemy powers' shipping is one large whole. It is therefore immaterial where a ship is sunk – in the end it must still be replaced by a new ship. The decisive question for the long term lies in the race between sinking and new construction.'[4]

The westward progress of Dönitz's boats caused consternation at the

Admiralty. The US navy's failure to introduce a convoy system threatened to breathe life into a U-boat campaign which had appeared almost dead. Rodger Winn's weekly Tracking Room reports made for grim reading:

> The number of U-boats in the Atlantic has now reached the record total of 53...a large proportion of the ships sunk have been laden tankers of substantial displacement. The tonnage lost in January will be found to amount to an ugly figure...no effective counter measures have been employed....[5]

The 'ugly figure' for January 1942 amounted to 106 ships or some 420,000 tons, the largest portion of this total claimed by U-boats operating in North American waters. Worse news was to follow.

In the first week of February Winn was obliged to admit that the Tracking Room could no longer predict with 'any confidence the present and future movements of U-boats'. The flow of 'Special Intelligence' had dried up. Furthermore, no one at Bletchley Park was confident that it could be restored. The first indications that a change in the Enigma codes was being prepared had come some four months before. In September 1941 Bletchley intercepted early tests of a new Enigma machine, with an additional fourth rotor. It was intended for use on the Atlantic net; the key cipher used for signals between U-boats on patrol and headquarters, Hydra, was to be replaced by a new cipher, Triton.

Dönitz had been repeatedly assured that there was no evidence that his codes were compromised. For all that, there were just too many 'coincidences'. Alarm bells sounded in September 1941 when a British submarine attacked three U-boats ordered to a rendezvous in the Cape Verde islands. 'A British submarine does not appear in such a remote part of the ocean,' Dönitz observed in his War Diary; 'either our ciphers have been compromised or it is a case of leakage.' This was followed by the sinking of two U-boat supply ships in the South Atlantic; more 'coincidences'.[6] The Admiralty had been careless with the use it made of some of its 'Special Intelligence'. As far as Dönitz was concerned the case for a change in the codes was proven.

Soon a virtual U-boat blackout descended on Bletchley Park's Hut 8. The key cipher for operational purposes, the Atlantic net, would defeat the best efforts of the cryptanalysts for months to come. This particular Ultra tap was turned off just when the United States most required its assistance.

Anxious to help prevent the disaster beginning to unfold on the east coast of the United States, the Admiralty offered to lend ten corvettes and twenty-four anti-submarine trawlers. At the same time the First Sea Lord, Admiral Pound, cabled his American counterpart, urging once again the swift introduction of a coastal convoy system. This was, King replied tartly, under 'continuous consideration'. For reasons that still remain obscure, he refused the corvettes but accepted the anti-submarine trawlers.

One of these was the veteran St Loman, commanded by Lieutenant Colin Warwick. Since joining her in spring 1940 he had earned a reputation as a tough and thoroughly capable officer. Captain and crew had a good deal of experience of escort work; the ship proudly sported two stars on her funnel for two U-boat kills. The St Loman was to make for New York from Greenock 'without delay': 'We loaded all the coal,' recalls Warwick, 'but it was a Saturday afternoon and the stores weren't going to open until Monday morning. We were without fresh meat and vegetables but we sailed all right, on Sunday morning. It was to be ship's biscuit and bully beef; "hard tack" to the United States.'

The St Loman quickly saw something of the destruction meted out by the U-boats. She was still a day and a half's steaming from Newfoundland when her watch spotted a large merchant ship that appeared to be in difficulties. This was found to be the Shell tanker Diala; a torpedo had blown her bow clean off back to the first watertight bulkhead. Remarkably, Diala had been torpedoed on 15 January by one of the first U-boats to attack the American coast; she had been drifting in the Atlantic for almost a month, an 8000-ton piece of steel flotsam. Warwick recalls:

'We went alongside and were able to get all the frozen chickens out of the officers' refrigerators there, which of course helped us out with our short rations. We got a tow line on her and sent a signal into St John's, Newfoundland to say that we had this tanker and they sent a tug out.'

The *St Loman* reached New York in early February. The security arrangements were still inadequate. Warwick remembers:

When we were coming into New York we saw a destroyer, so we flashed her with our Aldis lamp, and she took no notice of us at all. We went in a bit closer. There were some small patrol boats and we flashed them; no one replied. We made our way up through the passage and into New York Bay, and no one seemed to take any notice of this little British ship flying the white ensign.

Then out from Staten Island there eventually came a lamp signal, 'Come in here.'

So we said, 'Well, at least someone watched us.' We went in.

An American officer came down with orders for us and I told him of our journey into New York Harbour. I said, 'It's rather strange because, you know, no one took any bloody notice of us at all.'

The next day I went up to report to the base commandant and he was really quite worked up about this. He said, 'Now look, they're supposed to be out there on patrol and to report ships coming in. As a favour to me, next time you're out there and they don't reply to you,' he said, 'shoot 'em up. I mean that, shoot 'em up.'

So I said, 'Yes, sir. I will.'

A couple of nights later we were out there and one of these patrol boats was sleeping. We flashed him with the Aldis lamp and there was no reply; another flash and still no reply. So we fired a starshell with the 4-inch gun, which made rather a loud bang. And everybody woke up on that boat and they headed full blast for the Jersey shore.

Instead of being put to work as a convoy escort, as Warwick had expected, the *St Loman* was ordered out on 'hunt and destroy' operations – hours spent in fruitless sweeps of empty ocean. The Royal Navy, had used this tactic in the first months of the war to no more effect. The pointlessness of these operations was, the Admiralty told its American ally, 'one of the hardest of all lessons to swallow'. It was the instinct of every naval officer to seek out and destroy the enemy, but thirty months of war had taught that it was better to wait for the U-boat to come to the convoy.

On one of Warwick's first anti-submarine sweeps he was ordered to examine the buoys placed by local fishermen off the Long Island shore:

> I was told, 'We think someone is putting supplies for U-boats underneath those buoys for them to pull up.' My fisherman crew and I knew perfectly well what was underneath those buoys; we hadn't pulled them up because it would have been bad public relations. But the next time we went to sea I said, 'Now we have the authority.'
>
> So we picked them all up. The lobster nets were underneath them, and we took all the lobsters out and put the bait back and threw the buoys back over the side. We had over a hundred lobsters floating around on our main deck. I reported that there were no supplies for U-boats there at all.

The figures for February 1942 were grim; some 154 ships totalling 680,000 tons, most of which again were lost in the western Atlantic. Churchill took the matter up with Roosevelt, who told him that every vessel over 80 feet long was being pressed into service and there would soon be 'a pretty good coastal patrol'. This was nowhere near as reassuring as it sounded. Orders had been placed for sixty new anti-submarine ships, but in the meantime the backbone of Roosevelt's 'coastal patrol' consisted of a motley collection of fishing boats, yachts and motor cruisers, crewed by enthusiastic amateurs. Its official name was the Coastal Picket Patrol, but some of those who served in it dubbed it the 'hooligan navy'. A clerk in a New York steamship company, Jakob Isbrandtsen, signed up for service in the Coastal Picket: 'I knew a couple of people who were already, in and they said the sailing was good and the government would pay you and this sounded just great.' Isbrandsten and his seven crewmates aboard the yacht *Edlu* were not much more than boys, most of them from solid middle-class families: 'The son of the Chairman of Connecticut General Life Insurance was on board, a man by the name of Wilde. George Hart was the son of a major electrical contractor in New York. We also had the son of the manager of the New Yorker Hotel.'

It was Isbrandtsen, as 'boatswain's mate second class', who took command of the *Edlu II*. His orders were to take the yacht out of Greenport to a small box of sea off the Long Island coast. He remembers: 'We were to sit out there and keep the submarines underwater. The idea was if you plastered the ocean with enough boats like ours you could move them further offshore.' It is hard to tell what Isbrandtsen and his crew were to do if they came across a U-boat:

On the first trip on the *Edlu* the only thing we had was a .38 revolver, then later on we were issued a Springfield rifle and a Lewis gun, which was an air-cooled machine gun that you could either put on a tripod and fire or hold like a gangster. This was the armament that they thought we should have. Later we were given a depth charge which looked about the size of a gallon paint can, and it had a timing device in it and you were supposed to throw this.

Those yachts foolish enough to use this charge were often forced to limp home for emergency repairs. For all that, the crew of the *Edlu* took its job seriously and on one occasion detected what it took to be a U-boat on the yacht's primitive echo sounder. Isbrandtsen recalls: 'We had this contact and we reported it, and two days later a destroyer showed up. "Where is he?" the destroyer asked. Well, we had to say he'd long since gone.'

This was the U-boats' second 'happy time'. The hunting proved so good that U-boat Command was determined to fling every available boat at the US coast. That, however, did not amount to as many as Dönitz would have hoped. His repeated efforts to persuade Berlin that the U-boat fleet should be concentrated in the Atlantic rather than spread across different theatres of war came to nothing. Fortunately for U-boat Command it was able to squeeze a lot out of the medium-sized Type VII boats, due in no small part to the enthusiasm of the crews for 'the great American Turkey shoot'. Dönitz later wrote: 'In their eagerness to operate in American waters the crews... filled some of the drinking and washing water tanks with fuel. Of their own free will...they gave up such "comforts" as they had, and crammed their boats as full as it was possible to cram them. For weeks on end the bunks were stacked with cases of foodstuffs. Often there was hardly anywhere a man could sit.' In March, twenty Type VIIs and six larger Type IXs were to sail for American waters.[7]

The first of the larger boats to leave was *U-123* under the new Knight's Cross holder Reinhard Hardegen: 'As I was making for America I was lucky enough to receive a radio message from Dönitz granting me "freedom of manoeuvre". I felt at that time that I was Dönitz's favourite in a way, because I had made a success of my part in Operation Drumbeat. So nothing was laid down and I was given a free hand, and I said to myself, "I'll start at Cape Hatteras," which is where I had stopped.'

Hardegen remembers: 'I was very surprised when I got over there, because the Americans had begun to develop defences; some ships were beginning to sail without lights, and the coast was only brightly lit close to the big seaside resorts. There was also an astonishing number of "blimps", these small airships, flying about; they were carrying out reconnaissance, but they also had bombs on board. When a ship was sunk planes arrived relatively quickly. They had woken up a bit.'

By the time *U-123* reached the United States it had already claimed its first two victims; on the evening of 26 March a third, a disappointingly small freighter of just 3000 tons, presented herself:

I torpedoed her, and she seemed to be lying a little bit lower in the water. The crew abandoned ship and I could see she was smoking, but she didn't appear to be sinking. When the crew were all in the lifeboats and had moved away, I said, 'We'll carry on with the deck gun.' As we approached her, something struck me as strange. She was somehow still sailing, changing course towards me. I said to myself, 'How can she do this? They've all left the ship.' Then suddenly the hatches opened on her deck and she started firing and throwing depth charges at us.

I veered off on 'full speed both engines', which was lucky, because our diesels were smoking so much the ship couldn't see us. Nevertheless we were hit a number of times. Midshipman Holzer fell at my side – his right leg was shot off and hanging ragged. We were lucky that the boat's pressure hull wasn't damaged, only the superstructure. I don't know how many times we were hit. I dived. Holzer died – he was so seriously wounded an amputation just wasn't possible. I didn't have a doctor on board on this patrol so I could only give him morphine and try and make him as comfortable as possible.

We approached the ship underwater and torpedoed her once more in the engine room. As she began to sink I could see barrels, wood, cork floating out of her. She was a U-boat trap – she had been filled with all this stuff to make her as difficult as possible to sink.

Hardegen had been attacked by one of two American 'Q' ships. The USS *Atik* had been disguised as a merchantman to lure U-boats into a surface engagement. This was her first and last contact with a U-boat. None of her crew survived.

By the beginning of April the waters around Cape Hatteras were crowded with U-boats. Among the new wave of medium-sized boats was Erich Topp's *U-552*. It was his first war patrol off the United States coast and he was determined to make the most of it, sinking six ships in seven days including four large tankers. The Type VIIs were supported by the first U-tanker or 'milch-cow', an enormous sub-surface supply boat loaded with up to 700 tons of fuel, food, water and torpedoes: enough to enable twelve medium-sized boats to carry out further operations in waters as distant as the Caribbean.

Refuelling from a U-tanker was not without its risks. Although the rendezvous points were some distance from the coast, for two hours or more the U-tanker and the boats it serviced wallowed almost motionless on the surface as fuel pipes were passed back and forth. The boats were especially vulnerable to air attack throughout this time, but the Enigma code change had ensured that this would only be a chance encounter. In the spring of 1942 the existence of the 'milch-cows' remained a German secret.

It was apparent to Rodger Winn at the Admiralty that Dönitz was managing to refuel his medium-sized boats, but how? Although he did not know it a reconnaissance photograph of the first U-tanker in port had been among the intelligence papers that flooded into the Tracking Room daily. Because of the Ultra blackout there were no leads available from 'Special Intelligence' and it was identified as a minelayer. For a time Naval Intelligence suspected U-boats were being refuelled by surface tankers operating out of Mexico; its man in Washington, Peter Smithers, was sent to investigate, but found no evidence. Access to 'Special Intelligence' would of course have put all this beyond doubt. It might also have warned the Americans where the weight of the U-boat attack would be heaviest.

As it was, by shifting his attack up and down the coast from Nova Scotia to the Caribbean Dönitz ensured that the hard-pressed defence forces were stretched to breaking.

The figures for March 1942 were grim indeed; the Admiralty calculated that total losses in all theatres amounted to 273 ships, some 834,000 tons; again, the lion's share sunk in American waters. More than a third of the ships lost off the east coast were tankers, an alarmingly high percentage. Things were sufficiently critical for Prime Minister to demand 'drastic action' from President. In his reply, Roosevelt privately admitted that the US navy had been 'slack in preparing for this submarine war'.

It was a frustrating time; ships were being convoyed safely across the Atlantic, only to be sunk off the American coast. In his weekly report for 30 March Winn noted drily: 'there is some evidence…that the Germans are contemptuous of A/S measures on the other side of the Atlantic and consider that the only serious restraint on U-boat operations there is imposed by the torpedo capacity of their U-boats'.[8] By April some effort was being made to shepherd ships between safe anchorages, but this fell short of a proper convoy system. Remarkably, as Hardegen had observed, the shore still glittered with lights, silhouetting the ships. Ships were sunk and seamen drowned, the official American historian was later to write, in order that people might enjoy business and pleasure as usual.

The twinkle of shore lights served only to sharpen the acute anxiety felt by men like Frank Trubisz, who sailed these waters. 'It was like a shooting gallery,' he remembers. 'You were in a constant state of tension.' Trubisz had joined the American merchant marine the year before at the age of 22; it was the freedom and informality of life in the merchant marine that appealed to this New Yorker: 'I don't like too many guys telling me what to do. On a merchant ship there was none of this, "yes sir, no sir."'

Trubisz first learnt of the losses offshore from the local coastguard while at the Merchant Seamen's School in Florida. He recalls: 'They kept it pretty hush-hush. They used to tell the people that there was aircraft cover all over the Atlantic coast, and they were watching everything, but there was next to nothing. That was a bunch of baloney.'

Although he knew of the losses, Trubisz was still prepared to sign up on a tanker, the 8000-ton *Esso Baton Rouge*; the money was just too good. He remembers: 'They couldn't get enough guys to go on tankers. One guy told me, "Hell, 'I'm gonna go join the army, it's safer. Picture yourself sitting out there on about 120–140,000 barrels of high-octane gas. That's something to think about!"' It helped that Trubisz was joined on the *Baton Rouge* by his best friend, Billy Scheich.

Their first trip was down the coast from New York to Baytown, Texas to load 90,000 barrels of oil. Trubisz and his friend were unable to share a cabin; because Scheich was on the far side of the ship with the engine room seamen. By the night of 7 April the *Esso Baton Rouge* was off the Georgia coast near St Simons Island, more than halfway home. Trubisz remembers: 'That night I was standing on the poop deck and Billy came back to see me. He knew I wanted to get a job in the engine room, but that night he said, "Frank, I tell you what, you stay where you are, the next trip I'll leave the engine room and ship over on deck with you." Billy went down to go on watch at about 12 o'clock. He was on the 12 to four. I was supposed to go on the four to eight. I went down to my room to sleep but it was hot, hotter than hell, so I took my lifejacket up on deck and I lay down on top of it fully dressed – I must have fallen asleep.' At a little after midnight, as Billy Scheich was beginning his engine room watch, the shadow of the *Esso Baton Rouge* was spotted by lookouts on the bridge of *U-123*. Hardegen closed for an attack.

Frank Trubisz saw nothing of the approaching U-boat: 'I woke up on deck. It was cold and damp and I said, "Ah, God, maybe I'll go back down below again." Then suddenly, *Ba-woom!* I don't know how high up in the air I went – the explosion was almost right under me. It knocked me out. When I came to, my whole right side was hurting bad, my shoulder and my hip. You heard about religion in a foxhole? The first thing out of my mouth was, "Please God, help me now." I ran towards the stairs to the catwalk, and how I missed falling into the hole in the deck I'll never know. They said later on that it was large enough to drive three big school buses through it. The water was running into this big vacuum, which was the engine room. It rushed in so fast the ship had begun to list already and I was running uphill.' The watch on the bridge of *U-123* could see that the *Esso Baton Rouge* was sinking by the stern. The ship did not have far to go; the water beneath her keel was less than 15 metres deep. Von Schroeter remembers: 'The torpedo hit the engine room, and in a tanker that is usually a mortal wound – it's a large room, and because it's at the stern it drags the ship down.'

Trubisz managed to escape in one of the ship's lifeboats, but realized his best friend was dead: 'They didn't stand a chance in hell in that engine room. They were wiped out completely.' News that Scheich was missing, feared dead, reached his family in Jacksonville two days later. The Scheichs were a close family; 'My daddy died when I was ten and so really it was just a three-person family,' Billy's younger brother Louis recalls. 'Billy was kind of the clown of the family.'

The Scheichs lived in a small weatherboard house just a stone's throw from one of Florida's most beautiful beaches. Louis recalls: 'That night we were just sitting there talking about Billy with the family, when at a little after ten o'clock the whole sky suddenly lit up – like a flash. And we wondered, "What was that?" I ran down to the beach, and when I got there I could see this ship ablaze.'

The ship was the 8000-ton tanker *Gulfamerica* on her maiden voyage. Scheich could not know it, but she had just been attacked by the U-boat responsible for his brother's death two years before. Hardegen had taken *U-123* further south in search of even better hunting. He had hit *Gulfamerica* with one torpedo, but was anxious to seal her fate: 'She was burning fiercely, so I said to myself, "That isn't worth another torpedo, I'll sink it with artillery." She was lying so close to the coast I thought, "Well, I can't shoot at the ship from the sea because if I don't hit her, the shells could explode on the coast and innocent people might be killed. I've got to do this some other way. I'll have to get between the coast and the ship and shoot outwards, seawards." This was very risky. We had a wind off the sea, blowing us towards the land; the oil burning on the surface of the sea was being blown in our direction.'

A crowd had gathered on the beach. 'A rare show for the tourists,' Hardegen logged in his War Diary.[9] There was a big dance on the pier that night, but the angry orange flash of the explosion had brought the revellers on to the beach. Scheich stood among them: 'In the light from the flames of the ship you could see the silhouette of the submarine. The next thing I knew, there were tracers coming from it; they were shooting at the ship. I thought, "Why is he doing that? The ship is burning, the crew is helpless and they're definitely trying to get off." We had a very helpless feeling seeing this ship burning out there, being machine gunned and shelled, and there was nothing we could do about it. I felt very angry; he was a bloodthirsty Nazi. That was the first thing that came to my mind: why would he do that?'

Of the forty-eight men on board *Gulfamerica*, twenty-nine were eventually rescued. There is no evidence to suggest that Hardegen fired on the survivors; rather, he was intent on 'making sure' and he did. The ship sank in less than 20 metres of water but she was beyond salvage.

This time, however, *U-123* did not escape undetected. An aircraft sighted the boat as it was making for deeper water and its location was passed to a destroyer hunting nearby. 'Alarm!' was sounded and *U-123* went into a steep emergency dive; it hit the bottom with a jolt. The destroyer ran in and dropped a pattern of charges. Von Schroeter recalls: 'The engines stalled, there were hisses everywhere, water was coming in, the lights went out. It was really a bad situation. We were lying on the bottom at 22 metres and couldn't do anything.'

The destroyer sailed over the top again. Hardegen was on the point of giving the order to abandon the U-boat. The crew assembled with life-jackets and oxygen flasks; at this depth there was a chance they might make it. Hardegen remembers: 'The commander has to leave first, unlike in other vessels, because the one who gets out first usually loses his life. If a depth charge is dropped, he dies immediately from exploded lungs. Then the chief engineer remains underneath and organizes the escape of the crew, and he leaves the boat last. But every time I opened the tower hatch and felt the water down the back of my neck, I closed it again and gave it half a turn because I could hear the destroyer coming. She would come close time and again, but she didn't drop any depth charges. I couldn't understand why.'

Hardegen had no way of knowing but the destroyer had seen decking and oil float to the surface – she believed her job had been done. Many hours' work was needed on the diesel engines before the U-boat was capable of making the homeward journey. Of this narrow escape Hardegen observed in his war diary: 'Why the enemy didn't wait for the commander's cap as proof of its kill is entirely incomprehensible...it shows how inexperienced the defence forces are.'[10]

Louis Scheich visited Jacksonville beach at daybreak. There was no sign of the ship, but the white sand was black with thick tar. Those who witnessed *Gulfamerica*'s end were never to forget it: 'After that we were made to put in the blackout shades and they had blackout wardens walking the street. We had to paint half of the lens on our car lights on low beams. There were armed guards on the old Atlantic Boulevard, which was the only road to the beach then. The guards would board the bus and check us for identifications. Things changed.' By the end of April this sort of rude awakening had been inflicted on communities up and down the eastern seaboard.

On the homeward journey the crew of *U-123* prepared ten tonnage pennants to be hoisted up the periscope as they made their way into port. Dönitz was to learn of Hardegen's success from a radio report rendered in verse:

> For seven tankers the hour has passed,
> The Q-ship hull went down by the meter,
> Two freighters, too, were sunk at last,
> And all of them by the same
> Drumbeater! [Translation Professor Michael Gannon][11]

Hardegen's tally was ten ships, totalling about 54,300 tons; an impressive haul. It was his reward for being prepared to take risks, pushing his large boat close into the shore with only a few metres of water beneath its hull. Before the battered boat reached home the crew was to learn that the Führer had awarded its commander the Oak Leaves to add to the Knight's Cross.

Frank Trubitz has never forgiven the U-boat commander who sank the *Esso Baton Rouge*: 'I have a very bitter feeling, I'm sorry, but I do. Even though he was doing his job. Don't tell me they weren't Nazis, because if you weren't a Nazi what the hell were you doing there? What they did to my life – and I'm one of the lucky ones. I mean, nerves. Some of the other guys are worse off that I am, especially those that got burnt. But I still get nightmares, I get some doozies. One time I was running down the hall hollering, "Come on, it's general quarters." Would you believe it?'

By May the bones of a coastal convoy system were in place up and down the eastern seaboard. If senior US navy officers were reluctant to learn from the British experience, on the water there was no such reticence. The captain of HMS *St Loman*, Colin Warwick, recalls:

I took the first convoy from New York down to Norfolk, Virginia, and there was a captain of a brand-new American destroyer with us. I went to him and said, 'Well, sir, you're a captain in the US navy. You should be commander of the escorts.'

He said, 'No, sir. You people have been at this for two years. You know the business, and we've got to learn and learn fast. I am under your orders.'

I told our liaison officer this – he was a Commander English RN retired. I said, 'Commander, these people have got the right idea. Would you have willingly put yourself under the orders of a lieutenant of a foreign navy?'

'No,' he said. 'No, I wouldn't.'

I said, 'No, you'd have tried to bluff it out. But they're quite open about it, and they will learn fast.'

So it was to prove. By April the great wheels of American industry were turning; a programme of 'Sixty Ships in Sixty Days' had been promised to meet the shortfall in anti-submarine craft. A Subchaser Training Center was established in Florida to initiate new recruits into the mysteries of ASDIC. The first counter-blow was also struck; in the early hours of 14 April the destroyer USS *Roper* surprised *U-85* on the surface; a barrage of fire at almost point-blank range forced the boat's crew into the water. The *Roper* watched the U-boat sink by the stern; it was the first kill in American waters.

Unfortunately, blood was up; the *Roper* ran in and dropped a pattern of eleven depth charges over the sinking U-boat, killing all the survivors in the water. A sinking was, however, something to celebrate; it also offered the promise of a greater prize. The U-boat was lying in a little over 30 metres of water; vital intelligence materials that might help the Allies end the Ultra blackout were tantalizingly close. Over the next three weeks US navy divers made a number of attempts to enter the U-boat, but it was lying awkwardly and all of these efforts came to nothing.

Almost as soon as the convoy system was introduced, losses on the east coast started to decline; vindication, the Admiralty said, for the case it had been arguing for many months. Total losses were, however, to remain high; in May and June Dönitz shifted the weight of his attack to the Caribbean and the Gulf of Mexico. The climax came in June, when total monthly losses reached a staggering 834,196 tons or 173 ships, 144 of them sunk by U-boats.

Of particular concern to the British was the large number of tankers lost in American waters, 129 in the first five months of the year.[12] By the beginning of May British officials were predicting a serious oil crisis, with an end-of-year shortfall of some 2 million tons. The United States made good these losses but tempers in Washington and London were nevertheless frayed. The British placed responsibility squarely at the door of their American ally; as far as the Admiralty was concerned, defeat seemed to have been snatched from the jaws of victory. Support came from the US army Chief of Staff, General George Marshall; he wrote to Admiral King on 19 June: 'The losses by submarines off our Atlantic seaboard and in the Caribbean now threaten our entire war effort.'

Churchill delivered this same message to Roosevelt in person at the Argonaut Conference in Washington just days later. The British delegation was armed with Rodger Winn's latest projections for the size of the

U-boat fleet. Between fifteen and twenty-five new U-boats were being built a month, he estimated, which meant that by the end of year the fleet would number at least four hundred. Just eight had been sunk in six and a half months. Winn was also of the view that this U-boat fleet would soon be deployed again on the Atlantic convoy routes. Rerouting convoys around larger U-boat search groups would be difficult; without 'Special Intelligence' almost impossible.

On 11 May a specially formed U-boat pack had found and attacked Atlantic convoy ONS 92 and sunk seven ships.[13] The Royal Navy was critical of the performance of the American and Canadian escorts, judging the convoy lucky to have escaped without further damage. Yet the success of this attack owed much to a catastrophic security failure within the Admiralty: its codes had been comprehensively penetrated by the German Naval Intelligence service, *B-Dienst*.

By May, *B-Dienst* had gathered 'excellent' information on the routes and sailing dates of North Atlantic convoys. Its chief source was the Admiralty's Naval Cipher 3, used by all British, American and Canadian forces engaged in convoy work. It was a traditional book cipher, an altogether easier proposition for the German cryptanalysts than Enigma had been for their British counterparts. *B-Dienst* was to enjoy access to as much as 80 per cent of Allied traffic sent with this cipher.

It was not the first time the Admiralty's codes had proved vulnerable. *B-Dienst* had been reading Royal Navy traffic on and off since 1935; access to Naval Cipher 3 tipped the intelligence scales just as the war was about to enter its decisive phase. A secret report on British code security compiled by Naval Intelligence after the war suggested that this breach 'not only cost us dearly in men and ships, but very nearly lost us the war'.[14] Certainly *B-Dienst* was able to supply again and again what Dönitz described as 'timely and accurate information'.

The successful attack on ONS 92 was still fresh in Dönitz's mind when he visited Hitler at the Wolf's Lair on 14 May. There he repeated his view that the enemy's shipping should be treated as a whole; with every tanker sunk, the Allies did not lose just the ship and the oil, they also suffered a 'blow' to their shipbuilding and war production capabilities. The U-boat force was 'striking at the root of the evil'. The stated goal of the Allied shipbuilding programme was 8.2 million tons by the end of 1942; this figure, Dönitz told the Führer, was 'probably propaganda'. To keep pace Axis forces would need to sink 700,000 tons of shipping a month, which he believed was 'by no means a hopeless' goal. Soon the U-boat would need to return to the harder convoy war in the North Atlantic, but the task would be easier than hitherto because the U-boat fleet had grown in size and could rely on *B-Dienst*'s guidance. All in all, the outlook seemed 'promising'.

Among Hitler's other visitors at the Wolf's Lair that spring were Reinhard Hardegen and Erich Topp. The Führer wished personally to present these two heroes of the 'second happy time' with their Oak Leaves. Before Hardegen set off he received some friendly words of advice from Dönitz: 'He said to me, "If you go to the Führer HQ you have to go through two security zones, and when you've gone through the first zone you leave the ground of honest soldiering and step on to the polished floor of politics. Don't slip."'

After the presentation Hardegen and Topp were invited to have dinner with Hitler:

I sat on Hitler's right and Topp sat on his left. I was a bit annoyed because Hitler was given apple rice with sugar and cinnamon, which I would have much preferred to eat. We were given a whole lot of meat; we got enough of that on the U-boat.

I was surprised at how well informed Hitler was about the U-boat service. He always prepared himself, and this was his strength. If men came to be decorated with the Oak Leaves, he was careful to ensure they passed on the right message when they left. They were always asked by people when they returned, 'What did the Führer say?' And everybody said, 'He's so well informed, he knows so much, it's wonderful.' And that's what happened.

He also craftily wove a few sentences in which would somehow stick in your mind, which he wanted you to pass on. At the time, of course, you didn't notice this, but as a young lieutenant commander I was somehow fascinated, I openly admit it, by a man who knew everything.

By no means over-awed, Hardegen used the opportunity to lobby hard on behalf of the U-boat:

I said, 'My Führer, you're always looking to the east, standing with your back to the sea, and this war is a sea war. It will only be decided at sea, won or lost there, and not on land. If you're standing with your back to the sea and you look only landward, then this won't work.' The admirals and the generals sitting in front of me were really astonished and looked somewhat embarrassed.

When Hitler stood up and went out, they all said, 'Thank God', because they were then able to light their cigarettes or cigars. You weren't allowed to do this in Hitler's presence because he was a non-smoker. Then we went to the other room and we celebrated with sparkling wine. The senior officers told me there that I had been quite impertinent. I asked, 'Why is that? The Führer needs to know the truth. I have to say what I think. He asked me, and I had to tell him.'

It appears that Hitler took some of what his young visitor said to heart. So impressed was he by the successes of his commanders in this, the 'second happy time', he is reported to have predicted that 'the submarine could in the end decide the outcome of the war'.

CHAPTER NINE

THE SARDINE TIN

BY THE SUMMER OF 1942 Karl Dönitz judged himself to be in command of a U-boat fleet large enough to strike a decisive blow against the Allies in the Atlantic. The outlook was promising; some 330 U-boats were in service in July, of which almost 140 were frontline boats and the fleet was growing by more than twelve a month. After the breathtaking success of the campaign in American waters, the confidence of crews was sky high; Dönitz believed the time was ripe for a return to the convoy war. The U-boat had been deployed in American, African, Arctic waters – anywhere Dönitz thought success could be guaranteed, yet he was firmly of the view that the final 'issue' could only be decided in the North Atlantic. The busiest convoy routes passed through these waters; they were still Britain's main arteries to the west; along them, too, would come the arms and men needed for an attack on German-occupied Europe. Dönitz would now be able to maintain a continuous U-boat presence in the North Atlantic operations area. Larger packs could be deployed across the convoy routes; their search for targets would be easier thanks to the steady flow of quality intelligence from *B-Dienst*.

That the new campaign would be difficult and bitterly fought was evident from its opening shots. In June a U-boat pack was formed to attack a convoy homebound from Gibraltar. Almost six months had passed since the last attack on this route: in the battle for HG 76 five boats had been lost, including *U-567*, commanded by 'Oak Leaves' holder Engelbert Endraß. There were old scores to settle; what better place to signal the resolve of the U-boat arm to win the convoy war? Among the nine U-boats of group *Endraß* was *U-552*, 'the Red Devil' boat commanded by Erich Topp. The pack's target was HG 84:

twenty-three merchant ships protected by just four escorts from Captain 'Johnny' Walker's group. It was Walker's ships that had sunk Endraß; this time the screen was so small the odds appeared to favour the U-boats.

The *U-552* was first to find the convoy; Topp gave chase, broadcasting beacon signals for the benefit of the other boats. Pursuit was difficult; it soon became apparent that the small escort screen was extremely active. Topp managed, nevertheless, to stay in contact. 'June days are long days,' he recalled in his memoirs: 'any attack before midnight was out of the question. Wherever the sea was disturbed by the bows of U-boats and ships, or churned up by propellers, the water shone in silvery-golden cascades and trails – marine phosphorescence. At a distance of about 3000 metres we could barely make out the silhouettes of the ships, but all the more visible were their silvery wakes. Our boat, too, left behind such a brilliant trail.'[1] Topp nevertheless worked himself into an attacking position:

> It was from a distance of 3000 metres. I fired four torpedoes from the bow and then I sheered off and fired one from the stern, but almost at once, before they found the target, a corvette detected me. She pursued me at high speed; she came closer and yet closer, close enough for me to make out the details of her bridge. It was rough and the waves were coming over the conning tower. I had already ordered my crew below and I was ready to crash dive. I knew very well that we could expect a lengthy depth charge attack, but when the corvette was only 500 metres away from me she turned away and fired her depth charges. We'd escaped.

Topp was able to haul away and reload his tubes, but the other boats in the pack fared worse: one was seriously damaged and the rest beaten off; only *U-552* succeeded in penetrating the escort screen. Topp approached the convoy again, launching another salvo of five torpedoes; two were to find their mark, bringing his total to five ships sunk. Later that night

U-552 was subjected to a punishing depth charge attack, which cracked a fuel ballast tank; it left the U-boat trailing a film of oil that threatened to reveal its position. It was a disappointing return for Dönitz; only one out of nine boats had launched a successful attack on a convoy escorted by just four ships.

It was much the same story on Topp's next patrol. In July the 'Red Devil' boat was one of ten ordered to form a patrol line between Iceland and Greenland, where convoys would be beyond the protection of Allied aircraft. Yet in a month's hunting, group *Wolf* managed to sink just three ship; Topp claimed two of these. By 3 August Topp had just one torpedo left and yet he was still doggedly clinging to a convoy in the hope of a final opportunity to attack. Taking advantage of a dense Atlantic fog, he hauled off to load this last torpedo. What happened next is described in his memoirs:

> After taking a look at the charts, I decided to lie down for a nap while the chief engineer, after long hours of demanding work, retired to the boat's toilet for some private business. Suddenly a cry comes from the bridge: 'Alarm!' The shrill sound of the alarm bell jars everyone awake. I jump up and run into the central control room. When I arrive there the men of the watch are tumbling down the conning tower from the bridge…the Chief Engineer dashes by me to turn one of the valves. I see the terrified face of our chief navigator, the last man to slide down from the bridge into the control. His only word of explanation: 'Destroyer!'.[2]

The Canadian corvette *Sackville* had suddenly loomed out of the fog at a distance of 50 metres, hell-bent on ramming *U-552*. Her bow slipped by with just 5 metres to spare. As the U-boat struggled to dive, the corvette opened up with everything she had; 'Two shells hit, of all things, the Red Devils on my conning tower,' Topp recalls. As the U-boat dived, *Sackville* picked up a contact and pursued it with depth charges. Later that day she reported she had sunk a U-boat with two distinctive devils on its conning tower. But Topp was very much alive, if rather shaken: 'Our radio equipment was broken and we couldn't send signals to headquarters. We still had approximately ten or twelve days to go before we would reach St Nazaire. In the meantime the *Sackville*'s claim that it had sunk us had reached our families. They were of course devastated. When we ran in to St Nazaire it was to quite a welcome; my family heard on the radio that we had risen again from the dead.'

For all the members of group *Wolf* it had been a bumpy patrol; one boat had been lost and three damaged. The escorts had been able to find and attack the pack even in an Atlantic 'pea souper'. There could be only one explanation: Allied escort ships were equipped with radar capable of finding U-boats on the surface.

Why Dönitz and his staff had been unable to reach this conclusion before the summer of 1942 is a mystery. The Allies had been equipping ships with radar for two years; it had played its part in the sinking of Schepke's *U-100* in March 1941. Yet on 5 July 1942 Donitz logged in his War Diary that 'there is still no conclusive evidence of enemy surface radar. That boats were sighted and driven off was due in many instances to lack of caution on the part of inexperienced crews...'.[3] The evidence was now conclusive. No one would have the temerity to describe Topp and his crew as 'inexperienced'.

There was also a creeping awareness that U-boats were being attacked after sending sighting or beacon signals. Some of Dönitz's most experienced commanders were convinced that allied escorts were equipped with some form of radio direction finding equipment. The commander of *U-94* wrote in his War Diary that summer:

9 June 1942 16.45 to 17.15 transmitted beacon signals. Shortly afterwards a corvette is sighted steering straight towards us. She cannot have seen us by any visual means. On two previous occasions on transmitting signals I was approached by enemy escort vessels...

12 June 02.45 convoy in sight right ahead. Transmit sighting report and beacon signals. 03.20 a corvette and a destroyer come straight towards me. I at once stop transmission and 15 minutes later the enemy ships sheer off and return to the convoy. I do not suspect radar, for I would have detected this while shadowing and attacking during the past few days....[4]

If true, this was worrying indeed, for pack tactics required a good deal of signals traffic between U-boats and headquarters. No alternative had been found to what one senior British naval officer later called 'this constant chatter'. Dönitz and his staff were reluctant to admit that they had been caught out twice; they were prepared to accept the existence of radar, but found no conclusive evidence that escorts were also equipped with radio direction finding equipment. In fact the Allies had begun equipping escorts with HF/DF (High Frequency Direction Finding equipment) – 'Huff Duff' – the summer before. It was an invaluable tool; a bearing could be taken from a U-boat's radio signal and a ship sent in pursuit. The alarm bells should have rung at U-boat Command when boats were attacked at some distance from a convoy, outside the range of radar. There were plenty of warnings from senior U-boat men, for instance Jürgen Oesten, the former commander of *U-61* and *U-106*: 'It was quite obvious that the destroyer was in the position to take bearings from our short-wave messages. But when we came to the staff and told them that, they just laughed and said, "That's impossible. It can only be done with very elaborate antenna systems ashore. It cannot be done from a ship."'

There were further unpleasant surprises for U-boat Command that summer. The Bay of Biscay was like a funnel, some 400 miles wide through which the U-boats passed on their way to and from the operations area; the Allies were intent on making that passage as difficult as possible. In the spring of 1942 U-boat Command became aware of a puzzling increase in daylight attacks in the Bay. Aircraft were appearing out of the sun without warning; how had they managed to find and approach the boats undetected? The matter was put beyond doubt that summer.

On the night of 13 July *U-159* was homebound after a highly successful patrol to the Caribbean. Its commander was twenty-seven-year-old
Helmut Witte, who had served his apprenticeship as First Watch Officer
under Dönitz's son-in-law, Günther Hessler, on *U-107*. To avoid a brush
with Allied aircraft, Witte followed the general practice of crossing the
Bay of Biscay at night:

> That night we were sailing full speed ahead when suddenly we
> were caught in the glare of a huge light from a plane that was
> coming towards us at a right-angle. The anti-aircraft gun was
> manned and we fired at his cockpit. I turned sharply but he
> dropped his three depth charges next to the boat – they were
> pretty close. We saw him turn away, and then we dived. Everything
> was a mess: the radio room was in the captain's quarters, the cap-
> tain's quarters were in the radio room. We didn't know what had
> happened. All we could say for sure was that for the first time a
> plane had attacked us at night and managed to come straight at us.
> We later heard that two boats were destroyed that night. We had to
> bridge almost half the battery cells – they were nearly all cracked –
> just to get some emergency light.

It was clear that Allied aircraft were equipped with radar too; the small,
dark shadow of a U-boat was almost invisible from the air at night, yet a
Coastal Command aircraft had found and almost sunk *U-159*. The combination of radar and the 'Leigh Light', which was now being mounted
on to aircraft, threatened the foundations of Dönitz's strategy. 'The aircraft had suddenly become a very dangerous opponent,' he later wrote.
'In areas where air cover was strong our most successful method of
waging war would no longer be practicable.' If the Allies were able to
mount air patrols across the whole of the Atlantic, then 'the mobility of
the U-boats would vanish and their system of joint surface [pack] attacks
would be defeated'.

For Dönitz to describe this threat as 'sudden' is highly misleading. He was slow to appreciate the part that aircraft would play in the war at sea; slow, too, to recognize that they were being equipped with radar. The British had begun to fit aircraft with the first radar sets in the very first months of the war. Nor was a radar a mystery to the Germans; the Reich's scientists had made substantial progress in the development of their own sets. As early as 1938 one U-boat commander had tried to discuss with Dönitz the threat radar might pose to operations, but he was ignored.[5] On the eve of war, headquarters abandoned a version for use in U-boats because it was judged to be bulky and unreliable.[6]

Donitz was sufficiently concerned about the course events were taking to request an opportunity to broadcast to the German people. For six months they had heard of nothing but successes; now they must be prepared for the new conditions of the convoy war. Dönitz usually left his young aces to do the talking; the public wanted to hear tales of derring-do, of ships sunk and English destroyers outwitted. But on 27 July 1942 the admiral himself spoke of difficult times ahead; the easy successes of the previous months were at an end, the enemy's defences were stronger and the public must be prepared to accept greater losses.[7]

In May Dönitz had assured Hitler that the U-boat arm had 'faith in its equipment and belief in its fighting capability'. Yet the discovery of important Allied technical advances just weeks later shook his confidence in both. At the heart of all this was a failure of leadership; Dönitz and his staff neglected to act on the warning signs. The threat posed by combined sea and air support was clearly demonstrated in late 1941 during the pack attack on HG 76, yet no significant steps were taken to meet it. The convoy campaign resumed with the same boats and the same tactics.

Perhaps it is surprising that a crisply efficient, dedicated officer such as Dönitz should have presided over such a haphazard headquarters operation. Until the spring of 1942 U-boat Command was based at the Château Kernével, the sardine merchant's house on the outskirts of Lorient, known, on account of its size, as the 'sardine tin'. From here Dönitz and half a dozen staff officers directed the Battle of the Atlantic.

It was an intimate operation, because that was how Dönitz liked it; one of the six was his son-in-law, Günther Hessler. Many of the staff were, like Hessler, former commanders who had served with distinction before taking up posts ashore, but an aptitude for sinking ships was of limited use at Kernével. The staff were trained by and dedicated to Dönitz's methods, and fired with his enthusiasm. Their strengths were his strengths: they were good at making bold operational decisions, but not at identifying trends in the campaign. They were also reluctant to question his judgement.

Helmut Witte joined the staff later in the war; he remembers how abrupt Dönitz could be with those who disagreed with him: 'He had a very clear, harsh style of leadership. Short and clear. He always limited himself to the most important points. He could be very sarcastic, sometimes humorous.' Debate was encouraged, but Dönitz invariably predetermined its outcome.[8]

After the war Dönitz and senior members of his staff would blame the failure to keep pace with advances in Allied technology on the bad advice they received from 'experts in Berlin'. Yet Dönitz's decision to operate with little more than a skeleton staff imposed an intolerable burden on the individuals concerned. By summer 1942 there was no time to step back from the day-to-day conduct of the war, to assess the quality of intelligence and technical reports. One of the core six on Dönitz's staff remembered being reduced more than once to weeping into his pillow with fatigue. Ironically, in an effort to prevent intelligence leaks the size of the staff was at one point cut, although at the time the real spy at headquarters was the Enigma machine.

It is hard to escape the impression of an operation that relied chiefly on what one historian has described as 'inspired improvisation'. Dönitz's adjutant in 1940, Hans-Jochen von Knebel Doeberitz, remembers spending hours in his room at headquarters typing up orders; 'I was only a two-finger typist,' he admits. 'Once typed, the orders were checked and then stencilled, using water-soluble ink to prevent them falling into Allied hands if the U-boat was sunk. 'It was a joke in itself, how primitive this

whole thing was. For six months I used to have to hang out the operational orders to dry over the bunk in my little room. That's how it was –
we were all just doing things as well as we could, you know.'

That mistakes were made is hardly surprising; a particularly dangerous one involved a new search receiver, capable of detecting radar transmissions. Once it was established that Allied aircraft were using radar,
work began at once on equipping boats with this receiver. Fortunately for
the Germans no major development was required – an existing French
system known as Metox was capable of receiving signals at a distance of
30 miles, giving enough time for a boat to dive.

In August 1942 Horst von Schroeter had replaced Hardegen on
U-123; at twenty-three, he was one of the youngest commanders of a
frontline boat in the U-boat arm. He remembers the Metox system as
'unwieldy' and difficult to use:

It was really a wooden frame aerial in the shape of a cross – we
called it the 'Biscay Cross'. A cable led through the tower hatch
into the boat and to a receiver in the radio room. When it detected
something, the alarm sounded, and everything had to be brought
into the U-boat as quickly as possible.

Once we were returning from a mission, crossing the Bay of
Biscay submerged and then suddenly there came the cry
'Located!' from the radio room. It wasn't true, because location
wasn't possible through water, but it showed us that there were
breaks in the cable and when the ends brushed against each other
you'd get a sound in the receiver as if a radar was searching for
you somewhere. That's how primitive this detector was – but for
all that it usually worked.

For a time Metox offered U-boats some insurance against surprise attack
from the air. All the more remarkable, then, that a year later Dönitz
abandoned it. This decision was taken on the basis of a story told by a
captured British pilot to his German interrogators. Allied planes hardly

ever used their radar, he said, for they were able to home in on the radiation emitted by the U-boat's Metox receiver, which could be detected from up to 90 miles away. It was a clever deception, and for a time it left U-boats vulnerable once again to a surprise attack.[9] For Dönitz, Metox radiations appeared to offer an explanation for all 'the hitherto mysterious and inexplicable phenomena' that seemed to have beset the U-boat arm, 'such as the enemy's circumvention of the U-boat dispositions and our losses in the open sea'.

This episode demonstrates how little the 'Berlin experts' knew of Allied radar advances. Scientific and technical development in the Reich suffered from the rough philistinism of the Nazis: even those with brains had to do their bit at the front for the Fatherland, despite the fact that their talents could have been employed better elsewhere.

The danger of putting too much faith in the Kriegsmarine's specialists was exemplified by the whole 'torpedo fiasco'. After three years of war the U-boat was still struggling with its primary weapon. Countless Allied ships escaped because faulty torpedoes bounced off hulls or ran beneath them. Things first came to a head during the spring of 1940, when repeated torpedo failures forced Dönitz to withdraw his U-boats from the Norwegian campaign. The investigation unearthed a number of defects: one concerned the torpedo's firing mechanism or 'pistol'; another was a tendency for some torpedoes to run too deep. Heads in the navy's Torpedo Inspectorate rolled and improvements were made; but not enough – problems persisted. They were finally solved at the very end of 1942, but until then the torpedoes were no more reliable than those fired in World War I.

Dönitz and his staff cannot be blamed for the incompetence of the navy's torpedo engineers; yet they share some responsibility for letting the business drag on for more than three years. Inevitably the decision to base U-boat Command on the front line in France left its staff remote from the debate about technical and strategic developments in Berlin. In September 1942 Dönitz wrote to Grosssadmiral Raeder complaining that he had 'learned by mere chance of certain weapons developments which might be vitally important to the U-boat war'. It was incredible that such matters should be left to 'mere chance' when, in Dönitz's view, 'the whole issue of the war depends on applying the latest technical developments to help U-boats to overcome the ever-growing menace of the enemy's A/S [anti-submarine] devices'. It at last demonstrated to Dönitz, after three years of war, 'the lack of cooperation between operational interests and experimental establishments'. There were independent scientists and engineers who could have provided Dönitz and his staff with good technical assistance, but civilians were not welcome at U-boat Command.

What it amounted to was a huge technical and intelligence hole at the heart of U-boat operations. Dönitz was a brilliant front-line commander capable of inspiring great personal devotion in his men; his determination and judgement were admired by Hitler himself. Yet by the summer of 1942 the current of the war was sweeping him into dangerous waters.

In marked contrast to the 'sardine tin' and the tiny band that staffed it, the Allies devoted huge technical and operational resources to the tracking and killing of U-boats. The staff operations at the Admiralty in London and Western Approaches Command in Liverpool were mirrored on the other side of the Atlantic by the United States and Royal Canadian navies; in these establishments several thousand men and women were employed in intelligence gathering, technical development and training. In Britain Churchill, who leaned heavily on his adviser, Professor Frederick Lindemann, was anxious that the Admiralty's net should be cast widely to ensure that all those who could help did so. The part played by 'the brains' from 'civvy street' in the intelligence field at Bletchley has been well documented; less well known is the important work carried out by civilians within the Admiralty and RAF Coastal Command. The development of radar sets capable of detecting the dark slither of the U-boat's hull in an Atlantic night illustrates the success of this approach.

A good deal of work was done before the war on detecting ships and aircraft – next to none on U-boats. One of those charged with this task was a young scientist called Robert Hanbury Brown. The Air Ministry approached Hanbury Brown in 1936 while he was still at college and asked him to join a small research group led by Dr Edward Bowen. 'I heard of radar one day after joining the group,' he recalls. 'I think there were seven of us at that time and we were the only group in the world developing airborne radar'. At the end of 1939 Bowen's group was based in a draughty hanger at RAF Maintenance Unit number 32 in South Wales; for all that it was deemed work of the first importance to the war effort, conditions were extremely primitive. Through the winter of 1939–40 a steady stream of RAF aircraft arrived to be fitted with the group's ASV MK1 [Air to Surface Vessel] radar and work had already begun on a new improved set to be known as the Mark II.[10] At this time Dr Bowen received an unexpected call; one of the navy's most senior officers, Vice Admiral Sir James Somerville had tracked the group down to its remote hanger. Hanbury Brown remembers:

God knows how he'd got through to us, but he did. Bowen came over and said, 'Admiral Somerville wants to know if we can detect a submarine by radar, trimmed up or trimmed down.'

So I said, 'What's trimmed up and trimmed down?'

And Bowen said, 'Well, I'm not too sure.' He said, 'He's going to give us a submarine, and we'll have to do it in a week's time.'

We had done some experiments on trying to detect posts standing up in the Norfolk Broads, which we thought looked like submarine periscopes, but we hadn't managed to pick those up. Bowen thought we could detect a submarine, possibly trimmed down with just the tower above the water, at about 3–4 miles. But he didn't think we'd be able to detect the submarine end on – only broadside.

I fitted a Lockheed Hudson with the ASK MK1 and we flew down to Gosport and went out into the Solent to meet our submarine. We got ranges of about 3½–4 miles as we had predicted.

I spent about five days flying round this submarine in the Solent making the measurements.

A submarine had been detected from the air for the first time. In their report to the Admiralty Bowen and Hanbury Brown concluded that, with more powerful directional aerials, it would be possible to increase the range to 10 or 12 miles: good news indeed. The contrast with the way U-boat Command handled similar problems could not have been greater. One of the Royal Navy's most senior admirals had rung through to a bleak aircraft hangar in Wales to speak to the civilian employees of a different service. A week later the said employees were able to monopolize one of the few submarines in His Majesty's fleet for five days of trials.

Perhaps the first to recognize the contribution of civilian scientists was RAF Coastal Command. No service had further to travel; in September 1939 it consisted of just eighteen squadrons – a motley collection of ancient aircraft equipped and trained ostensibly for reconnaissance. By the summer of 1942 it was fast becoming the U-boat's chief enemy, an increasingly efficient killer. The speed of this transformation is apparent in the figures for successful attacks launched against U-boats from the air. In the twelve months between April 1941 and March 1942 aircraft managed just five; between April 1942 and March 1943 there were almost 50.[11] This was due in no small part to the groundwork carried out by Coastal Command's civilians. Their influence extended beyond the development of vital equipment such as radar into areas hitherto the preserve of military men.

By summer 1941 a team of eight scientists and mathematicians, led by the distinguished physicist Professor Patrick Blackett, was delving into every aspect of Coastal Command's operations with the aim of improving efficiency. These 'Operational Researchers' applied the principles of scientific analysis to the study of military operations. Nothing was beyond the team's reach: targets, tactics and equipment were all rigorously examined.

One of the first studies carried out by the Coastal Command

Operational Research Section was into the effectiveness of air attacks on U-boats: 'This showed that the pilots were rather apt to over estimate the success of their attacks,' William Merton recalls. Merton joined the Section in July 1941 at the age of twenty-three, poached by Blackett from the Admiralty's research section. The initial analysis demonstrated, Merton recalls, that the depth charges, dropped by Coastal Command aircraft, were set to explode at too great a depth to sink – less than one per cent of attacks resulted in a kill.[12] It highlighted the need for a wider spacing of the charges, shallower depth settings and an altogether more powerful explosive. From spring 1942 aircraft were equipped with new Torpex-filled depth charges which promised a 30 per cent more lethal punch. It was also clear that something more precise than the human eye was needed, and Blackett's team began to develop a bombsight suitable for low-level operations.

That a light was shone in every corner of Coastal Command's operations can be judged from Merton's first task as a member of the team:

> I was trying to determine the distance at which you could pick out an aircraft with the human eye. We used aircraft painted black underneath – the standard colour for bombers at that time – and aircraft that were painted white, and we were able to demonstrate that an aircraft painted white was able to get nearer to a U-boat without being seen than a black one. This was terribly important, because as soon as the U-boat saw the aircraft it dived, and it was only vulnerable to attack for a short time after it had dived.

Merton illustrated his report to the top brass with photographs of crows and seagulls; a black speck was more obvious than a white one against a grey Atlantic sky. Blackett's team was usually pushing at an open door, for it possessed a strong ally in Air Marshal Sir Philip Joubert de la Ferté, the officer commanding Coastal. 'He was fully persuaded that our research could have an impact on operations,' Merton recalls. 'Amazingly he gave us a complete run of the whole place and we could talk to anybody, go anywhere.'

The tweedy, bespectacled O.R. team stood out in the canteen at Northwood, on the outskirts of London, like crows in an Atlantic sky. Merton had studied Physics at Oxford University before the war but then taken up the Law: 'We were an amazing assortment of people,' he recalls. 'There was my old tutor from Oxford, Henry Whitehead, who was a mathematician. He was working on the optimum size of convoys and the cover they were given. There was a nutritionist – goodness knows what he did. There was an archaeologist and later, when it expanded, two chemists. I think the air force people regarded us as a different kind of animal to themselves, but they were extremely receptive – we ate with them, drank with them and we got along extremely well.'

Things could be a little harder out in the field, as Robert Hanbury Brown was to discover when he visited RAF Leuchars in Scotland to supervise the fitting and testing of a squadron's radar sets.

We thought we were taking them God's gift to reconnaissance because you could see through mist and cloud and dark and all that sort of thing. I said to this busy-looking squadron leader, 'I've brought you radar,' and I expected him to say, 'Ah, good, marvellous! Let's go down and look at it.'

But he said, 'I'm sorry, I'm too busy. You'd better go down to the hangars and show it to the flight sergeant.'

I said, 'Would you mind telling me why?'

And he said, 'Yes. You see all this paper on my desk? Those are reports of pigeon flights. We're testing pigeons as a method of sending messages back from our aircraft and I have to put in a report in duplicate on each pigeon flight we make.'

Nevertheless, it was clear that civilians were able to open doors that were closed to those in uniform. Hanbury Brown remembers: 'You have to collaborate with everybody, and this you can only do if you wear your suit as a civilian. You can't talk to an air vice marshal in the same way if you're a pilot officer, and you can't talk in the same way to a pilot officer if you're an air vice marshal. It was this collaboration between the scientists and the military forces that was so tremendously effective in promoting radar.'

In 1942 the Admiralty gave Professor Blackett the same brief to scrutinize weapons, tactics and strategy that he had enjoyed at Coastal Command. His influence was to extend into Number 10 itself, where he sat on Churchill's Anti U-boat Committee. His early work demonstrated that the number of ships sunk bore no relation to the size of the convoy attacked. By doubling the size of convoys it would in fact be possible to halve the loss rate.[13] With fewer convoys to escort, the protective screen could be twice its usual size. This flew in the face of received Admiralty wisdom, which held that forty ships in a convoy was good, sixty just possible, but any more was downright dangerous. Blackett's advice was, however, difficult to ignore and by the end of the war some convoys contained as many as 160 ships.

Operational Research made an immediate impact in the weapons field, too; a study into attacks carried out by surface ships on U-boats demonstrated the need for a new forward-throwing weapon. To drop the standard existing depth charges, a ship was obliged to pass over the U-boat, and at that point the ASDIC echo was lost. Maintaining contact as the sea rumbled with the detonation of the charges was almost impossible – for a few precious minutes the U-boat was able to manoeuvre undetected. It was hoped that a forward-throwing weapon would enable escorts to attack without losing the tell-tale echo. From this research sprang the Hedgehog, a square battery consisting of twenty-four 'prickles' – 65 lb bombs on the ends of spigots – which could be fired 200 metres ahead of the ship. The Hedgehog laid a pattern of charges within a circle some 30 metres in diameter, and each charge was set to explode on impact – just one lucky strike was all that was needed to sink the U-boat. The first ships were issued with this weapon in the summer of 1942; by the end of the year it had begun to prove its worth.

Improving the weapons available to the escorts was one thing, encouraging them to use these devices in an intelligent manner an entirely different matter. Yet in this, too, the Royal Navy demonstrated great foresight. The Western Approaches Tactical Unit or WATU was established in Liverpool at the beginning of 1942. Its brief was to develop tactics for the defence of convoys, building on the experience of those at sea and the work of the Admiralty's operational researchers.

At the heart of the operation was 'the Game', a great 12-metre-square floor upon which an imaginary convoy was laid out using model ships. Around this floor plot were a number of small curtained booths in which escort commanders and one or two of their officers sat with a chart. 'On this you'd plot your convoy, which was similar to the one on the floor,' remembers John Guest. The thirty-two-year-old Lieutenant Commander Guest was recruited on to the staff at WATU in 1943 after more than two years convoy escort work in the Atlantic. Guest helped organise 'the game':

> You would be told the time, visibility and speed of the convoy, and you could see through a little cubby-hole in the booth the distribu-tion of the ships. There would be a move every two to four minutes – the convoy didn't physically move, but the escorts and the enemy submarines did. The officers would get a little chit through the windows of their booths, perhaps saying that contact with a submarine was made somewhere. They'd have to make a decision what to do, put that on a chit and send it back.

The unit's WRNS mapped these moves on the floor in coloured chalks. When an imaginary night fell, the flap was dropped over the window and the escort officers had to rely on the chits sent in by the WATU staff and on their own record of the convoy's movements. At the end of 'the Game' they were debriefed by Captain Gilbert Roberts, the formidable head of the unit. Guest witnessed some painful scenes: 'He used to sum up what happened and he would say, "There's so-and-so's ship. What's he doing with himself? He's not paying attention to the signals and he doesn't realize he's got a U-boat alongside." Terrible criticism. I mean, you got murder if you made a mistake. And it didn't matter who got the stick – he would speak his mind to an admiral without hesitation, though he might say "sir".' Roberts knew that the price paid for a foolish mistake might be a ship and the lives of its crew.

It was not just a question of patrolling the perimeter of a convoy with ASDIC and radar; escorts needed to be active. Should most of the escort ships be stationed on the windward side of the convoy? Experience had taught that U-boats often preferred to attack, downwind; upwind, the spray was thrown back into the faces of the bridge watch, severely restricting visibility. What type of searches should be used in foul weather? Should the escorts pick up survivors if the convoy has no designated rescue ship? These questions needed to be addressed before an attack, so that the escorts knew what was expected of them. To help the escort ships coordinate their action Roberts devised a series of defensive moves named after fruit and vegetables, such as 'Pineapple' or 'Artichoke'. On the command 'Pineapple', for instance, the escorts were to fire starshells in an effort to spot U-boats attacking on the surface. Guest recalls: 'He was a master at it. At first we thought when there was an attack at night, all ships should turn outwards to face where the contact probably was and steam full at it. This was Pineapple. It wasn't always satisfactory, so there was another for dealing with submarines that torpedoed ships from inside the convoy – "Raspberry" – and in that case all escorts turned and went to the back of the convoy, hoping to meet the U-boat as it came out astern.'[14]

In the words of one distinguished escort commander, Roberts managed to 'instil a common doctrine of convoy defence, together with the team spirit and initiative which were the mark of a well-trained group'. Some five thousand Allied naval officers of all ranks from admiral to sub-lieutenant were eventually to play 'The Game'.

All of this amounted to a formidable Allied technical and staff effort, which promised to bear considerable fruit. The contrast with the haphazard operation at U-boat Command could not have been greater.

After the war British anti-submarine warfare officers, including Captain Roberts, interrogated senior members of Dönitz's staff. They noted with astonishment the poor technical and research support available, and their report concluded: 'We gave the U-boats more credit than we should have done for efficiency.'[15]

One further significant Allied advantage was beginning to emerge in mid-1942. The ragbag of junior officers, gentleman yachtsmen, merchant seamen and fishermen pressed into anti-submarine duties at the beginning of the war had spent nearly three years on convoy duties in the Atlantic; they were now tough and experienced. As the director of the Admiralty Anti-Submarine Warfare Division noted in May: 'Our A/S ships are increasing in confidence in their ability to defeat the U-boat.' Victory was assured; it was just a matter of time.

It was, of course, merchant rather than escort ships that bore the brunt of the U-boat assault, so the number of experienced escorts and men involved in anti-submarine warfare operations was growing steadily. Naval Intelligence was aware that the U-boat arm was growing too, by twelve boats a month, but it was clear that the training was not what it had once been. The captured commander of *U-353* grumbled to his British interrogators that 80 per cent of his crew were just raw recruits. This smacks a little of shifting the blame for the loss of the boat on its first war patrol; it was however true that the U-boat training flotillas were struggling to keep pace with the rapid growth of the fleet. There was always a U-boat waiting on the dockyard stocks for a new commander and crew to commission it.

By September 1942 Dönitz knew that time was not on his side. There were successes to celebrate; three hundred ships were sunk by German and Italian submarines between July and September, representing some 1½ million tons of shipping. This did not match the success rate achieved in American waters earlier in the year by fewer boats, but then the target was unprotected; more than half of the ships sunk that summer were in convoys. Happily for Dönitz, the intelligence advantage was still his;

information gleaned from Allied signals by *B-Dienst* helped lead U-boats to 21 of the 63 convoys that sailed in August and September. Yet losses were growing, as Dönitz had predicted they would; a total of 29 U-boats were sunk in all theatres in the first three months of the new convoy campaign.

That Germany's submariners were facing an altogether stiffer task was obvious to old hands like Erich Topp, who carried out his last war patrol that summer. In his two years in command of first *U-57*, then *U-552*, he sank 34 ships totalling 185,434 tons, which would make him the fifth most successful U-boat commander of the war.[16] Before taking up a shore appointment Topp made a special request: 'I asked Dönitz not to give my successor as commander of *U-552* a war patrol in the North Atlantic but to send him instead to the South Atlantic, where the crew would have a greater chance of survival.' Topp knew that he was leaving his crew in the hands of an inexperienced commander who would struggle in the tough new conditions of the North Atlantic convoy war. Dönitz agreed and *U-552* was sent south; Topp's men survived.

Dönitz was a fundamentally optimistic man whose first instinct was to accentuate the positive, but at the end of August he logged in his War Diary that enemy aircraft in particular had made 'the operation of boats very much more difficult'; indeed, in some cases no longer worthwhile. This worsening of the operational situation might, he noted, lead 'to insupportable losses, to a decline in successes and to our chances of victory in the U-boat war as a whole'.

He adopted the same tone the following month when, with Grand Admiral Raeder, he briefed Hitler on the Atlantic battle. In particular he stressed the difficulties his boats faced in attacking convoys and the threat posed by radar-equipped aircraft. To counter this, the Führer was told, the U-boat needed its own air support, not just to scout for convoys as before, but to attack the Allied long-range bombers that threatened to strangle pack operations. Furthermore, work needed to begin at once on the development of a true submarine – one with high underwater speed that would be capable of outrunning and outmanoeuvring escorts beneath the surface. Without progress in these areas, Dönitz asserted, the danger was clear: a time would come when the U-boat would be 'crushed and eliminated' by the Allied defences. Only four months earlier, Dönitz had assured Hitler of his faith in the equipment and fighting ability of his forces; but this new request was tantamount to an admission that the existing U-boat types were almost obsolete.

If this was not bad enough, the German Naval Staff had reappraised American shipbuilding capacity and concluded that, to stand any chance of winning the tonnage war, a staggering 1.3 million tons would need to be sunk each month. This was almost twice the estimated figure quoted by Raeder and Dönitz in their May briefing to the Führer, and more than twice the existing monthly rate. Yet there were no searching questions; Hitler was supportive and full of praise for the achievements of the U-boats. It was impossible to promise new aircraft, he told the admirals, because there were too many calls on the German aircraft industry; but the construction of a faster submarine with good underwater speeds was something that he whole-heartedly endorsed. This judgement was no doubt influenced by Dönitz's claim that early development work promised a U-boat that would transform the war at sea. In truth the project had been inching forward for nearly ten years, neglected and underfunded.

Hitler dismissed the American shipbuilding estimates as pure propaganda. He was confident, he told his admirals, that the U-boat's monthly sinking rate would outpace the enemy's new construction. Even if the Allies were capable of building more ships than the U-boat could sink, they would still need men to crew them. It was unfortunate, Hitler observed, that the crew of most sinking ships had time to take to the lifeboats and were soon at sea again in new vessels. This was a familiar theme; he had first suggested the targeting of survivors from merchant ships some nine months before. 'Shooting up the lifeboats' would act as a deterrent, he had argued; the Allies would be hard put to find enough experienced men prepared to run the risk of a final meeting with a U-boat. His admirals were able to dissuade him from this course, promising instead a more destructive torpedo warhead to ensure greater loss of life on the ships. Hitler was placated for a time, but the idea lingered.

The last decisive phase of the war at sea would be fought in the 'black pit', the seven hundred miles of ocean between Iceland and Greenland beyond the reach of Allied air cover. Here, the odds appeared to be weighted in favour of the U-boat. From October 1942 Dönitz was able to deploy at least two packs in a relentless hunt for Allied convoys. In his judgement the Atlantic battle was yet to be decided, for whilst Allied technical developments had stolen a march on the U-boat, the fleet was growing, sinkings remained high and the morale of the crews was 'steadfast'. Yet victory needed to be grasped in the coming months, for the 'distant future, when examined as a whole, caused me much anxiety'.[17] Everything was to be thrown into a last, all-out effort to destroy the vital convoy run to the British Isles. It was impossible for those involved in the Battle of the Atlantic to imagine that this struggle could become harder and more brutal, but so it was to prove.

CHAPTER TEN

SURVIVORS

FOR ALL ITS INHUMANITY there was an undeniable logic in Hitler's proposal that U-boats should turn their guns on survivors in the water. It was a warped tribute to the merchant seamen playing such a vital part in the Allied war effort. They wore no uniform, they were officially non-combatants, but it was these men who bore the brunt of the U-boat assault from the first to the last day of the Atlantic battle. Morale never broke. Nearly ten thousand of them lost their lives in British ships in 1942, but there was no shortage of those prepared to come forward for this dangerous, uncomfortable and badly paid job.[1] It took a very particular sort of courage; these men were at risk for weeks at a time, almost powerless to influence their own fate. Some were torpedoed twice or three times and yet chose to return to sea. They were united by a common sense of purpose, a determination to see it through no matter what the risks; by the summer of 1942 these were greater than they had ever been.

In the first months of the war Dönitz had issued Order No. 154, urging his U-boat commanders to 'Rescue no one and take no one with you. Have no care for the ships' lifeboats...we must be hard in this war.' This bleak, uncompromising order was one which many commanders chose to ignore. It was not uncommon for the survivors of a torpedoed ship to be confronted by the architect of their misfortunes. On 4 August 1942 the 8000-ton freighter *Richmond Castle* was torpedoed in mid-Atlantic; she went down in seven minutes. 'It was like walking across Brighton Beach – there was a slight incline down the side of the ship and you just walked into the sea,' John Lester recalls. Just seventeen, Lester was serving on the ship as a cadet: 'We'd been on that ship since April.

It was then early August, so it felt as if your home had gone.' The sea was covered with a thick film of diesel oil: 'It just floated on the surface like a carpet. You swallowed it because you were in a state of high shock and you weren't thinking what you were doing.' To make matters worse, the surface of the sea was littered with great beef carcasses which had burst from the ship's holds as she sank: 'Hundreds of them, covered in meat gauze, like a butcher's shop.'

Lester and some of his shipmates scrambled into an empty lifeboat, only to be faced with a new danger:

> I looked up and about a hundred feet away was this thumping great U-boat. All the machine guns were manned and we sat there waiting for him to open fire. But he didn't. Instead, the commander asked one of the other lifeboats to come alongside. He spoke good English and he asked if there were any wounded, and there was one chap terribly burned in the second officer's boat – his skin was all off. The U-boat commander said: 'We can't do anything, you know.' But he handed out some first aid dressings and big tins of bread and he said, 'You're 700 miles west of Newfoundland and we will report your position after dark. Good luck.' Then he took off.

The survivors of the *Richmond Castle* were struck by the U-boat commander's concern, but for all the sympathy they still had to endure a terrifying nine-day journey in an open boat before they were rescued.

'We were waging war against merchant ships, not against the crews, and there is a great difference,' Reinhard Hardegen recalls. At the end of its first 'Drumbeat' patrol to America in February 1942 his *U-123* sank the tanker *Pan Norway*; a number of her crew were left clinging to wreckage in the Atlantic swell with little hope of survival. Hardegen pursued a neutral vessel, the Swiss *Mount Etna,* and forced her to return with him to pick these survivors up. Conventional wisdom had it that there was no room on a U-boat for compassion, Hardegen and others proved this was not always the case. Ships sunk were celebrated but there was a natural sympathy for the plight of their crews. Most U-boat men would have been horrified to learn that their Führer was prepared to murder survivors in the water. Although his orders were to 'rescue nobody' Dönitz was prepared to ignore acts of common humanity, for there was clearly no weakening in the resolve of his commanders to 'pursue, attack, sink'. In September 1942 an incident occurred that changed all this; a new, tougher instruction was given to U-boat commanders, one that would achieve notoriety as the Laconia Order.

Before the war the old Cunard liner *Laconia* had worked the trans-Atlantic passenger run between Southampton and New York, but in 1939 she was taken into service as a troop ship and for almost two years her decks had been filled with khaki.[2] The cabins had been ripped out to create mess halls, where soldiers could sling hammocks. It was still possible to breathe something of her former, grander air in the altogether more comfortable berths enjoyed by officers and civilians. On the morning of 12 September the *Laconia* was some 900 miles south of Freetown, steaming for home at a respectable 16 knots.[3] Battened below were 1800 Italian prisoners of war, up top 900 Allied servicemen and civilians, including 80 women and children. On the journey out to the Middle East her decks had been crowded with British troops and she had been escorted by a veritable fleet of warships; homebound she was on her own.

Almost two years had passed since Frank Holding had watched from a lifeboat as his ship the *Beatus* slipped away. After convoy SC7 he had resolved to work on larger, well-escorted ships and was delighted when a vacancy for a kitchen porter came up on the *Laconia*. Now, at twenty-one, with three years' convoy work behind him, he was a wiser, more cautious seaman: 'I knew the U-boats would be waiting for us up around Freetown, so I used to sleep with my gear on. To that point I'd always had a drink in the bar every night with my mate Harry Randall. But I said, "I'm not going into the bar of a night now, Harry. It's getting too near the danger zone. If we get a few ales inside us we've had it."'

"Ah," he said, "it'll be all right." "No," I said, "That's it.'"

Mrs Janet Walker was travelling home from South Africa in one of the smarter cabins with her five-year-old daughter Doreen. Her husband John, a soldier in the Black Watch regiment, had been captured in Crete the year before and was now behind the wire in Germany. Doreen had been reluctant to board the ship at Durban, but quickly made friends with a little boy called Freddie Moore; 'His mother was in the same position as me – she was also going home to Scotland and her husband was in the forces,' Janet Walker recalls. The two women shared a table at dinner; 'We talked, but never once did the possibility come up that anything could go wrong. We just weren't afraid.'

That same morning the *Laconia* was spotted by the bridge watch of Werner Hartenstein's *U-156*. A 19,965-ton liner, perhaps loaded with British troops, was a rare opportunity. The U-boat tracked her until dark and then ran in for a surface attack. Janet Walker remembers:

> It was eight o'clock. I'd decided to have an early night and was putting my little girl to bed when I heard this awful crash, then another loud crash and I felt the ship listing to one side. I opened the door. Water was pouring down the corridor and there were people running everywhere, crying hysterically. The children were still in pyjamas and bare feet. I ran back into my room and put a lifebelt on my little girl. She didn't utter a word, although she must have sensed something was wrong. I managed to get out of the cabin again and stood there bewildered; everyone was pushing and it was hard to keep our feet. One of the crew saw me standing there with Doreen in my arms – he grabbed her and told me to follow him.

Frank Holding was in his quarters aft when the first of the torpedoes hit the ship: 'I heard this bump. It shook the ship, and the people around me said, "What was that?" Well, I knew what that bump was; I'd heard it before. I didn't want to panic them all, so I said, "I don't know, we might have hit another ship in the dark." Then another torpedo went right into us.' The second of Hartenstein's torpedoes was a mortal blow amidships. The ship was plunged into darkness. 'The Italian prisoners of war were crying because they were nailed down below. They were all panicking, crying. It's a terrible thing, men crying,' Holding recalls.

'The ship was leaning to port, so most of the boats on that side were all swung in. And they're heavy – you couldn't push them out.' Holding continues: 'I went round looking for a place in a lifeboat on the starboard side but there were too many other people there. There were women, and some of the prisoners were running round trying to get on the boats and getting pushed back – I suppose our fellas wanted preference over them. I couldn't get a place in one.'

Janet Walker recalls:

People were screaming all around us, but I was just numb with shock. There was one lifeboat in the water with room for a few more. The sailor told me to climb down the rope ladder.

'I'm not going to climb down,' I said. 'You've got my little girl – she's got to go first.'

He said, 'You go first and I'll hand her down to you.'

When I got in the lifeboat I looked up and he wasn't there. And I started screaming. 'My little girl's up there!' I said. 'They're not moving this boat till I get her.'

I panicked and tried to go up the ladder again, but this RAF man said, 'Don't worry. I'll go up and get her – you sit in the boat.' When he came back down again he said: 'The sailor must have thought this lifeboat had gone, because he's taken her to another one. Don't worry – you'll see her in the morning.'

Holding felt his best chance would be back on the port side: 'It was a moonlit night and I could see these lines hanging down, but before I jumped I could see ahead of us a low vessel. It was a submarine and it had a lamp on, and it was picking people up. Then I jumped and I slid right down a line and when I got to the bottom there was the lifeboat. It was practically full – there were about forty people in it.'

The *Laconia* had enough lifeboats and rafts for the 2700 people aboard, but it was impossible to get them all away.[4] As the ship began to go those left on her were forced to jump. Holding remembers:

> We heard the Eyties shouting: '*Aiuto! Aiuto!*' I found out later it meant 'help' in Italian. We were told to put all cigarettes out, because if they saw a glow they would come straight for the lifeboat and overload it. In fact, one fellow said, 'If any of them hang on to the side, call out and I'll give you the hatchet so you can chop their fingers off.' I wasn't thinking like that, though. There were sharks about – you could hear the screams. The next day we looked down and you could see big shapes, dark shapes cruising round beneath us.

Hartenstein, too, heard the desperate cries for help in Italian; from the survivors whom he pulled out he learned that his torpedoes had exploded in the pens where many of the PoWs were held.[5] His attack was within the rules of war; Dönitz's instructions in such cases were also clear: 'Rescue no one.' Yet Hartenstein could not abandon so many people to a grisly fate. He notified U-boat Command of the situation and Dönitz agreed; one Italian and two German submarines were directed to help with the rescue operation.[6] With the dawn it was possible to make out scores of survivors clinging to bits of wreckage – and even more bodies. 'All I wanted was to see my little girl,' Janet remembers. 'There were about five lifeboats around us with people in them and the boys in my boat were very good, they kept calling out to the other boats, "Is she there?". They said, "You'll get her. There are a lot of lifeboats, you might find her on another one."'

The officer in charge of Frank Holding's lifeboat was for sailing towards the African shore:

He said we were about 900 miles away, but that we should make it if we organized what rations we had: water, malted milk tablets, chocolate. We put the sail up and we were going to do that when the submarine came up and told us to take it down. The commander [Werner Hartenstein] said we'd got no chance – it was too far, and we shouldn't move out of the area.

We didn't believe him – you know, just a German telling lies. But then he said if any of us had got any wounds he would help us. I had these rope burns from getting into the lifeboat, so I went aboard and they put dressings on my hands.

I said to one of them, 'Cigarette?' And this German took some cigarettes out and he said '*Kamerad*, give these to your mates.' I thought, 'This is a funny German. Not the way I've been brought up to think about them.' They were brilliant. They put us back, and one of them said, 'Have you got room in your boat?' He had all these Eyties on his deck and he asked us if we had room for four or five of them.

The deck of *U-156* was soon crowded with survivors; its cook worked hard to give as many as possible a bowl of soup. Hartenstein had managed to round up more than twenty lifeboats and a large number of small rafts; he had also fished four hundred desperate people from the sea, many of them suffering shark bites. It would be another two days before the U-boats sent by Dönitz were able to reach the scene.

On the afternoon of 15 September a cry went up in Janet Walker's lifeboat: 'A ship! A ship!' 'We were all laughing,' she recalls. 'This was great – a ship had come to help us.' But as the dark hull drew closer it proved to be a U-boat; it was Harro Schacht's *U-507*.[7] 'He said, "The women and children must go in the submarine."'

'One of the men said, "They're not going in."'

But he said, "Don't worry. They'll be all right."'

Despite their fears, the women and children went aboard. Janet told Schacht about Doreen: 'He was very sympathetic. Every time a lifeboat was sighted he called me up to the conning tower and gave me his binoculars to see if she was in any of the boats before bringing the survivors on board.'

Inside the *U-507* Janet Walker found Doreen's playmate from the ship, five-year-old Freddie Moore; he was alone and very frightened. 'I said, "You come with me Freddie." The Germans gave up their bunks for us, and Freddie lay in the bunk with me. Above my head there was a photo of Hitler.'

Acting on his own initiative, Hartenstein broadcast an appeal in English, giving his location and promising, 'If any ship will assist the shipwrecked *Laconia* crew I will not attack her.' The message was picked up by the British in Freetown but dismissed as a trick. On the morning of 16 September, an American B-24 Liberator spotted *U-156* on the surface. It reported that the U-boat had draped a large Red Cross flag over the conning tower and appeared to have four lifeboats in tow; the squadron commander knew nothing of the *Laconia*, the Liberator was ordered to 'Sink Sub'.[8] One depth charge fell amongst the lifeboats, throwing survivors into the sea; another dropped close enough to damage the U-boat. The following day the same American Liberator attacked another of the U-boats engaged in the rescue.

Holding's lifeboat had drifted away and he missed the air attacks: 'They found us again later and said, "You've got to keep together." He made us tie ourselves to the submarine and said, "If you hear any aircraft engines cut yourself loose because I'll have to submerge."'

Janet Walker and Freddie Muir had been returned to one of the boats: 'The Germans reassured me my little girl would be in another lifeboat, because there were a number of submarines picking up survivors. I just had to wait and pray Doreen would be safe.'

By 17 September three Vichy French ships were approaching the site of the sinking. Holding remembers: 'The commander of the U-boat said, "I've got to leave you", and he passed a tin of bread into the boat, soup and a bottle of wine. He told us to wait there, and we had no choice but to take his word for it.'

The Germans were as good as their word and six days after the sinking they were rescued by a Vichy French ship sent to the scene at U-boat Command's behest. Janet Walker was picked up by the French too; she searched amongst the survivors for Doreen and for Freddie Moore's mother but they were not there. 'Even when I went back home I still didn't give up. I thought maybe she'd been taken to some island. I used to spend money on fortune-tellers, hoping they would give me some clue.' After a year of searching she spoke to a survivor who had seen a young seaman climb into a lifeboat with a little girl very like Doreen. As the lifeboat was being lowered down the side of the ship it had overturned, throwing everyone into the sea.

Frank Holding has never shaken off the memory of that first night in the lifeboat, the cries of those left in the water: 'For a time I was a fucking nutcase – I was crazy. It still comes to me at times.'

Of the 2700 people aboard the *Laconia* when she was torpedoed, 1600 lost their lives; perversely, but for Hartenstein and his fellow commanders it would have been much worse. Yet this effort was to provoke a stern rebuke from Dönitz; he believed three of his commanders had shown bad judgement in allowing their humanitarian instincts to endanger the safety of their boats. What made it worse was that no distinction had been made between Italian allies and British enemies. After the air attack on *U-156* Dönitz had come under pressure from his staff to abandon the rescue operation, but he had told them: 'I cannot put those people into the water. I shall carry on.' Nevertheless the whole affair had, Dönitz argued, taught the U-boat arm an important lesson: a commander should be given no discretion in deciding whether or not to rescue survivors, and the safety of his U-boat should not under any circumstances be compromised.

The last survivors were still being picked up when Dönitz issued new tougher orders to his commanders: 'All attempts to rescue the crews of sunken ships will cease forthwith.' No one was to be helped into a lifeboat, seamen were to be left in the water, and under no circumstances could food and water be offered to survivors; 'Such activities are a contradiction of the first object of war, namely, the destruction of enemy ships and their crews.'

To what degree the Laconia Order was influenced by Hitler's view that survivors should be shot in the water is a matter of conjecture. It was the centrepiece of the case against Dönitz at the Nuremberg Trials after the war; the British prosecution team in particular endeavoured to prove that the order was nothing short of an injunction to murder Allied seamen. It argued that this was implicit in Donitz's contention that the 'destruction' of crews as well as ships was the 'first object of war'. The former commander of *U-123*, Karl-Heinz Möhle, testified that he had interpreted the Laconia Order as a subtle instruction to kill survivors and had briefed new commanders to this effect. No one else broke ranks. Some historians argue that Dönitz was prepared, in the words of one, to 'throw overboard every seamanlike and moral code' in pursuit of victory;[9] but the judges at Nuremberg found very little credible evidence that would support this contention, and nothing significant has emerged since then to suggest they were wrong.

It was Dönitz's instinct from the first not rescue survivors; the Laconia affair confirmed this. 'Be harsh,' Dönitz urged his commanders. 'Think of the fact that the enemy has no regard for women and children in his bombing raids on German towns'. Dönitz had a point; the Allies were bombing cities all over the Reich, and the ordinary people who lived and worked in them. The Laconia Order was an injunction not to help survivors; it was not a licence to kill. It did, of course, demonstrate a ruthless disregard for the lives of the helpless. It is worth noting, however, that Allied submarine commanders adopted much the same policy. For all that there were isolated acts of humanity, submarine warfare was a brutal, uncompromising business. 'You couldn't help survivors really,' the former commander of *U-61* and *U-106*, Jürgen Oesten recalls. 'You didn't have the space. It was just a matter of bad luck, that's the feeling you had.' One incident from the winter of 1942 was to demonstrate just how grim this reality could be; it again involved an elderly ocean liner – the *Ceramic*.

A veteran of World War I, the 18,700-ton *Ceramic* had been pressed into service again in 1939, carrying passengers and cargo across the Atlantic and out to Australia. She boasted a distinctive profile, with one funnel and four masts, which had made her the tallest ship to pass under the Sydney Harbour Bridge.[11]

On 23 November *Ceramic* set out from Liverpool on the long haul to Cape Town and then Australia; amongst the passengers was twenty-year-old Sapper Eric Munday. It promised to be a comfortable voyage. The ship's company numbered 656 in total: 278 crew and 378 passengers, of which 226 were classified as 'military' personnel, the remaining 152 were civilians.[12]

At first *Ceramic* sailed westwards in convoy, but in mid-Atlantic she turned south. About midday on 6 December the bridge watch of Werner Henke's *U-515* picked up the outline of the ship. The U-boat then chased her wake in an effort to work itself into an attacking position.

Munday had volunteered to do a watch on the ship's anti-aircraft guns. That evening he came off watch at 7.30pm, washed, changed and went up to the ship's lounge for a beer. 'We were playing solo and I was having a drink – I can remember it was a Scottish brewer's bottle of beer. I'd picked up my hand and was looking at it when the first torpedo struck. It was a muffled sound, quite a way from where we were, right up fore'ard. Nobody moved. Nobody could believe it. My first thought was, "Will she be able to keep going?"' The first torpedo was followed by two more. The order was given to go to boat stations and soon after that to abandon ship.

'The lifeboats were lowered and people were getting into them in quite an orderly fashion,' Munday recalls. 'I had to go down a rope, which took the skin off the palms of both hands. There were about fifty people in my boat – two or three women and one child, and the rest were mainly ship's crew and some army personnel.'

All the boats managed to get away before the ship, which was finished off with a final torpedo from *U-515*. The *Ceramic* was lost some 600 miles northwest of the Azores; there were no ships close enough to mount a rescue operation. Munday remembers the first hours after the sinking as unrelentingly bleak; his lifeboat pitched and rolled through the winter night in a sea that was becoming steadily more restless. 'A lot of people were just sitting. I didn't mind rowing – I was quite glad just to have something to do.' With the dawn the wind worsened and a great Atlantic swell began to toss the boats about: 'We were bailing furiously with whatever we could get hold of. There were some who had obviously given up hope, who were doing nothing. They had reached the conclusion they weren't going to be saved. I never reached that stage.' Munday, a former choirboy, knew how to pray; as the wind and sea built to storm force it became clear that only a miracle would save them: 'The waves were coming over the side. We were trying to keep the lifeboat into the wind, to prevent it from capsizing, but we couldn't bail the water out quickly enough. I was one of the first out when it capsized, and I had great difficulty getting to the surface because the others were all tumbling out on top of me. We righted the lifeboat and some men got back in – but it was hopeless. I found some loose pieces of timber and just clung to them.'

Munday remembers seeing and hearing others in the sea around him; there were also bodies, still supported on the surface by their lifejackets. Even in this most desperate of situations he had faith that he would be saved, and he was: 'I saw something big in the water about 100 yards away and swam towards it. I couldn't really believe my eyes – it was a submarine.' This enemy U-boat was his one hope of salvation: 'Two of the crew came down on to the deck and threw ropes. I missed them. One chap gave up and went back, but the other stayed and threw his once more and I caught hold of it.'

Munday had been pulled from the Atlantic by *U-515*. It was midday on 7 December; he was cold, wet and exhausted, but safe. It was his army uniform that had saved him: a soldier could provide information. The U-boat's commander, Werner Henke, had actually been searching for the captain of *Ceramic*.

From the bridge Henke watched the struggles of those still in the water. At one point a lifeboat was tossed towards the *U-515*; in it was a woman holding a small child. He knew that most of the survivors would die; rescuing just one, he later observed, was like playing God.[13]

Munday was given food and dry clothes and allowed to sleep; the following day he was interrogated by Henke and one of his officers: 'They wanted to know if it was a troop transport so that they could say they had claimed the lives of so many hundred fighting troops.' It seemed altogether less heroic to have torpedoed a ship carrying a few military personnel, nurses and civilians with children. 'They didn't want to hear that. That's why they kept on, asking me over and over who was on the ship.' One of the officers threatened to throw Munday back into the Atlantic if he did not give him the correct information, but Henke accepted there was no more to tell.

Henke had acted entirely within the rules of war accepted by both the Allies and the Axis. The *Ceramic* was travelling under war conditions, armed and blacked out; a legitimate target. What of the survivors? Henke had simply obeyed the Laconia Order, one prisoner was enough to provide him with the information he needed; Munday was the only survivor of 656 men, women and children. 'I know it's sad, but if they had taken half a dozen people, would people have thought more of them?', Munday says. 'I suppose I was just grateful that they had fished me out. I never lost sight of the fact that I'd been very, very lucky.'

The crew of *U-515* was good to its only prisoner; four days after the sinking Munday marked his twenty-first birthday with a cigarette on top of the conning tower: 'One of the chaps came and said, "Happy Birthday".' Munday understood well enough that he had been exceptionally fortunate, but it would be many weeks before he learned he was the only survivor.

The British public was told nothing of the fate of the *Ceramic* although the families of those lost were officially notified. Munday's parents received a telegram baldly informing them that their son was missing, presumed drowned. It was Goebbels who broke the news; on the night of 17 February Munday's parents received a telephone call from a friend who had been listening to a German propaganda broadcast; the troopship *Ceramic* had been sunk and Sapper Eric Munday saved. The British government finally confirmed the details some ten months after the sinking.

The crew of *U-515* was to experience something of the fear and desperation felt by those lost with *Ceramic*, a little over a year later. In April 1944 American warships depth-charged the *U-515* to the surface; Henke and 43 of his crew were fished out of the Atlantic, 16 were lost. American naval interrogators threatened to hand him over to the British to stand trial for the sinking of *Ceramic*. Rather than face this humiliation, Henke chose suicide. There were in fact no plans to put him on trial, for the sinking fell squarely within the accepted rules of war and he was under no obligation to help survivors. Henke had acted 'correctly'.

During the war there were many stories told of Allied seamen shot in the water, but Allied investigators were able to establish only one indisputable instance. On the night of 13 March 1944 the large U-cruiser *U-852*, commanded by Heinz Eck, sank a lone Greek freighter southwest of Freetown. Conscious that a number of these large, awkward U-cruisers had been lost to Allied aircraft, Eck decided to conceal the evidence of the sinking. For five hours *U-852* subjected the liferafts and wreckage of the *Peleus* to a barrage of machine gun fire. Eck was utterly indifferent to the lives of the seamen left clinging to this debris, but three survived to bear witness against him. Just weeks after the sinking, Allied aircraft attacked *U-852* and forced it aground on the Somali coast; Eck fell into British hands. His interrogator, Lieutenant Commander Colin McFadyean, was struck by his inexperience. In his estimation, Eck had panicked: 'If you do set out to do something drastic like that, which is against all the rules of war and so forth, you might as well do it properly. He didn't even do that.' At the post-war Nuremberg Trials the prosecution attempted to demonstrate that Eck was acting on Dönitz's orders, in particular the Laconia Order. It failed, which came as no surprise to McFadyean; in this case, U-boat Command was guilty, but only of a serious misjudgement: 'They should never have sent an inexperienced

Above and left: Aircraft from the USS *Bogue* caught the supply boat U-118 on the surface as it was preparing to refuel a U-boat on the 12 June 1943. Just 16 of its crew survived, 43 were lost with the boat.

Below: U-117 was attacked on the 7 August 1943 with the loss of all 62 crew members.

Right: The lone survivor of a merchant ship torpedoed by U-124 in the spring of 1941, is left to drift in the Atlantic. U-boats were under orders from Dönitz to rescue no one.

Below: Survivors from the *Laconia* crowded on to the deck of U-507, one of the U-boats sent by Dönitz to help with the rescue; 1,600 men, women and children lost their lives when the ship was torpedoed in September 1942.

Above: The survivors of the *Richmond Castle* torpedoed in August 1942 are, after nine days in an open boat, on the point of being rescued by the corvette HMS *Snowflake*.

Below: The commander and crew of U-571 watch the final moments of the ship they have just torpedoed.

Opposite page: The USS *Spencer* depth charges the U-175 to the surface in April 1943; 41 of its 54-man crew were rescued.

Right: The face of defeat; an exhausted U-boat man is helped up the scramble nets of an Allied ship.

Below: The boarding party from the USS *Pilsbury* secure a towline to the ill-fated U-505. The U-boat was depth-charged to the surface in a combined escort ship and air attack on 4 June 1944; valuable Enigma intelligence was captured with the boat.

Above: Grossadmiral Dönitz and Hitler discuss the attempt on Hitler's life in July 1944 with the Italian Fascist leader, Benito Mussolini. Dönitz urged his men to 'ruthlessly destroy' anyone they suspected of sympathy with the plotters.

Right: The crew of U-249 troop aboard a Royal Navy ship and into captivity at the end of the war; Allied officers reported the morale of the U-boat men to be unbroken.

Above: Admiral Max Horton and his staff are guided across the deck of U-532 by a German officer; this U-boat was one of a token force that surrendered to the British at Londonderry in May 1945.

Two damaged U-boats lie in a Hamburg pen that has been hit by a 12,000-lb RAF 'cookie' bomb. A total of 1,167 U-boats were commissioned during the war, of which 859 saw service as front-line boats. Of these, 757 were lost; a third on their first war patrol. More than 30,000 men of the U-boat Arm are listed as missing.

commander on that journey, and he paid for it with his life – Eck and two of his officers. We executed them after the war.'

At the heart of the Laconia Order and its injunction not to help the survivors was a recognition that the Atlantic would often complete the task. The three seamen who survived *U-852*'s attempt to sink the 'wreckage' of the *Peleus* drifted on a raft for twenty-five days before they were rescued.[14]

The war at sea claimed the lives of more than 32,000 merchant seamen[15] from Britain and the Empire; some 75,000[16] seamen serving in British merchant ships were casualties of a U-boat attack. The number killed by the initial torpedo impact represents only a small fraction of this total; most were lost to the sea. The fate of those who survived an attack on a lone ship sunk in distant waters was especially uncertain. Nor could those who sailed in convoy be sure of rescue. By the winter of 1942 the weight of the U-boat assault on the convoy routes was falling in the mid-Atlantic air gap many hundreds of miles from land. Although the 'rescue ships' attached to the convoys did a remarkable job, seamen were inevitably lost. Those cast into the Atlantic in winter could hope for little; losses from Allied merchant ships in late 1942 and early 1943 regularly exceeded six hundred men a month. US navy gunner Albert Becker's ship was sunk at this time; his remarkable story of survival in an open boat is not untypical of an ordeal endured by thousands of Allied seamen.

It was Becker's first voyage. Born and raised in Iowa, the 19-year-old chose the US navy because it seemed 'a clean life' and altogether less dangerous than a 'foxhole' on a battlefield. On 15 December 1942 he marched up the gangplank of the 5000-ton freighter *City of Flint*. Becker and his 23 navy comrades were responsible for guarding the ship, which meant manning the 5-inch and 3-inch guns; the smooth-running of the ship was left to her merchant crew. The *City of Flint* was to join convoy UGS 4, bound for Gibraltar with supplies for the Allied troops in North Africa. Her holds were packed with gasoline, a cargo that made some of the more experienced crewmen nervous.

From the first the convoy was battered by a winter sea, which tossed ships out of formation and made watch duty an ordeal. After nearly ten days the *City of Flint* was forced to drop out of the convoy. 'We had a cargo of telegraph poles on deck and they'd begun to break loose – we were losing them and leaving a trail behind us,' Becker recalls. The ship was given instructions to rendezvous with the convoy once it had secured its cargo. It was an anxious time, for a lone ship was an easy target; but by 25 January she was making good speed back. Becker recounts what happened next:

> It was just past sunset, which is the most dangerous time because it's very hard to adjust to the darkness. All eyes were on the water. I was on the poop deck with the 5-inch gun, and that's when we heard that there was a torpedo coming. The fellas up in the bow hollered over the phones and you could see the wake, the phosphorescence on the surface of the water. The ship lurched, trying to miss it, but we were too slow and it didn't miss.
>
> There was a big boom – we were hit right where we had the gasoline in the number one and number two holds. As it exploded the ship ploughed right on into the flames. They mushroomed out and engulfed the whole ship. It was such a massive explosion it ripped the bridge right off. There was fire on the water that lit things up, and you could see these telegraph poles going up in the air and coming down into the sea like matchsticks.

Becker remembers that at first the engines were still driving the ship forward – past members of the crew who had already jumped into the sea:

> You could hear your buddies in the water hollering. You knew you were going by them, but there was nothing you could do. Anything you saw that you could throw, you threw. Then I jumped.
>
> There was a lot of fuel on the water, patches of it. You tried to

get it away from you so it didn't burn you, but it stuck to you. It got hotter than hell, and you struggled to keep it from burning your face or your clothes. I could see from the flames that there was nothing but telegraph poles, and you can't last very long in the water with nothing to get on to. But I saw this rope ladder from the ship and I scrambled back on deck again. The only fire aft was caused by the gasoline that sprayed back from the explosion; the canvas and rope was burning, but the ship was not on fire there. My buddy Steve Kubik was on deck, and we decided to get this big plank raft down in the water.

From the liferaft Becker watched the stern of the ship lift out of the sea, the screws still turning, and then with a great hiss of steam slip away.

That's when we saw this lifeboat come out of the smoke towards us. They'd spotted our raft – did we want to get in with them? They only had nine men in there. We took the food from the raft, and got in, and that's when we ran into this machine gun fire. We figured the sub had to be firing. It was going right over our heads – I surmised they were going to make a good job of it and do everybody in. We got the heck out of that boat and into the water, and we stayed there until things quietened down.

The *City of Flint* had sailed directly into a U-boat patrol line; it was *U-575* that claimed her in the end. The first torpedo sealed the ship's fate but, impatient to see her gone, the U-boat attacked the burning wreck with its deck gun and one more torpedo. Becker and his companions thought the firing continued after the ship had gone and that they were the target, but in the smoke and darkness it was difficult to be sure. The survivors did not see the U-boat and there is nothing to suggest the U-boat saw the survivors. Nevertheless the U-boat's gunfire was to have a profound effect on the fate of Becker and his comrades. 'We had two oars in that boat and they must have been red-hot, because we were rowing all night just to get away. That was probably the mistake we made, because the other lifeboats hung together and were picked up three days later.'

The next morning the survivors took an inventory of the lifeboat. It was just 18 feet long but that was room enough. Its rudder had gone but there were a mast, canvas and a little rope. Emergency provisions included thirty cans or so of pemmican, malted milk tablets and about 15 gallons of water. Pemmican was a concentrate of meat and fruit extract, packed into something the size of a sardine can; only to be recommended in extremis. The popular American survival guide *How to Abandon Ship*, first issued in June 1942, advised seamen that they could survive in an open boat without food for fifty days; water was the key to life and had to be carefully rationed.[17] The men in Becker's boat divided the food and water to ensure supplies for three weeks – they felt sure that by then they would be rescued: 'When you opened this pemmican can the food would come out as a slug and you'd take your knife and each man got a quarter. Then each man would get two malted milk tablets and a little container of water about the size of a shotgun shell. We got that twice a day, mid-morning and late afternoon. And that was our rations. Everybody took their share when it was given to them, and nobody tried to take more.'

The men split into two camps, the merchant seamen and the navy armed guard: 'We had words with a couple of the seamen. They didn't like the way we were doing things and we didn't like their attitude: they were at one end of the boat, we were at the other end. There were six navy men and five of them and we had the government-assigned .45 revolver, so we let them know that we were going to man the boat and we wanted all the help we could get. We had a Norwegian, a Puerto Rican, a Spaniard and a coloured guy.'

It soon became clear, however, that one of the merchant seamen, the Norwegian Rohmar Johansen, knew more than anyone about sailing an open boat. It was 'the Norwegian' who became the navigator and prepared a sail and a makeshift rudder. Becker admits the navy boys were relieved to find someone who knew what he was doing. The greatest fear was the sea itself and the unrelenting gales:

You could see them coming. The clouds form and then the ocean starts getting choppy, and the next thing you know you get the big swells and these 30–40-foot waves, and you're right in them with this little 18-foot boat. I've sat there and looked straight down and there'd be nothing under that boat. The next thing you'd just fall. That was the worst. The boat rolled like a cork. Those times we headed into the wind and thank God we had the Norwegian.

They were constantly bailing out water with two army helmets they had on board. All the men took turns holding the rudder, which at times threatened to tear their arms off. All differences were forgotten as everyone fought to stay alive.

The men were left drenched, exhausted and very, very cold. Through the night they would huddle together and share the warmth of each other's bodies. In one respect they were lucky, for the *City of Flint* had been sunk on the mid-ocean convoy route where the sea was warmer. Those left drifting in open boats in winter waters south of Greenland or in the Denmark Strait knew they needed to be rescued quickly before frostbite and hypothermia carried them off. The authors of *How to Abandon Ship* urged all seamen to have a rubber life suit, which 'would all but eliminate the possibility of death from exposure'. It would also 'prevent blood from a body wound getting into the water and attracting sharks'. But steamship operators were not obliged to provide them and seamen were often reluctant to buy their own, preferring to trust to luck.[18]

Becker and his companions assiduously counted each day at sea; at dawn the man at the helm would scratch a mark on the boat's side. Within three weeks they caught sight of their first ship; rescue seemed at hand. 'We were waving and hollering and we fired two or three flares, but the ship either didn't see us or wasn't going to pay us any attention. That was a real heartbreaker.' Some of them cried; the youngest of the survivors was 'probably about seventeen at the most, and that poor kid was scared to death. This gunner's mate that we had in the boat used to just mother that kid and try to console him and keep him going.' It was too much for one of the merchant seamen, Becker remembers:

> Mentally he was not with it. He'd lay his money out in the boat, he'd dry it and he'd give somebody a five-dollar bill and tell them to call a water taxi – he wanted to go ashore. Sometimes he'd imagine a boat out there selling crabs – he'd want somebody to go out and get him a bucket of crabs.
>
> We had a rubber life suit in the boat and we figured if we kept this guy dry, maybe he would be a little safer. But he wouldn't let us tie the drawstrings on the suit. We had to be careful, because he'd picked up this hatchet and he'd never let go of it.
>
> Then we got into this terrible storm. As we were all doing our bit, baling, steering, he jumped out of the boat. We never saw that man again. We assumed that with the drawstrings open that suit filled up like a big bucket and he went right down. He just decided he'd had it.

Keeping up spirits was hard enough after three weeks in an open 18-foot boat; the loss of this seaman was another blow to this company's morale. Becker recalls: 'No one moved about; men would sit in the same place for hours on end. They did have a copy of the New Testament: 'We'd read that two or three times a day, weather permitting. It settled your mind, gave you something to look forward to.' The Bible was passed from man to man; every reading would begin with the 23rd Psalm, 'The Lord is My Shepherd': "Yea, though I walk through the valley of the shadow of death, I will fear no evil: for thou art with me.'"

It was clear before the three weeks were up that the boat's rations were not going to last out: 'We realized we were really in trouble and that we had to make them go further yet. We just kept cutting back. But we also had to replace them with something, so we went after fish.'

At their first attempt they caught a barracuda:

> He had some set of teeth. We couldn't kill him because we were
> afraid if we chopped away and missed we'd punch a hole in the
> boat – then we would really be in trouble. So we waited most of
> the day for that sucker to die. He was bouncing all over the boat. It
> was a banquet. You took the skin off it and cut up the meat. It was
> raw fish but it tasted just like steak. Afterwards we felt guilty – we
> eat too much at once. Any fish we caught after that we rationed
> just like the rest of the food. That was the only fish we ever caught
> on a line, but there were sharks round the boat. We'd go for three
> or four days and we wouldn't see a shark, and then we'd go for
> days and they wouldn't leave us. They brought all these fish with
> them and they looked like a pretty easy catch. When the sharks
> swam near the boat these pilot fish would swim real close. We took
> out our sheath knives and we would just pitch them in the belly
> and throw them in the boat. You probably missed fifty of them
> before you got one.

When the storms came the survivors were able to collect a few precious ounces of rainwater in the sail. There was never enough, but no one
lost control of their thirst and drank seawater. This was one of the golden
rules of survival drummed into every seaman. The second cook of the
torpedoed British freighter *Anglo Saxon* was reported to have drunk can
after can of seawater; it drove him out of his mind. The authors of *How
to Abandon Ship* also warned seamen against drinking their own urine:
'Its toxic waste products will add to the agony of thirst...and will cut
down your survival time.'

After a month at sea Becker and his companions were still sure they
would be rescued: 'You don't quit if you've got an ounce of strength and
if you're all pulling together.' The weather improved, which helped, and
the colour of the sea changed; Rohmar Johansen told them they were
nearing land. Seagulls began to follow the boat, and seaweed drifted pass

them. Johansen showed Becker how to pick little 'berries' of fresh water from the weed: 'You'd pull the seaweed in by the armful and you'd sit there like a monkey picking these little berries out. When they picked us up the lifeboat looked like a hay wagon because we'd got so much seaweed in it.'

There were forty-six little scratches on the side of the lifeboat when at dawn on 12 March 1943 its crew saw the plane. 'We had been seeing a lot of seagulls,' says Becker, 'and we saw this thing on the horizon – and, it looked at first like an awfully big seagull.' The men in the plane waved but promptly disappeared. It was dusk before smoke was spotted on the horizon: it was the destroyer HMS *Quadrant*. The survivors were too weak to help their rescuers; 'We were one hell of a mess, unshaven, our hair was a foot long, shirts white from the salt and very emotional.' The crew pressed food and rum on the men, but the ship's doctor insisted it was to be liquids only, and no alcohol at first. Everyone suffered from painful saltwater boils caused by constant soaking, and their tongues were black and swollen with dehydration. But for all that the ten survivors were in remarkably good health; they had been luckier and more resourceful than many who endured this ordeal.

Becker and his companions made the journey home from Gibraltar to the United States on a fast troopship; at no point did they venture below the ship's waterline. Their families had all but given up hope; Becker called his mother from Chicago to tell her he would be arriving on the one o'clock train the following morning. 'All she said was, "Oh, my God, no, no."' Becker was back from the grave. At first his thoughts constantly turned back to the lifeboat: 'I'd dream about the storms, because that scared the living hell out of me.' Now the memory of it all returns only at difficult times, but as a comfort; for if it is possible to keep body and soul together through such an experience, then he believes there is nothing left to confront but death itself.

CHAPTER ELEVEN

COLLAPSE

IT WAS ACCOUNTED ONE of the worst storms in the North Atlantic in living memory, and on 16 December 1942 outbound convoy 153 sailed into it. On the destroyer *Firedrake* Ordinary Seaman Donald Coombes watched as the convoy danced across an unforgiving ocean. 'It was just a boiling, frothing mass,' he recalls. 'The waves were twice the height of a normal suburban house. We'd climb to the top of the first one, and then drop into an abyss and hit the second one about halfway up. So you had this tremendous weight of water on the bows of the ship.'

The B-7 escort group had joined ON 153 some four days earlier in a westerly gale, which built steadily and by the 16th was storm force 12. It was difficult for all the ships of the convoy, but especially uncomfortable for the little corvettes in the escort group. One of these, HMS *Pink*, was pitching awkwardly on the starboard side of the convoy; her captain was Lieutenant Robert Atkinson: 'The ship is rolling like a son of a gun, and you can't go on deck because of the weather. And you take your watch, and it's cold, and your clothes are still wet, and there's no decent food, and you have to have a strong inner spirit to say, well, can we get through this lot?' The 26-year-old Atkinson had seen more than his fair share of tough times in the Atlantic since the beginning of the war; short, wiry, with boyish looks that belied his experience, he had earned a reputation as a fine seaman and a conscientious officer: 'A commanding officer is supposed to be on duty 24 hours a day, he has to be there. I thought it best to have a little mattress put in the wheelhouse and I slept there at sea all the time, because there's no time for yawning and climbing up the companionway and getting one's eyes accustomed to the dark.'

The *Pink* was Atkinson's second command, his fourth corvette;

he knew better than most the pressure of constant convoy work in these most difficult of ships: 'I had a couple of cases of people going berserk in the stress – screaming, crying like children,' he recalls. 'If you have men in action and one of them is screaming and shouting, he's destroying the morale of the others so he's got to be removed. You haven't got time to pause for these things – panic spreads quickly. So the chief purser's mate thought the best way to remove him was to slug him, which he did.' There was plenty of sympathy for shipmates who momentarily collapsed under the strain; everyone felt it.

By December 1942 the new convoy campaign in the North Atlantic was entering its sixth ferocious month. That the battle was reaching a crescendo was clear to all involved; Allied shipping losses were edging upwards again – in November a staggering 807,754 tons. A steady flow of intelligence gleaned from the allied codes had helped Dönitz's packs to land a series of heavy blows on convoys crossing the 'black pit' south of Greenland, beyond the reach of aircover. The growing U-boat fleet (by December some 400 boats of which 212 were operational), supported by the 'milch cows', allowed Dönitz to maintain a continuous presence in this inhospitable stretch of sea.

Gale force seas had on occasion offered convoys some protection from attack – not, however, ON 153. Dönitz deployed two packs in the air gap in December; boats from the one he had christened *Raufbold* (Brawler) were quick to make contact with ON 153. The convoy was put on its mettle when U-boat signals were picked up on the high frequency direction finding set carried by *Firedrake*, the escort leader. The pack struck in the teeth of the storm in the early hours of the 16th, claiming two tankers; that evening it claimed a freighter. The *Firedrake* carried out a sweep on the port side of the convoy but this pursuit came to nothing.

At about six o'clock on the evening of the 16th *Pink* received a signal from the senior officer escort on *Firedrake*. 'He called me and said, "The attacks are coming from your side – change places with me. I was a bit disappointed at that,"' Atkinson admits. The *Firedrake* then took up a position some 4 miles off the starboard side of the convoy in the hope of intercepting U-boats closing from the north.

At 20.00 hours Donald Coombes went on watch at the stern of *Firedrake*. He had joined the ship as a raw twenty-year-old recruit some eight months before; in that time he had seen a good deal of the Atlantic, but no real action. As far as he was concerned, his chief enemy that night was the sea washing knee high over the quarterdeck where he stood. Then at about ten o'clock he heard a dull thud: 'Nothing spectacular at all. I turned to my colleague, who was an old salt, and I asked, "What was that?" And he just said, "Torpedo."'

Coombes moved out from the shelter of the ship's superstructure and glanced forward: 'There were bits of the ship flying everywhere. It was obvious if I stayed there I might well be hit by something, so I ducked down out of the way until the clatter subsided and then came out to have a closer look. I was just in time to see the whole of the bridge structure lean over to starboard and fall into the sea.'

The ship had split in two; the bridge, the wheelhouse and the bow section was torn clean off by the impact of the torpedo. It happened in mere seconds, allowing no time for the men sleeping on the mess deck to escape from the heaving darkness below. Coombes watched in disbelief as the bow drifted into the stormy night, taking with it all but 35 of the 194 men on board:

The predominant sound was the howling wind – I suppose it was like watching a silent film. The only indication we got that there was anybody still alive in that part of the ship was when this chap started signalling from somewhere. As he flashed we could just see the outline of a piece of ship. How many of them were there I've no idea. They obviously had no power to move, and there was nothing we could do about it. We were completely at the mercy of the sea.

Within half an hour the fore'ard half of the ship had gone, overwhelmed by the unrelenting storm. One of the engineers went below with a party of stokers to shore up the engine room bulkhead, which was now bearing the full force of the oncoming waves. Only one lifeboat remained but this was too close to the torn, twisted front of the hulk to launch. The survivors' only hope lay in attracting the attention of one of the other escorts. The corvette *Sunflower* responded to these signals, but it was too rough for her to do anything but keep a watching station. 'It was grim,' Coombes recalls. 'One minute the *Sunflower* was towering above us at a great height, the next minute she was down there in the depths. So it was decided that we ought to wait until daybreak.' But the sea was too unforgiving; the forward bulkhead began to buckle under the constant pounding of the waves, and it was soon clear that the hulk was sinking.

'You just have to get on with it. I climbed over the rail and dropped into the sea,' Coombes remembers. But for the seamanship and persistence of the crew of the *Sunflower* everyone would have been lost. Coombes reached her side only to be washed away by the storm, and for a time he lost sight of her. 'I managed to get on to another carley raft, where I was entirely on my own for some while. That was when I thought, I'm going to meet my Maker any minute now. But it was strange, because still at that stage I seemed to have an assurance that I would survive.' Coombes was eventually fished out after nearly two hours, one of just twenty-six who survived. Nine of those left on the quarterdeck with him were washed away. 'They would have either drowned or perished with the cold. Some of them were stokers – they came up from the boiler room with just boots, trousers and singlets, no real protection.'

The torpedo that sank the *Firedrake* was fired by *U-211*, which had just surfaced to recharge its batteries. Its commander had been amazed to find himself presented with a plum target, a lone destroyer unaware of the U-boat's presence. Over the next few days *U-211* and the rest of the pack chased the convoy westwards, but managed to sink only two more ships. The losses to the convoy as a whole might have been much worse but managed to sink nothing more, thanks to the timely arrival of a half dozen American and Canadian escorts.[1]

It had nevertheless been a bruising encounter for the B-7 escort group; the Admiralty was privately critical of the decisions made that night. The position taken by the captain of the *Firedrake*, was, to say the least, 'risky'; a destroyer on a steady course, in a heavy moonlit sea, presented the most tempting of targets for a U-boat. This error of judgement cost the captain his life; with him went 168 of his crew.[2]

As ON 153 was emerging from the 'black pit', ONS 154 was preparing to enter it. Acting on the advice of its Submarine Tracking Room, the Admiralty diverted this convoy on to a southwesterly course intended to take it away from the Atlantic storms and the waiting U-boats. This time the Tracking Room had got it horribly wrong; the route chosen took ONS 154 across the path of two U-boat groups. Contact was made on Boxing Day 1942 and Dönitz immediately ordered both packs in pursuit. The convoy was to be harried day and night for four days by some twenty U-boats. The Canadian escorts were overwhelmed by the weight of the assault; 14 ships were lost and with them 500 seamen. Rodger Winn had followed 'this grave disaster' on the Tracking Room plot; it was, he observed, 'a grim demonstration' of the vulnerability of a typical escort screen of six ships to a large pack attack of the kind now frequently mustered in the North Atlantic. Winn once again emphasized the pressing need for air support at all times: 'Heavy concerted attacks by considerable numbers of U-boats can and usually have been prevented if aircraft are in company with the convoy.' In this regard, the sorry story of ONS 154 could, Winn suggested, be contrasted with another December sailing, convoy HX 217.[3]

A chasing U-boat pack had made contact with this fast homebound convoy on 7 December some 300 miles south of Greenland. On that first night, seven U-boats attacked HX 217 in a howling gale, sinking just the one tanker. By the following morning twenty-two boats were on the trail of the convoy, but so too was a long-range B-24 Liberator of Coastal Command. In the pilot's seat was Coastal's leading ace, twenty-seven-year-old Squadron Leader Terence Bulloch. By December 1942 this combative Ulsterman had managed to track down no fewer than nineteen U-boats – more than any other RAF pilot, more than most squadrons; 'the Bull' had attacked most of them, sunk one and severely damaged a number of others. Bulloch's Liberator was one of a handful of very long-range aircraft stationed in Iceland that winter to offer some support to convoys crossing the air gap.

On 8 December the seven-man crew of Liberator B120 was turned out of bed at the ungodly hour of 2am. Ahead lay a five-hour flight out to the convoy; the first challenge would be finding it in hundreds of miles of dark, featureless ocean. 'Often when we got to where we were told they should have been, they just weren't there,' Bulloch recalls. 'We used to start a search on their track until we picked them up on radar. A big convoy of about 50 ships would show up very clearly on the radar screen at about 30 miles so we could home in on that.'[4]

The crew was to spend a draughty, noisy seventeen hours in the air. 'You couldn't really move about,' Bulloch recalls. 'You could just about crawl aft to go to the toilet. The radioman was in a special place on the left-hand side halfway back. We had a navigator up front, the flight engineer sat between the two pilots, and there were three or four wireless operators/air gunners who used to take it in turns on the equipment. They needed to get some sort of a rest, because it was very hard on the eyes looking at a radar screen for any length of time.' When time allowed, a member of the crew would heat up a meal on a paraffin stove. 'It was always hot, which was the great thing – though if we spotted something it usually ended up on my knee and that was my lunch for the day gone,' Bulloch recalls.

Fortunately, no time or fuel had to be wasted in searching for HX 217, which Bulloch found just as dawn was breaking. He began an immediate sweep of the perimeter. The radar played its part, but there was no substitute for what Bulloch calls the 'Mark I eyeball': 'You couldn't actually see the U-boat in the North Atlantic with the swell and the waves. You'd pick up its wake first – a big stream behind it – and then if you were lucky you'd see the hull. It was always a horrible grey colour which sort of matched the sea.'

At a little before 11.30am [Iceland time] Bulloch spotted a U-boat's wake at the stern of the convoy. The crew went to Action Stations at once – every second counted. 'I used to fly in and out of the cloud base so they wouldn't see us until we were committed to the actual attack,' he remembers. Bulloch chose to deliver six of his eight depth charges: 'In those days you had to drop them within 10 to 12 feet of the hull to be lethal.'

The U-boat's crew would have been surprised to see a plane in the air gap. As the Liberator approached, the boat began a crash dive: 'If they got down before you reached them, you'd aim slightly ahead of the swirl the U-boat left as it disappeared,' says Bulloch. The individual bombs in the stick of charges were timed to drop about 50 feet apart; as the Liberator reached the bottom of its dive Bulloch pressed the switch on his control stick and down they tumbled. The explosions threw up a great dome of water as a chunk of metal was ripped from the U-boat and sent flying up towards the Liberator. As the sea settled back, a slick of dark brown oil began to spread across its surface. It was always difficult to be sure from the air, but one of the convoy's escorts investigated and sent a morse signal back to the aircraft: 'You killed him.' 'We were hoping we had – that was what we were trained to do – and we felt a lot of satisfaction that we'd made a good attack.'[5]

A little over an hour later Bulloch spotted two more U-boats in pursuit of the convoy. He attacked and damaged one of these with his two remaining charges. Yet this was by no means the end of the patrol; the crew were called to Action Stations five more times that day. 'We attacked the other U-boats with our cannons and made them submerge, and of course the convoy didn't lose any ships that day at all,' Bulloch recalls. There was no hope of sinking a U-boat with cannon fire, but forcing it down allowed the convoy to outstrip it. Bulloch was relieved by another Liberator from Iceland, and this in turn detected five boats and forced them under. The pack continued its pursuit for another two days, but the threat from the air in support of a vigorous defence mounted by the escorts ensured that only one more ship was lost from HX 217. The

Admiralty was understandably delighted: twenty-two U-boats beaten off and just two ships lost. Bulloch's 'epic defence' turned him into something of a celebrity; 'The Bull gets a U-boat' read one newspaper headline.[6] As Rodger Winn observed, it was an object lesson in what could be achieved with air support and just served to underscore the importance of closing the gap.

But despite this success for Coastal Command, the losses from convoys ON 153 and ONS 154 in December marked a disastrous end to a disastrous year for the Allies. Total losses at sea in 1942 amounted to 7,790,697 tons or 1,664 ships; German and Italian submarines were responsible for 6,266,215 million tons of this and the largest part by far, 5,471,222 tons, was sunk in the North Atlantic.[7]

Even before these bleak end-of-year totals arrived in Downing Street, the Prime Minister had resolved that 'action this day' was called for. His Statistical Branch was predicting a crisis at home, with imports of food and raw materials dropping to dangerously low levels. The pre-war total of 60 million tons a year had fallen to an uncomfortable 30.5 million in 1941 and in the last months of 1942 was estimated to be little more than 23 million.[8] By mid-December there was only 300,000 tons of commercial fuel in Britain and yet consumption was running at about 130,000 tons a month.

Losses to U-boats in the Atlantic were exacerbated by Operation Torch, the Allied landings in North Africa. The Germans had been caught off guard, and within weeks Axis forces began a retreat which would end with their expulsion from North Africa. It was a welcome Allied success, but supporting this effort imposed a great strain on shipping. Donald MacDougall was Chief Assistant in the Statistical Branch at this time: 'We were sending something like 120 ships a month round the Cape of Good Hope to Egypt, and a lot of American ships were sailing to North Africa,' he recalls. 'It wasn't possible to use the Mediterranean but the voyage round the Cape was taking eight months – a ship on convoy duty in the Atlantic could have done three or four round voyages and brought in an awful lot of imports in that time.' MacDougall took his fears to the head of the branch, Churchill's friend and personal adviser Professor Frederick Lindemann:[9] 'I doubt whether you realise the gravity of the UK import outlook,' Lindemann wrote in his minute to Churchill. '[Imports are running at] a rate of only 17 million tons per annum – less than two thirds of our consumption! Imports at this level will reduce our stocks to very near the danger point by April, and it seems unlikely that sufficient American tonnage will be available in time to prevent a further fall thereafter.' Whilst it was possible to make an immediate cut in the number of ships committed to the Middle East, the long-term objective could only be the defeat of the U-boat peril itself.

In an effort to focus attention again on this all-important struggle, Churchill convened a new cabinet Anti U-boat Committee made up of ministers and service chiefs. It was charged with the task of carrying out a thorough review of all aspects of Allied strategy in the Atlantic. At its first meeting, on 4 November, it was told that the Admiralty estimated U-boat production to be running at twenty to thirty new boats a month; the Allies were destroying less than a third of these. The number one priority was the sealing of the mid-Atlantic air gap. There were very long-range aircraft capable of rising to this challenge – the new Mark III Liberator could be fitted with extra fuel tanks to give it a range of almost 800 miles, two score of these would be sufficient to close the gap. But extracting them from RAF Bomber Command was to prove an altogether harder task than might have been expected. The head of Bomber Command, Air Marshal Arthur Harris fought to prevent any diversion of aircraft from what he considered to be their war-winning role, the destruction of the Reich from the air. None of the eighteen merchant aircraft carriers under construction would be available for convoy escort duty until the spring of 1943. A direct appeal from Churchill to Roosevelt elicited a promise of two additional long-range Liberator squadrons, but these would not be available for some months. Nor were the prospects brighter for an immediate increase in the number of escort ships. The huge naval effort in support of the landings in North Africa left the Allies dangerously exposed in the Atlantic. Until the spring at least, more would have to be wrung from the existing escort groups. The responsibility for that rested on the shoulders of a new man at Western Approaches Command – Admiral Sir Max Horton.

An ex-submariner with thirty-five-years' experience, Admiral Horton was just the man to pit against Dönitz. Following hard on the creation of the new cabinet committee, his appointment helped to rekindle the energy and resolve the Prime Minister deemed to be lacking in Atlantic operations. The contrast between Horton and his urbane predecessor, Admiral Noble, could not have been more marked; Horton was ruthless, rather distant, on occasions downright rude. The staff at Derby House were at first flummoxed by his unusual habits. Lieutenant Commander John Guest was a member of Captain Gilbert Roberts' team at the Western Approaches Tactical Unit; under Horton he was called on to perform additional, less conventional duties. He remembers:

I was in the mess alone one night, waiting to do rounds, and a captain came in and said, 'Are you alone?'

I said, 'Yes.'

'Do you play bridge?'

And I said, 'Yes.'

'Right! Down to the plot – the admiral wants to play.'

That was my first meeting with Max Horton. He said, 'Are you any good?'

'Oh, I'm all right. I play quite a lot.'

And we went into this private room he had at the side, with a bunk and everything, and played until four o'clock in the morning. Then he said, 'Well, we've got a quiet night, no attacks tonight. We can stop, turn in…. Do you play golf?'

I said, 'Yes.'

He said, 'Oh well, you might have a game of golf with me.'

I said I'd be delighted. 'You've got your clubs?'

And I said, 'No.'

'What, a naval officer who doesn't carry his clubs with him?

Where are they?'

I told him my wife had taken a furnished house outside Woking and they were there. The next day Horton's secretary rang me up to say, 'Your clubs are here. The Admiral had them picked up from your house.'

Horton's office overlooked the main plot at Derby House, so he could read at a glance the state of affairs in the Atlantic. On a busy night all thoughts of bridge were abandoned and the Admiral's mind bent on the battle in progress. 'His approach was to kill the enemy by any means whatsoever, and he was dedicated to that,' John Guest recalls. Horton was to lobby the Admiralty on an almost daily basis for the formation of more support groups, to act when necessary as reinforcements to convoys under, or at risk of, attack. These new groups would, he believed, help increase the number of U-boat kills. As for the existing escort groups, these were to be trained and retrained; more would be asked of them and captains deemed to be falling short would be weeded out. Guest noted: 'If Horton thought a man wasn't doing his job, God help him.'

Although Horton brought a new vigour to the conduct of business at Derby House, the blocks on which he would build were already firmly in place. Chief among these was the vital intelligence link to the Admiralty's Citadel in London. Horton knew and respected Rodger Winn; he understood well enough the mountain he was obliged to climb daily. On one occasion he expressed dissatisfaction with some of the interpretations of the situation in the Atlantic, sent to him by the Tracking Room and was challenged by Winn to carry out his own assessment of U-boat movements. Horton stepped into the Tracking Room to be confronted by a mass of special intelligence signals, D/F fixes and sighting reports; it was not long before he admitted defeat. He left the Tracking Room with what Winn's deputy described as a 'cat-like' smile, his parting shot, 'Goodbye, Roger – I leave it to you'; and so he did.[10]

The Tracking Room's task had been made all the more difficult for most of 1942 by the Enigma blackout. Winn and his small team were obliged to assemble 'the Admiralty guess' without access to the Triton cipher used by U-boats on patrol in the Atlantic. But the year was to end on a positive note. On 13 December word reached the Admiralty that the cryptographers at Bletchley Park had at last succeeded in breaking the four-wheel Enigma settings used by Triton. Great was the rejoicing. Yet the decrypts were often three days old and of limited operational value. This was just the case with HMS *Firedrake* and convoy ON 153. On the morning of December 14 a British listening station had picked up a signal from Dönitz revealing the position of group *Raufbold*. It took Bletchley Park more than forty-eight hours to decrypt this signal, which meant it was too late to save *Firedrake*; the *Raufbold* boats found ON 153 on the 15th. If the 'special intelligence' had been available to the Tracking Room within twenty-four hours there might have been time to reroute the convoy. It was the same story just days later with ONS 154. It would be another nine months before Bletchley was able to read the Triton signals without interruption; by then the Battle of the Atlantic was effectively settled. But if it was not the key to victory that some have suggested it was undoubtedly an invaluable product.

In this, the decisive phase of the Atlantic campaign, the intelligence honours were more or less even. The German naval intelligence service, *B-Dienst*, was working at the peak of its efficiency decrypting a steady flow of signals to and from the convoys at sea. Of particular interest to the Germans was the daily update on U-boat dispositions which the Tracking Room prepared for all British warships at sea. Access to this gave Dönitz an excellent insight into the thinking of Winn and his team, enabling him to anticipate Allied attempts to reroute convoys around U-boat patrol lines. It was 'a game of chess', his first staff officer, Günther Hessler, later observed. 'We had reached a stage when it took one or two days to decrypt the British radio messages, and on occasions only a few hours were required between the time of original transmission and the arrival of the message...and we could sometimes deduce when and how they would take advantage of the gaps in our U-boat dispositions.

Our function was to close those gaps just before the convoys were due.'[11] Winn knew nothing of this breach of security, but he was all too aware that the rerouting of convoys was a much stiffer task than before – for one thing, there were just too many U-boats in the North Atlantic. In the end everything depended on the quality of defence offered by escorts and aircraft.

In the first weeks of 1943 news reached the French Atlantic ports of a defeat in the east that would have a decisive impact on the course of the war. After many weeks of bitter fighting the German 6th Army, trapped in the frozen ruins of what had once been the city of Stalingrad, had been forced to surrender. More than a quarter of a million Germans were killed or captured by the Red Army. The news was no better from North Africa, where the British were driving German and Italian forces westwards; defeat seemed inevitable here too. Yet for most of the men of the U-boat arm there was only one campaign that mattered, and that was the one being fought at sea in the west. Here, at least, there were victories to celebrate.

The 'first importance' of the U-boat in the Battle of the Atlantic was acknowledged in January when Dönitz replaced Raeder as Commander in Chief of the Kriegsmarine. It had been a meteoric rise; captain to commander in chief in a little over three years. Dönitz had once warned Reinhard Hardegen to tread warily on the 'polished floors of politics'; this was now to be his world, in which he was to prove remarkably sure-footed. Above all he was to enjoy a warm relationship with Hitler, who admired his restless energy and his unflinching determination to succeed. Dönitz had a gift for presenting his ideas in a way that would, in his own words, 'excite Hitler's vivid powers of imagination instead of merely tickling him';[12] this paid dividends, for his judgement in naval matters was almost always accepted without question. In return Dönitz proved himself a true disciple with an absolute faith in his Führer – the man who, he believed, had rescued a weak and humiliated Germany and led it to victory.

In his first broadcast to the navy, Grossadmiral Dönitz promised that, in spite of his new responsibilities, he would 'continue personally to command the U-boat war'; it was to be pursued with renewed vigour until 'victory and peace shall have been won'. To this end he was able to win Hitler's approval for another significant increase in U-boat production. What precisely Dönitz meant by 'victory at sea' in January 1943 is not clear; the hope that Britain would be forced to surrender was long gone, and the chief objective was now to prevent the United States deploying its vast fighting strength in Europe. The relentless pursuit of Allied convoys in the North Atlantic was, in Dönitz's estimation, the best – the only – way of restricting the American build-up in Britain.[13]

For their part, the Allies recognized that the defeat of the U-boat was a necessary precursor to a second front in Europe. In January 1943 Roosevelt and Churchill met in the Moroccan city of Casablanca to settle on the priorities for the coming year. It was agreed that 'first charge' should be given to the battle in the Atlantic. Allied bombers would intensify attacks on U-boat bases and construction yards; a minimum of five new support groups were to be deployed along the convoy routes on hunt-and-destroy operations; and air cover was to be stepped up in the 'black pit'. On the eve of the conference, President and Prime Minister were given a timely reminder of the need for these measures. An all-tanker convoy with fuel for US forces in North Africa was set upon by the boats of Dönitz's *Delphin* group and seven of its nine ships were sunk; 'A brilliant success,' crowed the Kriegsmarine staff. More were soon to follow.

In March, exceptionally precise intelligence from the code-breakers at *B-Dienst* led the U-boat packs to one of their 'greatest successes' of the convoy war. U-boat Command was able to direct some forty boats from groups *Raubgraf* (Robber Baron), *Stürmer* (Daredevil) and *Dränger* (Harrier) against homebound convoys HX 229 and SC 122. Contact was made on the morning of 16 March with the thirty-eight ships of HX 229, and by midday the first boats of *Raubgraf* had begun harrying the convoy; over the next three days the pack sank thirteen ships. As the U-boats of *Stürmer* and *Dränger* were racing westwards to join this battle,

SC 122 was sighted just 120 miles away. It was well protected, with nine warships in close escort and air support; U-boat Command nevertheless ordered the pack to chase, and nine ships were sunk before the attack was beaten off. There was much gloating in Berlin, where the attacks on these two convoys were treated as a single engagement; the Propaganda Ministry claimed 32 ships sunk for 186,000 tons, an 'unprecedented' success that was all the more satisfactory because only one U-boat was sunk.[14]

The actual figure for the two convoys was 22 ships lost for 146,596 tons, which was nevertheless worrying enough. Allied losses in all theatres in March amounted to 120 ships for 693,389 tons, the fifth highest monthly total of the war. Nerves at the Admiralty were frayed; writing some nine months later, the Anti-Submarine Warfare Division staff recalled that at this time 'there seemed real danger that the enemy would achieve his aim of severing the routes which united Great Britain with the North American continent'. Some were even prepared to think the unthinkable: an end to the whole convoy system.[15] The author of the Royal Navy's own official history concluded that 'in the early spring of 1943 we had a very narrow escape from defeat in the Atlantic'.

Desperate times called for desperate measures; perhaps it was time to cut off the head. A secret report on operations behind enemy lines recommended 'the assassination of Admiral Dönitz'; this, it was argued, 'would profoundly affect the morale of U-boat crews and the efficiency of U-boat operations'.[16]

No attempt was made to take this proposal further.

The Tracking Room's assessment of the March losses was much more measured. Winn and his team were inclined to view the attacks as a 'gambler's last throw'.[17] One month's figures should not obscure significant trends; Winn noted in particular that Allied aircraft and escorts were sinking a record number of U-boats – thirty-eight in the first three months of 1943. Dönitz's increasingly tetchy exhortations to his boats demonstrated a lack of confidence in his commanders; one signal picked up and read by the Tracking Room reminded them that 'the man who allows his healthy warrior and fighter instincts to be humbugged ceases to have any powers of resistance to present day enemy defences'.[18] Nor was the general air of gloom at the Admiralty in March mirrored at Derby House; Admiral Horton confided to a friend that 'although the last week has been one of the blackest on the sea, so far as this job is concerned I am really hopeful'.[19] Through the smoke Horton could see that the tide of battle was still flowing decisively in the Allies' favour. In this month, later judged by some commentators to be the one in which Britain's vital lifeline to North America came closest to being cut, important attacks were made on just four of sixteen convoys; hardly enough to shake the foundations of the convoy system.[20]

The monthly figures were none the less shocking: fathers, sons and brothers lost; nearly three hundred officers and seamen from convoys HX 229 and SC 122. The captain of the corvette *Pink*, Lieutenant Robert Atkinson was on escort duty with the B-7 group in the Atlantic on 5 March when he picked up a distress signal from a merchant ship just 17 miles away: 'We could listen but we weren't allowed to transmit. It was from the *Richard Bland*; my brother was serving on the ship. I read the signal, she'd been torpedoed, split in two. One half sank and one didn't. I found out on return to harbour that my brother was on the wrong half and was lost.' It was the second brother Atkinson had lost at sea during the war. By the end of March 1943 nearly four-and-a-half thousand merchant ships had been lost in three and a half years of war. The losses were, in Churchill's words, 'final proof that our escorts are everywhere too thin'; the Battle of the Atlantic should have first call on the Allies' ships.[21] Accordingly, the decision was taken to suspend convoys to the Soviet Union; this released a small fleet of escorts hitherto committed to the gruelling icebound run to the Arctic port of Murmansk. Western Approaches was finally able to deploy both the five support groups it had been promised and the first of the escort carriers. For all that March was a bleak month, the prospects were in Horton's estimation much brighter. 'I really have hopes now that we can turn to another and better role – killing them.'[22] The next series of convoy battles promised to settle matters; they would be fought, as before, in the 'black pit' of the Atlantic; a key role would be played by the ships of one escort group in particular.

Escort group B-7 was in new hands. In the three months that had passed since the sinking of HMS *Firedrake* she had been all but rebuilt by a new 'brass hat', Commander Peter Gretton. The thirty-year-old Gretton was cast from the same flinty mould as Horton; he too could be downright rude, ruthless and unreasonable, but he was also a dedicated professional with an impressive track record as a convoy escort captain. Gretton put the seven ships of the group through a punishing training routine. Robert Atkinson recalls:

He was very severe on all his commanding officers. He would send signals around the group clockwise – A, B, C, D, E, right back to himself. They'd be in Latin and you were required to produce those signals on return to harbour, so it was immediately apparent who had made mistakes. He would send you an instruction to take up a new position and would watch you and on return to harbour he might say, 'When I gave that signal it took 34 seconds before I noticed the change in the alignment of your masts. Why should it take 34 seconds for my instruction to change station to take effect? Were you on the bridge? If you had a good reason for not being on the bridge, why didn't your officer change the helm?' Nothing was allowed to escape. He was a brilliant leader – a very hard man but a fair man. One captain was removed for incompetence – he was as hard as that. But he was right – there was no question about it.

All ranks were subject to this training regime. There was the requisite course for the officers at the Western Approaches Tactical Unit playing Captain Roberts' 'game', but time too with the ship's companies at their base in Londonderry on depth-charge and ASDIC trainers and at a new establishment known as the Night Escort Attack Teacher. Here radar and HF/DF operators, the navigation and communications specialists – those whom Gretton referred to as 'the brains of the ship' – could run through realistic attack drills in night-time conditions.[23] Gretton could also rely on a small staff, his eyes and ears in the group; first amongst these was his navigator and operations officer, a twenty-six-year-old reserve lieutenant, Graham Bence. Gretton later described him as his 'tower of strength'; as keeper of the automatic plot his was undoubtedly a key role. This glass table, some 5 feet square, dominated the chart room immediately below the bridge of Gretton's ship, the destroyer *Duncan*. The course of the ship was automatically logged on the plot by a moving light, and around it Bence marked in pencil the position of the convoy and the escort screen. This vital aid promised to bring some order to the chaos of a night battle fought across a front of ships some 7 miles wide. Bence recalls:

> Gretton would talk to me down the voice pipe from the bridge. He'd say, 'Where is *Pink* at the moment?' and I'd say, 'Well, *Pink*'s over on your starboard side, about two miles'. You could glance at the plot and see where everyone was reported to be. And then if a report came through from the HF/DF that they'd heard a U-boat transmitting on bearing three two zero you could put that on to the plot and Gretton could decide whether he should send somebody from the screen to investigate. Everything that happened was translated on to the plot.

Things had moved on in the escort groups since convoy SC 7 some two and a half years before.

The group's first three months under its new commander were for the most part uneventful. Convoys were attacked ahead and astern of the group, but B-7 sailed through with 'nothing to show for it but rust'. Such was no doubt the expectation when, on 29 March 1943, the group set out from Canada with fast convoy HX 231.[24] It was, in Gretton's estimation, rather too large for B-7 to be escorting alone – 61 ships stretched across an 8-mile front. On 3 April the Admiralty alerted Gretton that a

U-boat close to the convoy had sent back a sighting report, and during the night a steady stream of signals was also picked up by the group on HF/DF. There was no doubt about it: a pack was assembling for an attack.

By the 4th HX 231 was in the 'black pit' and could no longer count on air support. During the day U-boats were sighted three times on the edge of the convoy and forced under; but it was clear that, come the night, they would be back. The first attack came almost as soon as it was dark. There was a flash on the starboard side of the convoy: the lead ship in the twelfth column, the 5529-ton British freighter *Shillong*, had been torpedoed. Within two minutes she was gone; the little red lights on the lifejackets of survivors were later spotted bobbing about the ocean. 'We went through a whole group of poor lads struggling in the water, and we shouted out to them, "Hang on, we'll be back," Graham Bence recalls. But the first priority was the protection of the convoy. 'It was very dangerous to stop and try and pick up survivors, because it meant leaving a gap in the screen when you had a hell of a lot of U-boats around. It was an appalling position to be in.' The survivors of the *Shillong* were unlucky; 'We never found them again,' Bence recalls. Gretton later admitted that the memory of those red lights left in the wake of his ship was his most painful of the war.

In the hours following the loss of *Shillong* the convoy was beset by a pack of sixteen U-boats. A stout defence over the next three days kept losses down to six ships – three stragglers and three in the convoy. By the afternoon of 5 April B-7 was able to count on some air cover, and on the 7th it was joined by the ships of Support Group 4. It was, Gretton later wrote, 'the blooding' of the group; two U-boats were sunk and five more damaged in the defence of HX 231 – a creditable performance.

There was concern at U-boat Command that the momentum gained by the March successes was beginning to slip away. An unprecedented 87 U-boats were to sail against Allied convoys in the North Atlantic in April; yet from the first the returns were poor. After HX 231 came ON 176, from which only two ships were sunk, and from the next two convoys just four more ships. These disappointments were put down to inexperience and the growing threat from aircraft in what had once been the air gap. For all that, Dönitz saw no reason to change his strategic goal, which, he told the Führer on 11 April, was still to sink more than the enemy could build. The lessons of the previous summer seem to have been forgotten; then, he had warned that losses might soon become 'insupportable', successes almost impossible.[25]

On the afternoon of 22 April 1943 the B-7 group rendezvoused with slow convoy ONS 5 for the journey out to Halifax.[26] The convoy consisted of forty-three rather elderly ships, most sailing in ballast. It was supposed to be capable of 7 ½ knots, but it was clear it was not going to rise to that. The first four days were uneventful; the *Duncan* took up station in the middle of the convoy to conserve fuel; the other members of the group busied themselves shepherding ships back into formation. Persistently poor weather bounced the ships in ballast out of position and reduced the speed of the convoy to little more than 2 knots. On the night of 26 April two ships collided in the gale; one was forced to make its way unescorted into Reykjavik in Iceland.

On 27 April a small window in the weather allowed *Duncan* and her fellow destroyer *Vidette* to refuel from one of the two escort tankers. By now the convoy was about 250 miles southwest of Iceland. At a little after 11am the following day a U-boat signal was picked up by the HF/DF sets on *Duncan* and *Tay*; the enemy was close and directly ahead of the convoy. Another transmission was picked up an hour later; the pack was gathering. Gretton ordered the convoy on to a new course in an effort to throw off its pursuers, but at a little after seven in the evening a U-boat was sighted on the port bow. By now Gretton had, he later wrote, 'a horrible sinking feeling' that ONS 5 was in for a heavy attack. To make matters worse, the weather was too bad for air support to arrive from Iceland.

Convoy ONS 5 had sailed into the northern tip of a 250-mile search line formed by group *Star* (*Starling*) between Greenland and Iceland. It was *U-650* that had spotted the convoy on 28 April; it clung on tenaciously through the day, transmitting beacon signals to the other *Star* boats. It was unfortunate that just two days before this sighting the Allies had suffered another Enigma blackout; the Tracking Room knew nothing of *Star* and no warning was sent to B-7. The sixteen boats of *Star* were now in pursuit of ONS 5; two more groups, *Amsel* (Blackbird) and *Specht* (Woodpecker), lay to the west – an additional concentration of thirty-four boats. By nightfall on 28 April five of the *Star* boats were in close contact with ONS 5. The sea was rough, the wind picking up. Gretton judged that the U-boats would probably choose to attack with a following sea, which meant the blow would fall on the port side of the convoy. He arranged the escorts accordingly, leaving the starboard side completely unprotected. It was well judged; the first attempt was made on the port bow at a little before midnight. The U-boat was picked up on the radar of HMS *Sunflower*, which ran out and forced it down; no ASDIC contact was made, so the corvette returned smartly to her station. The second attempt came half an hour later, followed by four more, of which the last was made at 03.39 on the morning of 29 April when the corvette *Snowflake* sighted a U-boat and gave chase. The U-boat managed to fire a torpedo, which only narrowly missed its pursuer, but was then forced under and pasted with two salvos of ten depth charges. In his report on the action Gretton wrote, 'The night had been a busy one, the convoy unscathed, and I felt that the U-boats must be discouraged by our night tactics.' He was right; two of the four U-boats that attacked the convoy that night were so badly damaged that they were obliged to turn for home. The rest of the pack remained in pursuit.

By daybreak on the 29th the weather was again making life difficult for the escorts. The depth charge crews, Gretton recalled, had a particularly tough time as they struggled to lift heavy charges into position on a quarterdeck that was pitching and rolling mercilessly. At a little before 07.30 (GMT) Gretton left the bridge of *Duncan* and went below to get some sleep. His head had barely touched the pillow when the alarm bell summoned him back; a ship had been torpedoed in the fourth column. The group executed the set ASDIC sweep known as *Artichoke*, but this yielded nothing. The rescue trawler went alongside the American freighter *McKeesport* and took off the survivors. She was afloat, but beyond redemption.

By now it was clear at Derby House that ONS 5 was involved in a running battle; it was a very slow convoy and the chances of shaking off the pack were slim. There was also a risk that the convoy would be targeted by what it believed to be a large concentration of U-boats in the waters south of Greenland. Admiral Horton gave orders for the destroyer *Oribi* to leave homebound convoy SC 127 and join Gretton at once; four more destroyers from support group 3 set out from the escort base at St John's, Newfoundland.

It was, however, the weather that was to do most damage to the convoy over the next four days. The Atlantic battered the convoy without respite. On the morning of the 30th the *Oribi*, which had found the convoy during the night, managed to refuel from one of the escort tankers, but attempts by the other B-7 ships to do the same were defeated by the heavy seas. There were no attacks that day and the chief preoccupation was station keeping. 'The weather just got worse and worse,' Gretton's operations officer, Graham Bence, remembers. 'The convoy had to heave to, facing the wind. You just put the ship's head into the wind and kept the screw turning. You were all but stationary.' By the afternoon of 1 May force 10 winds were beginning to pull merchant ships out of the convoy. A watchful eye was kept on stragglers from the air by two long-range Liberators, but there was no sign of any further U-boat activity. The frigate *Tay* and corvette *Pink* were left astern of the main convoy to round up those they could.

By the morning of 3 May *Duncan* was in trouble, with only enough fuel to make Newfoundland at an economical 8 knots. She was a fleet destroyer, a fuel guzzler without the legs for the Atlantic, and all attempts to 'oil' from the escort tanker had come to nothing. Stretching a hose between two ships was tricky in calm seas; in a gale it was all but impossible. Graham Bence remembers: 'We'd had a couple of days of attacks and we knew there were still more U-boats homing on to the convoy.

Gretton had to decide whether he stayed and risked running out of fuel and having to be taken in tow, or whether it would be more sensible to go. In the end we decided that the only thing to do was leave.' Gretton would later write of his 'depression' and 'shame' at having to 'leave the group in the lurch', but any blame attached to the pre-war naval staff who had approved designs for a destroyer without the fuel capacity necessary for Atlantic service.[27]

Command of the group now fell to the captain of *Tay*, Lieutenant Commander Robert Sherwood. This was the same Sherwood who, as captain of *Bluebell*, had witnessed the slaughter of convoy SC 7 in the autumn of 1940. He faced quite a task: there was no longer just one convoy but two, a main body of thirty ships and astern of these four stragglers protected by the *Pink*. By the morning of 4 May the main escort force was made up of just *Tay*, *Vidette*, *Sunflower*, *Snowflake* and *Loosestrife* from B-7, and the destroyers *Oribi* and *Offa* from the 3rd Support Group. Little had been heard or seen of the enemy for five days, but on the morning of 4 May the HF/DF sets on *Tay* and *Oribi* began to buzz with U-boat traffic; ONS 5 was steaming into trouble.

Ahead of the convoy was the largest concentration of U-boats ever assembled in a patrol area: two groups comprising fifty-three boats.[28] U-boat Command had abandoned the fruitless pursuit of ONS 5 on 1 May and the remaining *Star* boats had been withdrawn westwards to form group *Fink*. A search line of twenty-nine U-boats nearly 400 miles long was positioned across the convoy routes south of Cape Farewell. To the west of *Fink* were the twenty-four boats of group *Amsel*. In London the Tracking Room knew from the extraordinary volume of signals that there was a large enemy concentration between Newfoundland and Greenland, but it was impossible to say precisely where because of the partial Enigma blackout.

On the afternoon of 4 May ONS 5 sailed into the middle of the *Fink* patrol line; almost at once three U-boats reported contact. U-boat Command responded quickly, directing forty-one of the *Fink* and *Amsel* boats on to the convoy. Conditions could not have been more favourable for an attack: wind strength 2, visibility good, the calm before the U-boat storm. Hungry for success, at a little after eight o'clock GMT that evening Dönitz sent a signal to the pack: 'I am certain that you will fight with everything you've got. Don't overestimate your opponent...strike him dead!' The pack began with the stragglers; the first was the 5666-ton freighter *Lorient*, lost with all hands, the second the 4635-ton freighter *North Britain*, which was limping along 6 miles astern of the convoy. Then attention turned to the main body of the convoy. At a little after midnight GMT on the 5th the *Vidette* picked up a contact on her radar and gave chase; a pattern of fourteen charges was dropped over the swirl left by the U-boat as it dived. A second radar contact was picked up minutes later and a U-boat sighted just 1000 yards ahead; *Vidette* closed at ramming speed as the boat struggled to clear the surface; again the destroyer arrived in time to drop a pattern over its swirl. At almost the same time there was an explosion on the starboard side of the convoy: the freighter *Harbury* had been hit and wrecked.

At this point seven U-boats were in contact with ONS 5; one was *U-264*, commanded by Hartwig Looks. It was the twenty-five-year-old Looks' third patrol as commander of *U-264*. After escaping from a staff post to the U-boat arm in 1940, he had served as watch officer aboard *U-375* in the Mediterranean. From his first two patrols with *U-264* Looks had one confirmed sinking to his name; ONS 5 presented an opportunity to improve on that. His chance came just before one o'clock on the morning of 5 May: 'A gap opened up between the escorts, so I turned towards the convoy and ran in. I launched two double shots at the convoy and then turned and fired a stern torpedo as well. Two torpedoes hit one ship. The detonation caused a wall of water to rise to mast height, and the steamship sank immediately on an even keel. I also hit the other steamship, and as far as I know this one went as well.' Looks was not given an opportunity to confirm his successes – the escorts were on to him at once. Sherwood had instantly ordered a Half Raspberry – a set pattern of triangular sweeps on the port side of the convoy. The *Snowflake* quickly picked up *U-264* on her radar and gave chase;

Looks was forced down, and for a time lost contact with the convoy.

The fencing between U-boats and escort screen continued, as Sherwood's log demonstrates, through the night:

02.15 Sunflower detected and attacked a submarine on the port bow....

03.42 Snowflake detected and chased a submarine on the port beam – she could not overhaul and requested assistance from *Oribi*. Both ships carried out attacks.

05.06 An HF/DF warning of a submarine close on the port bow was passed to the group and at 05.15 [two] ships were torpedoed. 'Half Raspberry' was ordered and at 05.18 *Loosestrife* detected and attacked a submarine. At 03.28 *Tay* on the starboard quarter attacked a good ASDIC contact.

During the night the pack claimed five ships from the main body of the convoy and two stragglers. Any hopes that dawn would bring an end to it were lost in an increasing buzz of U-boat traffic; 'Heavy HF/DF activity', Sherwood logged, 'indicating U-boats on the port bow.' The *Oribi* surprised three on the surface ahead of the convoy, and forced them to dive. It was clear from the constant 'chatter' picked up by *Tay*'s HF/DF that the pack was growing by the hour. Among the pursuers was Looks' *U-264:* 'I was able to position, myself in front of the convoy, but getting there took almost the entire day. During that time, we could hear all the other U-boats signalling and we thought, "Oh God, this will end up in a 'night of the long knives' if they all rush at the convoy."'

There was another convoy. A band of four stragglers was being shepherded along in the wake of the main convoy by the corvette *Pink*. The *Pink*'s party was 80 miles adrift, with no hope of catching up. It had steamed through the night without incident, but on the morning of the 5th its luck ran out. At a little before midday *Pink* picked up what Atkinson described in his report to the Admiralty as 'a first-class ASDIC contact', the echoes were 'the clearest and sharpest I have ever heard'. Sixty years later he remembers: 'It was a difficult decision: should I remain with the convoy, or go after this submarine that was shadowing us? I chose to attack.' It quickly developed into a deadly game of cat and mouse. 'The ASDIC operator was watching his graph. Ping, ping, ping; he could tell from the quality of the sound whether the submarine was coming towards us or going away. He was the key man, he called continuously: "Ship approaching, 1500 yards. Sharp echo. Ship turning to starboard, sir. Ship stopped, sir. Ship turned away from us, got his wake." Then we ran in.' The *Pink* attacked with the new 'hedgehog' forward-throwing weapon and with depth charges. The U-boat swung backwards and forwards, diving ever deeper. Meanwhile, '*Pink*'s party' steamed on unprotected; this, Atkinson logged, was a risk worth taking because the prospect of a kill was good. 'We were persistent – we never let the submarine go,' he recalls. 'After about our fifth attack huge quantities of oil came to the surface. We could hear him trying to blow his ballast tanks.'

'Tangible evidence of destruction was greedily and most enthusiastically searched for,' Atkinson reported to the Admiralty later. The *Pink* ran in for one final attack; this time 'a most powerful underwater explosion shook the ship, low in note and like a deep grunt.' The *Pink* was later credited with the destruction of *U-192*; recent analysis of U-boat records, however, suggests her barrage was directed at *U-358*. It was not the kill Atkinson had hoped for, but *U-358* had been badly battered and its commander was left with no choice but to turn for home.[29]

The attack had taken the best part of an hour and a half to complete, by which time *Pink* was some 10 miles behind her party. Atkinson was desperate to regain contact and gave the order to make best speed, but the corvette was still 3 miles short when a huge column of smoke began to rise from the port side of the group. 'My worst fears had materialized,' Atkinson recalls. 'The American ship *West Madaket* had been torpedoed. She went up in smoke and immediately began to settle. We circled around and dropped depth charges to put the U-boat down, and then picked up the survivors.' Picking up survivors with a U-boat close by was a dangerous operation. 'I was rather disgusted, actually, because they brought their suitcases with them. The gunner's mate said to me, "Look at that lot!" They were alongside passing up suitcases, and we called down, "Come on board or stay in your boat, but leave your luggage." They were quite disgruntled about it.' The *Pink* picked up one further contact before nightfall, but lingered only long enough to deliver a warning five-charge pattern. Atkinson expected more trouble and, he judged, his place was with the rest of the 'party'.

The main body of ONS 5 had suffered losses too. During the daylight hours of 5 May the pack had picked off another four ships. It was a depressing tally, but B-7 had struck back; an accurate depth charge attack by the *Sunflower* had sent the remains of *U-638* to the bottom. As night closed in a Liberator from Iceland appeared, and for an all too brief time made its presence felt patrolling the perimeter of the convoy. At 20.38 it was obliged to signal to *Tay*, 'Don't want to go, but have to'. The B-7 group was left to find its way through the night as best it could. Sherwood reported later: 'The visibility has closed down to half a mile...HF/DF indicated that submarines were all around...'. To the captain of *Offa* the weight of U-boat signals traffic suggested that the convoy was 'threatened with annihilation'.[30]

Dönitz certainly had high hopes for that's night's attack; all U-boats were urged to 'make the most of a remarkable opportunity'.[31] Speed was essential, because the convoy would soon be out of the 'black pit' and would then be able to count on air support. When the pack had finished with the merchant ships it was, in Dönitz's words, to 'sink the escorts'.

It is impossible to rescue the battle that ranged around ONS 5 on the night of 5–6 May from the Atlantic fog in which it was fought. Some have tried, notably in recent years the American historians Professor David Syrett and Professor Michael Gannon.[32] These are the bald facts as stated by the acting senior officer escort, Lieutenant Commander Sherwood, in his report to the Admiralty: '23 ships in about 10 columns...speed seven and a half knots. Calm sea, no wind, drizzle and heavy mist...at 00.41 (GMT) the first of about 24 attempted attacks from every direction except ahead was detected and the battle continued without stopping until 06.20....'

The convoy ploughed on as best it could. From time to time the commodore of the convoy ordered an emergency turn in an effort to shake off the pack, but with at least fifteen U-boats in pursuit everything rested on the speed with which the escorts could close down the enemy and force him under. Here the weather played its part. At one point visibility was cut to just a few hundred yards: the U-boats were practically blind, but shipborne radar shone a great light through this fog. The advantage rested with the escorts. The battle around ONS 5 was fought and won on a boxed screen. As the radar swept through 360 degrees it picked up familiar 'blips', the solid echo of the merchant ships in their columns and the escort screen around them. But then there might be a new echo, less distinct: 'Bearing 270, range 4 miles.' A signal would be sent to the senior officer on *Tay*: 'Smell 270'; minutes later, perhaps, there would be confirmation of a radar contact from one of the other escorts. Then the chase was on.

Looks' *U-264* was hunting on the edge of the convoy: 'It was a pea-souper; dreadful. While we were chugging about in it, trying to achieve something, we were almost rammed by a destroyer which suddenly appeared behind us, lighting up the stern of our U-boat with a big search-light. It thundered past with about 3 metres to spare. I dived immediately.'

One of the escorts threw a few depth charges at Looks, but there was no time for a long ASDIC hunt; B-7 had been schooled by Gretton to 'hit all submarines quickly and hard and then rejoin the convoy at full speed'.[33] It would be a disciplined performance by all the escorts; it needed to be. For a time the battle was fought at an astonishing pace. This is an extract from the log *Sunflower*:

22.40 (GMT) Radar contact picked up on port bow; closed to investigate at 14 knots.

22.47 The radar echo faded but was picked up on Asdic [the submarine had dived]

22.48 Attacked.

22.52 10 charge pattern was dropped set at 150 feet. This was considered a most promising attack. Immediately before firing depth charges [another] radar contact was picked up ahead at 3400 yards. Course was continued, to attack the next submarine.

22.55 Asdics reported torpedo fired from Red (Port) 20. Turned towards it and torpedo passed down port side. Radar picked up [a second] contact at 2800 yards about 30 degrees from the other bearing. Continued in pursuit of nearest submarine which had just fired the torpedo....

23.00 Opened fire [with deck guns]....

The *Sunflower* could now see two U-boats on the surface; she had fired on the first but was unable to catch it, so her captain had decided to concentrate on the second:

23.05 ...turned to starboard towards other submarine to try and drive him under.

23.07 A full salvo of torpedoes was reported from the [first] submarine that we had been pursuing. Helm was put to hard-a-port to point back...torpedoes passed down port side....

At this point the corvette *Snowflake* came to her aid, but for a time contact was lost. Yet in just half an hour *Sunflower* had intercepted three U-boats; one she had shaken with a depth charge attack, two had been driven away from the convoy.

First blood went at 23.30 to the destroyer *Vidette*; second an hour later to *Loosestrife*; to be followed by two more successes. The most dramatic kill that night was shared by *Snowflake* and *Oribi*. At a little before 03.00 *Oribi* picked up a radar contact and closed at a brisk 22 knots; 'I saw a submarine slide out of the fog,' her captain later reported. The *Oribi* was just yards away and well placed to ram the U-boat: 'The force of the collision slewed her round to port and she passed down the port side, heeled over with her bows and conning tower out of the water.' The captain of *Oribi* pronounced himself satisfied beyond doubt; that was, the end of another U-boat. He was mistaken. Somehow *U-125* had managed to escape, though not for long. At 03.54 *Snowflake* picked up a faint 'blip' from what appeared to be a stationary vessel; the ship's radar operator was sure it was a U-boat low in the water. The fog was so dense that *Snowflake* was obliged to close to within 100 yards before she could be sure; 'Switched on starboard searchlight to reveal a 500-ton U-boat swinging rapidly to starboard,' her captain, Lieutenant Harold Chesterman, logged. Here is his account of the end of the crippled *U-125*: 'Wheel was put hard-a-starboard in an attempt to ram and all guns that would bear opened fire. Ship turned inside U-boat's turning circle and came up alongside her starboard side with only a few feet separating the two. By this time the enemy was being illuminated by port searchlight and was seen to be in a sinking condition...as the ships drew apart the stern of the U-boat settled with constant streams of air bubbles rising from the after hatch. The crew were seen to be abandoning ship but they made an attempt to man the forward gun; this attempt was defeated by accurate shooting from the two pounder and port Oerlikon [gun] plus some intimidation from the four inch, which missed. Some of the crew waved their arms, presumably as a signal to cease fire, this was ignored.'

Commander and crew jumped into the sea and minutes later scuttling charges detonated in the U-boat; *Oribi*'s task was accomplished. What of the survivors? In the beam of the ship's searchlight Chesterman could see them struggling in a large patch of oil. Permission to pick them up was sought from Sherwood on *Tay*; the answer was shockingly blunt, 'Not approved.' *Snowflake* turned back to the convoy and left the survivors of *U-125* in its wake. It was, of course, a death sentence, but the battle was still in progress and the convoy came first.

Dawn on 6 May brought a most welcome sight; four of the five ships of Support Group 1 joined the screen around ONS 5. By then the battle was all but won; B-7 had taken the convoy through the night without loss. The *Pink*, too, had shepherded her small flock through the pack.

'Most satisfactory,' was Sherwood's typically understated assessment of B-7's performance. It was, in fact, a famous victory; the escorts had harried the enemy tirelessly, four U-boats had been sunk and a number damaged. The final balance sheet for ONS 5 was very much to the credit of the British; whilst thirteen ships were lost from the convoy it was at the price of six U-boats sunk, with a further four seriously damaged. This is the conservative estimate; another three U-boats were sunk en route to and from the convoy by aircraft and other escorts, bringing the total losses to nine. For the Germans it was an unsustainable rate of loss – one U-boat sunk for every two Allied merchant ships.

The B-7 ships were showered with well-deserved praise; Churchill sent his 'compliments' to all for their 'unceasing fight against the U-boats'. Admiral Horton observed, 'The skill and determination of all escorts engaged in this operation leaves little to be desired.' Commander Peter Gretton had listened to his group's signals traffic as he steamed away from the battle. 'Poor Peter was tearing his hair out,' Graham Bence remembers. 'We could hear all the chattering going on, but could do nothing about it.' Gretton would later write of his pride in the group's performance, but admitted, 'I shall never cease to regret that I did not risk the weather and stay with them until the end. This decision has haunted me ever since.'[34] It was, of course, Gretton's work in forging his group into a tough professional unit that had paid off with ONS 5.

The Royal Navy's own official historian was to write later that the seven-day battle fought over ONS 5 stood comparison with the great victories won by Admirals Hawke and Nelson in the eighteenth century. It 'has no name by which it will be remembered; but it was, in its own way, as decisive as Quiberon Bay or the Nile.'[35] This is overstating the case, for it was a significant rather than a decisive victory. Nevertheless it did mark just how far the tide of battle in the Atlantic had turned.

Dönitz blamed the failure of his boats on the poor weather conditions and above all radar, which the U-boat Command War Diary noted, had robbed the U-boat of its most important tactical advantage – its ability to remain hidden.[36] If no mention was made of shipborne HF/DF, the other great search tool in the Allied armoury, it was because U-boat staff still stubbornly refused to accept the evidence for its existence. It was impossible, however, not to notice the dramatic fall in the efficiency of the U-boat fleet; Dönitz's measure of success was, as ever, the average tonnage sunk per U-boat per day at sea. Having fallen from a peak of 438 tons in 1942 to just 160, it made the official goal of sinking more ships than the Allies could build seem a pipe dream. The commander of *U-264*, Hartwig Looks, remembers the black atmosphere of the U-boat messes in St Nazaire at this time: 'We knew some of the commanders who'd lost their U-boats – some were friends. So within our circle of fellow crewmembers, of U-boat sailors at the base, we were pretty worried. We'd noticed the British had made colossal technical progress and that was really quite ominous.'

After ONS 5 the convoy battles seemed to follow a new pattern: U-boats sunk for little or no loss. Good intelligence from *B-Dienst* in the first half of May led large U-boat packs to eastbound convoys HX 237 and SC 129, but just five ships were sunk; in return escorts and aircraft sank five U-boats.

Days later, the attack on ONS 7 cost the U-boat arm another five boats; just one ship was sunk. In an attempt to reassure his crews, Dönitz sent a signal urging them to pit their ingenuity and toughness against the enemy's 'tricks and technical developments, finally to finish him off'. There was also a promise: 'I believe I shall soon be able to give you better weapons for this hard struggle of yours.'[37]

On 14 May B-7 set out for home with slow convoy SC 130, Gretton back in command. This time the group could rely on good air cover and on the ships of Support Group 1 for much of the journey. It kept a clean sheet: no ships were lost, but three U-boats were sunk; one was *U-954*, on which Dönitz's son Peter was a watch officer. 'Dönitz kept this entirely to himself and dealt with it himself,' senior staff officer Hans-Rudolf Rösing remembers, 'but I would say he was really in despair because he could see how things were going with the war.' The news from the Atlantic was unrelentingly bleak, and yet no one at U-boat

Command was ready to accept that the convoy war was over. 'The cause of failure had not been clearly established and we still hoped that the timely and accurate reports from *B-Dienst* would enable us to attack a convoy successfully on the first night,' First Staff Officer Günther Hessler recalled after the war. 'It was the irony of fate,' he added, 'that in this phase when the boats were barely able to sustain the battle, our radio intelligence was giving us the location of most of the convoys heading for Britain.'

On 21 May 1943 U-boat Command was able to direct twenty-seven U-boats from two search groups against homebound HX 239. This time Dönitz decided to throw down the gauntlet to his boats with an extraordinary personal message: 'Now if there is anyone who thinks that fighting convoys is no longer possible he is a weakling and no true submarine captain. The Battle of the Atlantic is getting harder but it is the decisive campaign of the war. Be aware of your great responsibility and understand this, you must answer for your actions. Do your best with this convoy. We must destroy it...do not dive for aircraft but fight them off. Wherever possible make your escape from the destroyers on the surface. Be tough! Get ahead and attack. I believe in you.[38]

The cajoling, the bullying, counted for nothing; HX 239 was protected by a hefty close escort screen and Support Group 4, with the merchant carrier HMS *Archer* providing continuous air support. Passing close by was ON 184 shielded by its own escorts and the merchant carrier USS *Bogue*. Any U-boat commander who was foolish enough to take seriously Dönitz's injunction to fight it out on the surface would be signing his own warrant. It was the same story; the pack circled both convoys purposefully, but hardly managed to get within striking distance of the merchant ships. No ships were sunk, but two more U-boats were lost. Between 9 and 23 May large U-boat packs had found and attacked six out of seven convoys in the North Atlantic, but managed to sink just six ships. In that time the Allies accounted for fifteen U-boats. There were also losses en route to and from the operations areas and in other theatres, taking the final monthly figure to forty; most of these U-boats went down with all hands. It was, Dönitz later declared, 'a frightful total, which came as a hard and unexpected blow'.[39]

On 24 May Dönitz accepted the inevitable and ordered the withdrawal of all U-boats from the North Atlantic convoy routes. In a signal to his officers he acknowledged the overwhelming technical superiority of the Allies, but promised that a day would come soon when the U-boat could deploy 'newer and sharper weapons…to triumph over your worst adversaries, the aircraft and destroyer'. On a personal note Dönitz added, 'believe me, I have done and will continue to do everything to catch up with this enemy leap forward'.[40]

This was special pleading, there had been no 'enemy leap forward', for the writing had been on the wall since 1941. Even now Dönitz and his staff seemed to have only a partial understanding of the technical and material superiority of the Allies. The U-Boat Command War Diary described the withdrawal from the North Atlantic as 'a temporary abandonment'; as soon as 'new weapons' became available the battle would be resumed.[41] This promise did not amount to a great deal. The new weapon that Dönitz most needed was a new 'true' submarine with high underwater speed, but this was many months away from production; in the meantime, the shipyards would continue to churn out obsolete boats by the score.

Looking back some fifteen years later, Dönitz acknowledged the true significance of what the U-boat crews called 'Black May': 'Radar, and particularly radar location by aircraft, had to all practical purposes robbed the U-boats of their power to fight on the surface. Wolf-pack operations against convoys in the North Atlantic…were no longer possible.' Dönitz might well have mentioned shipborne HF/DF as well, but in the harsh, bright light of hindsight he was clear about what it all amounted to:

'We had lost the Battle of the Atlantic.'[42]

CHAPTER TWELVE

SACRIFICE

IT WAS TO BE 'the most difficult decision of the whole war', Karl Dönitz wrote in his *Memoirs*, the bitterest of choices: fight on regardless, or withdraw?[1] The losses were insupportable; almost a third of the Atlantic U-boat force had been wiped out in the spring of 1943. Dönitz knew that the balance of advantage in the technical war rested with the Allies; until the existing U-boat types could be replaced with a new, 'true' submarine with high underwater speeds it seemed inevitable that losses would rise to 'an appalling height'. Would any purpose be served by struggling on against overwhelming odds?[2]

It is hardly surprising that the man who had endeavoured from the first to instil in his crews a 'spirit of selfless readiness to serve' now chose to fight on whatever the cost. Germany was on the defensive everywhere; its armies on the Eastern Front were engaged in costly holding actions; at home the Allied bombing campaign had begun systematically to reduce the Reich's cities to rubble; the navy could not, in Dönitz's estimation, 'stand aside as a spectator'. He knew too that Hitler would not permit it; 'The Atlantic is my first line of defence in the west', the Führer told him in May, 'even if I have to fight a defensive battle there that is better than defending myself on the coasts of Europe'.[3] Less certain was whether the U-boat arm would accept the need for this 'certain and deliberate self-sacrifice'.[4]

At the end of May 1943 Dönitz summoned the commanders of the Biscay combat flotillas to a conference at the headquarters of the senior officer in France, the Führer der U-Boote (West), Hans-Rudolf Rösing. 'He did something really quite unusual,' Rösing recalls.

He said, 'Now every one of you should tell me, without any regard for what I might perhaps think about it, how he judges the terrible situation we find ourselves in, and what we should be doing about it.' Well, our view was that even if we could no longer expect to have a decisive effect, as long as Germany was fighting, we would still have to keep up the pressure. When everyone had had his say, myself last, Dönitz said, 'OK, you have simply confirmed what I also think – as long as there is fighting the navy has to fight too.'

It was unusual for U-boat officers to do anything more than 'confirm' their commander's opinions, such was the force of Dönitz's personality.[5] Yet Dönitz was to make much of this meeting when he wrote his *Memoirs* fifteen years later; he was anxious to present it as an endorsement by the U-boat arm of his decision to fight on regardless. How representative the views of Rösing and the five flotilla commanders were of general opinion in the arm is difficult to judge. It was some time before those beyond the Biscay bases learnt of the spring losses. In the summer of 1943 Erich Topp was commander of the 27th Training Flotilla in Gotenhafen (Gydnia) on the Baltic, preparing crews for combat in the Atlantic; 'U-boat Command kept the bad news about the losses under wraps,' he recalls. 'It did not want to paralyse the willingness of new crews and commanders to go into action.' Among those who doubted the wisdom of Döntiz's decision to press on with the war in the Atlantic was Jürgen Oesten, who at the time was senior staff officer with special responsibility for U-boats in Arctic waters; 'We knew that it would lead to nothing in the end and of course that it would be deplorable to risk people further.' This was 'defeatist' talk, only to be discussed *sotto voce* with like-minded officers; and certainly most U-boat men fought on without question. 'We were told that we would tie up aircraft that would otherwise be used to drop bombs on Germany,' the former commander of *U-264*, Hartwig Looks, recalls. 'We weren't exactly enamoured with the idea, but you just accepted it in those days.'

Tying up aircraft was to prove a costly business. The Allies had begun to pursue the U-boats to the threshold of their bombproof bunkers. By June 1943 a 'Bay Offensive' was in full swing, with British and American aircraft and ships on a round-the-clock hunt for U-boats en route to and from the Biscay ports. Most boats were ordered to far-flung waters where Allied anti-submarine defences were less severe, but first they had to cross the Bay. 'It was distressing for the men', Günther Hessler, the first staff officer at U-boat Command, later observed, 'that their home waters should have become the most dangerous part of the whole Atlantic with the Luftwaffe powerless to intervene.'[6] Dönitz's response was to order the boats to cross the Bay in groups, in the hope that a com-bined flak barrage would beat off allied aircraft. First results were not encouraging: of the seventeen U-boats sunk in June, eleven were lost to aircraft; two more were claimed in the Bay by the ships of Captain Johnny Walker's 2nd Support Group. The twenty-nine U-boats that did make it to African and American waters sank just 17 merchant ships between them.

It was an unequal struggle; Allied aircraft were now fitted with a bat-tery of new weapons including rockets and a homing torpedo, Fido, designed to pursue the U-boat beneath the surface. The U-tanker was particularly vulnerable because it took at least a minute for it to dive to a depth of 10 metres. Hartwig Looks' *U-264* rendezvoused with a supply boat and its escort on 4 October 1943:

While I was lying alongside, still connected, the group, which con-sisted of the U-tanker, my boat and two others, was attacked by a carrier-based plane. I tried to stay on the surface with the U-tanker to ward off the plane, but while we were trying to deal with this one four more arrived. When I saw those, I said to myself, 'Right, the time has come.' I raced over to the U-tanker and shouted across with a megaphone, 'Come on, dive!' but the commander just stood there and shrugged. I couldn't make sense of it; he hadn't given any indication that he couldn't dive. I dived with the other boats. When a ship sinks, the bulkheads break. You can hear the cracking sound underwater – you know that someone's 'gone for a burton'. After six hours I surfaced, at the exact place where it must have happened. I thought there was a chance we might find survivors.

There were no survivors; the *U-460* and her crew of sixty-two were lost – the eleventh U-tanker sunk in five months, all but one from the air. The loss of all but three of its operational supply boats would severely restrict U-boat Command's ambitions for patrols in distant waters. Dönitz abandoned his reckless 'group' strategy on 2 August, but the threat from the air remained. 'We had one song which went; "Give me a new little U-boat, a U-boat that can no longer be located, Karl Dönitz," Horst von Schroeter recalls. In November 1943 his boat, *U-123*, was attacked by an RAF Coastal Command Mosquito as it was making its way back to Lorient. 'We were hit on the tower. Armour-piercing shells penetrated the hull and one man was killed, two more were wounded, and the U-boat was unfit to dive.' Von Schroeter was close enough to limp home safely. In the three months following the withdrawal from the North Atlantic convoy routes seventy-eight U-boats were sunk, more than half by Allied aircraft. Losses were high and successes few even in remote corners of the Atlantic hitherto judged by U-boat Command to be chinks in the Allied anti-submarine armour.

To underscore Anglo-American victory, in July 1943 the rising curve of Allied merchant ship construction crossed that of total war-time losses to enemy action and never again sank below it.[7] It was final confirmation that the tonnage war had been won; in July alone the Allies launched two hundred ships. New Liberty ships were racing down the slipways of American yards at a rate of more than two a day. Mass-produced to a standard 10,000-ton design, the prefabricated parts of a new ship could be built from the keel up in just 40 days.[8] Churchill's 'measureless peril' had been overcome. 'The convoys came through intact, the supply line was safe', he later wrote; 'our armies could now be launched across the sea against the underbelly of Hitler's Europe.'[9]

Dönitz had taken his decision to fight on to the bitter end, no matter how bleak the prospects. The devastating Allied bombing raids that summer only stiffened his resolve. 'You young men are alive at a great time', he told naval recruits in July, because you 'belong to a community of committed warriors' who stand in 'the frontline in the battle against the Anglo-Saxons'. 'I believe in youth. I have always believed in youth,' he assured them. 'The English may mock at the young crews I have. They say, "You've got commanders who are infants." These infants will show them what infants are capable of…in this hour we want to pledge our loyalty, our love, our obedience to our Führer.' The same spirit of defiant optimism characterized Dönitz's decision to resume the convoy war in the North Atlantic. In a radical shift of tactics U-boats were instructed first to 'decimate the escort' and then to attack the merchant ships. Hopes rested on the new anti-destroyer weapon, the *Zaunkönig* homing torpedo. The U-boats were also equipped with additional anti-aircraft armament and a new radar detection set, the *Wanze*, which promised to give some warning of the enemy's approach.

In September 1943 the twenty boats of group *Leuthen* returned to what had once been the air gap between Greenland and Iceland. They were left in no doubt as to the importance of their task: Dönitz sent a message informing them that the Führer himself was 'watching every phase of your struggle'.[10] So too was Admiral Horton at Western Approaches Command. Naval Intelligence had detected from Enigma decrypts that a new convoy campaign was planned; by mid-September it was clear that a large pack had assembled southeast of Greenland and that two convoys in particular, westbound ON202 and ONS18, were in danger. Horton ordered these to merge, ensuring a combined escort screen of twenty-two ships including a merchant carrier; the enlarged convoy could also count on support from very long-range aircraft.

The battle began on 20 September with a successful *Zaunkönig* attack on the frigate HMS *Lagan*; in the next four days the *Leuthen* boats claimed to have sunk between twelve and fifteen escorts. Dönitz was able to report to a delighted Hitler that the attack had been 'a complete success'; 'the new weapons proved their worth in every respect', the 'outer' and 'inner' rings of the escort screen had been destroyed and nine merchant ships sunk.[11] Not for the first time, Dönitz had been blinded by hopelessly optimistic claims; the true figures were three escorts sunk and only six of sixty-eight merchant ships. *Zaunkönig* was not the 'decisive weapon' Dönitz hoped it would be. The Allies had anticipated that the Germans would at some point develop an acoustic torpedo; within two weeks of the first attacks escorts were being equipped with an effective counter-measure, the Foxer. This simple noise-making device was towed in the wake of a ship to attract a homing torpedo. After less than four months of the new convoy campaign Dönitz was again obliged to admit defeat. U-boats had made a hundred war patrols but managed to sink just nine ships. Losses remained high – fifty-nine boats had been sunk. It was Dönitz's last effort to regain the initiative in the decisive North Atlantic theatre; the end, too, of the old-style pack attack. 'All we could hope to do was to fight a delaying action,' Dönitz later admitted.[12] It was the same story on all fronts: Hitler's Italian ally in the west had deserted him, whilst his armies in the east had embarked on an inexorable retreat to the borders of the Reich. In the autumn of 1943 Jürgen Oesten was preparing to return to sea after almost two years in staff positions ashore; one of the visitors to his new boat during its work-up period was the Reich Armaments Minister, Albert Speer. Some months later, over dinner in Berlin, Oesten asked Speer – one of Hitler's most trusted lieutenants – what the future held for Germany; 'He said to me, "Well, I guess we'll be defeated by the autumn of 1944."' When on 20 April 1944 Oesten set out on his first and last war patrol in *U-861* it was with a heavy heart: 'I had a rather bad feeling because I basically knew that it was all for nothing – what we would sink and kill was really not necessary.'

It was not a thought Dönitz would have countenanced. Helmut Witte was serving on the staff at this time: 'He spread necessary optimism and you could hardly contradict him in such a circle, although we all knew that everything was about how to end the war in a more or less acceptable manner.' The question was, how could the war be brought to an 'acceptable' end when the Allies were committed to a policy of 'unconditional surrender'? The leaders of the Third Reich believed they had to fight on regardless of the cost. At such a time Dönitz's accent on the positive was especially welcome at the Führer's headquarters; in particular there was much talk here of the new 'electro-boats' with high underwater speeds that were being developed. When Erich Topp visited the Wolf's Lair that autumn Hitler 'entertained' him with a monologue about the great advances of German technology, of which a 'true' submarine to wrest back the initiative from the Allies in the Atlantic was just one.

The same bunker fever was evident at U-boat Command. Commanders of front-line boats like Hartwig Looks were aware of a gulf growing between Berlin and the Biscay bases, intensified when in December 1943 Dönitz and his staff sought refuge from Allied bombing at a new headquarters in woodland outside Berlin. In the U-boat messes in France, 'staff talk' of new weapons to transform the war at sea was taken with a large pinch of salt. 'We scoffed about it among ourselves,' Looks recalls. In December he was asked to take part in a morale-raising broadcast: 'I received an order from the flotilla commander to do this hook-up radio transmission. I was connected with the Technical Institute in Brunswick, with a Professor Esau. I told him about my last voyage, when we lost the stern of the boat to an aircraft that had fired an anti-submarine homing torpedo. He said to me, "Ah, all that will be improved! We have amazing things in development, and these will soon be at the front and then you'll see, things will look up again." It was all froth. There wasn't any substance to it.'

A former *U-154* diesel mechanic, Heinz Kuhlmann had volunteered for the U-boat arm the year before at the age of seventeen, after a spell in the naval Hitler Youth movement: 'If it had been necessary we would have given our lives for the Führer, the People [*Volk*] and the Fatherland – that was our ideal.' Yet by December 1943 the war had become a 'shitty' affair; 'We said to ourselves, "For God's sake, it can't go on like this – that we only suffer losses and don't manage to sink a single ship".'

It is an oft-repeated myth that U-boat crews fought on to the end, united in their eagerness to lay down their lives for Germany and its people. Dönitz certainly wanted to believe it. The story of the last two years of the U-boat war is told in just twenty-five of the five hundred pages of his *Memoirs*, but much is made in these of 'sacrifice' and 'sacred duty', of the unshakable morale of the men. He saw in their willingness to set out on near-suicidal missions an endorsement of his own narrow sense of 'duty' to country. Allied intelligence papers tell a different story. In the summer of 1943 the Royal Navy's interrogators at NID 1 reported that prisoners had indicated that 'defeatist conversion' was common at the U-boat bases, and that 'their disinclination to go to sea is becoming evident...the ritual, including band playing, to welcome an incoming U-boat has been abandoned and at Lorient recently the usual bouquet was presented to a departing boat, whereupon the captain cast it into the sea and left the port without making a farewell signal'.[13] An intelligence source within the U-boat base at Bordeaux reported that punishments were becoming stiffer and there was good evidence that some crewmen had been imprisoned 'for refusing to go to sea'.[14] In September 1943 Naval Intelligence minuted 'proof' from 'our French organisation' that 'in order to delay their departure they [crews] damage various pieces of machinery and they hope for sabotage by the French'. More than one source reported that crew men in the Biscay bases had delayed their boat's war patrol by putting sugar in the diesel.

These secret reports were circulated to just a privileged few within the Admiralty, and were by no means written for use as 'black' propaganda. There is considerable evidence from within the U-boat arm itself that morale amongst crews in France was now close to rock bottom. Military court papers indicate that insubordination and desertion were on the increase. Slogans such as 'Victory at all costs' and 'Who has the better morale shall win' were dismissed as *Dönitz-Scheisse* (Dönitz crap).[15] By the end of 1943 231 frontline boats had been lost to all causes. Even experienced crews felt the pressure; on the eve of its next war patrol, in February 1944, some of the crew of *U-264* wrecked the

French villa that had been set aside for their use. 'They'd been drinking and they destroyed everything,' their former commander, Hartwig Looks, recalls. 'I was livid. I gave them, a real dressing down and they came back to their senses, but when I went to the Flotilla Commander and reported to him that I was due to set out again, I told him that this time I wouldn't be coming back. I told him I knew this would be my last patrol. He was shocked and tried to calm me down, but I had an instinctive feeling that this was my last voyage.' The *U-264* was the first equipped with the *Schnorchel*, a long periscope-like tube that drew air to the diesel engines when the boat was submerged. It was not a new invention – the Dutch had developed the device before the war – but there had been a general reluctance to use it because submarines at periscope depth were almost blind. These were changed times, however, and the freedom to operate below the surface almost indefinitely afforded the U-boat significant protection from the ever-present air threat. That was some comfort for the commander of *U-264* and his crew when on 5 February they set out from St Nazaire on their fifth patrol.

A year had passed since the Allies had agreed at Casablanca that mastery of the U-boat threat had 'first charge' on their resources. Those whose job it was to anticipate the enemy's next step fussed about the electro-boat programme, but beyond Naval Intelligence the issue was felt to be all but settled. As if to demonstrate that the dogs were in full cry, the famous Walker group put to sea at this time on what was to be the most successful anti-submarine cruise of the war in the Atlantic. Under Captain Johnny Walker, the 2nd Support Group had already notched up an impressive five U-boat kills. On 29 January 1944 the group set out from Liverpool to the strains of 'A-Hunting We Will Go', played, as was customary, over the speakers of Walker's own ship, HMS *Starling*. 'It *was* a hunt to him,' one of the group's officers, Bryan Butchard, recalls. 'Sometimes he would treat it as a sport. We sank one submarine and there was oil and debris on the surface, and he signalled to the captain of the ship which had sunk the submarine, "Come over here and look what a mess you've made." That was his jocular way of treating it.' Butchard was First

Lieutenant of HMS *Magpie,* and by 1944 a seasoned anti-U-boat cam-
paigner. 'We used to operate as a group with one escort carrying out a
slow, creeping attack, dropping depth charges with a very deep setting on
the course of the U-boat, whilst the other ships would use their ASDIC
sets to maintain contact. It was what Walker called "holding the ring" – if
the U-boat tried to escape, one of the other ships would sink it.' If the
enemy was proving especially elusive the attack was carried out by three
ships, a creeping barrage. Operation Plaster was usually directed by
Walker himself. It called for close cooperation between the six ships of the
group; once contact was made the hunt was relentless, escape rare. Acting
on good intelligence from Enigma decrypts, Western Approaches Command directed the Walker group to a U-boat concentration some two
hundred miles off the west coast of Ireland.

The group claimed its first victim on 31 January: *U-592* was lost with
all hands. Another four U-boats were sunk between 8 and 11 February;
again, there were no survivors. 'One had very little feeling about sending
men to their deaths,' Butchard recalls. 'It was a U-boat, and that was
good enough.' Peter Eustace was a nineteen-year-old radar operator on
the *Starling*; 'There was a great feeling of elation amongst all of us:
"We've got another one!" We had the feeling we were almost invincible.'
The Admiralty required proof of a kill, so a ship's whaler was often sent
to furnish it. 'It was a rather gruesome thing, picking up human remains
and putting them in the whaler,' Eustace recalls. On 19 February the 2nd
Support Group picked up another ASDIC contact, *U-264*: 'Walker
worked on me for ten hours and that was the end,' Hartwig Looks
recalls.

We got around two hundred depth charges and they exploded
beneath the U-boat. We were accustomed to depth charges
exploding above us, but the full wave of the explosion came from
below. I tried to shake them off by taking evasive action, but that
didn't work. Equipment broke away from the pressure hull, and
there were various leaks. The water reached above our ankles and

a fire was reported in the electric motor room, and when you're submerged and there's a fire on board that's the end. I thought, 'There's nothing doing – we have to surface.' We shot out of the water like a champagne cork, and found ourselves inside the circle made by Captain Walker's submarine chasers. The crew jumped in the sea. I was on the tower holding on to an antenna to stop my legs being pulled into the tower hatch, where a whirlpool was forming. Then the U-boat sank below me.

The entire crew of *U-264* was fished out. 'I was hanging on the scramble nets limp as a lettuce leaf,' Looks recalls. 'Then a British sailor jumped over the rail, climbed down the net, got hold of my collar and said, "Come on, sailor!" and hauled me up on deck.' Looks was a prisoner on board HMS *Woodpecker*; 'I was taken to the officers' mess where they bombarded me with questions, and one of them said, 'That was a very, very clever fight." That wasn't quite the impression I'd had.' But the war was not over yet for Hartwig Looks: 'They put me up in a cabin below decks. I thought, "There are other U-boats around – they're packing acoustic torpedoes. This could go very wrong!" And so it did.' There was a huge explosion, and I jumped straight out of my bunk, stood there in my socks, the ceiling lamp fell down and I didn't know where I was. I felt my way along the walls, trying to find a companionway; there was a bulkhead across from me. When I opened the door I saw the Atlantic Ocean spilling through a gaping hole in the ship's side.' The *Woodpecker* was badly damaged but survived another week; she was eventually lost in heavy seas en route back to Britain. By then Looks had been transferred to *Magpie*; 'We used to have a drink together and exercise out on the quarterdeck,' Bryan Butchard recalls. 'I can remember him saying, "Well, they're saying, in Berlin now, 'Oh, where is Hartwig Looks?'" Of course Hartwig Looks was very, very fortunate – he'd been rescued twice, and his war now was over.'

The remaining ships of the 2nd Support Group were accorded an ecstatic welcome on their return to Liverpool; six U-boats in twenty-seven days was quite extraordinary. 'We sailed in line ahead up the Mersey,' Eustace recalls. 'The other ships were sounding their sirens – you know, we felt pretty good. Both sides of the Gladstone dock were lined with hundreds of Wrens and people cheering us as we came in.' Admiral Horton and the First Lord of the Admiralty stood among the crowd. Captain Walker's 'run of six' marked the climax of what the Royal Navy's official historian called the 'bitter offensive by the convoy escorts against their cunning and ruthless enemies'.[16] Under his command the 2nd Support Group sank sixteen U-boats. But this tireless pursuit of the enemy took its toll. A little over four months later Walker died of a stroke brought on by nervous exhaustion, as much a victim of the Atlantic battle as the hundreds of U-boat men he had so efficiently dispatched in his three years of war service at sea.

The loss of fifty-four front-line boats in the first three months of 1944 did nothing to improve morale. At least one in five boats setting out on patrol at this time did not return; crews who did were exhausted by the constant strain of life inside what they called the 'iron coffin'. Dock-side bunting and bands were a distant memory; only survival mattered. U-boat Command noted that many commanders had no appetite for action and deliberately avoided pressing home attacks on convoys or stragglers for fear of being intercepted. Just two ships were sunk in the North Atlantic in February, seven in March; a dismal return that served only to point up the madness of fighting on with the old U-boat types.

The official justification was still that 'vast enemy resources' were being held down by the U-boat campaign. Dönitz believed this to be important, but he knew too that failure to actively engage the enemy at sea would severely undermine his bargaining position in the inter-service battle for the Reich's scarce resources. Steel and manpower tied up in the construction of the new electro-boats was needed for the campaign in the east, where the German armies were struggling to hold the line in the Ukraine; it was surely on land, Hitler's generals argued, that the war would be decided. Even if the new U-boats proved effective, they could hardly save Germany from defeat.

Yet, remarkably, Dönitz managed to fend off most claims on the Kriegsmarine's resources, and in this Hitler's support was decisive; that Dönitz was able to count on it demonstrates the two men's mutual respect. The Reich Armaments Minister, Albert Speer, remembered Hitler observing: 'Dönitz is a National Socialist through and through and he keeps the navy free of all bad influences. The navy will never surrender. He has implanted a National Socialist concept of honour in it.'[17] In February 1944 Karl Dönitz became Nazi party member no. 9,664,999.[18] Sitting at Hitler's conference table as Commander in Chief of the navy had strengthened his faith in National Socialism and demonstrated 'how very insignificant we all are in comparison with the Führer'.[19] Jürgen Oesten witnessed something of Hitler's hold on Dönitz's imagination at first hand: 'When I was on his staff I flew to Berlin with him for an interview with Herr Hitler. I was with him until just a quarter of an hour before that interview, and I met him immediately after it. There were a number of points he wanted to discuss at the meeting and some were very negative points, ones he wanted to have something done about. When I met him after the interview I said, "Well, did you succeed?" Dönitz said, "No, it is quite different, you know. It's not like we thought. No, I saw in his eyes and I knew everything would be all right." Dönitz was full to the brim with an emotional sauce, swimming in that emotional sauce, and facts were quite uninteresting.'

It was hardly surprising, then, that the U-boat arm was expected to fight beyond reason; hardly surprising, too, that anything but unquestioning loyalty to the Führer was deemed dangerous defeatism. One case above all stands out from this time: that of the commander of *U-154*, Oskar Kusch. A devout Christian, with a fine intellect, Kusch is ironically thought to have chosen the Kriegsmarine because of its reputation as a non-political service. He quickly demonstrated himself to be, in the words of one of his commanders, 'an excellent young officer' who was 'very well qualified' to take over his own U-boat.

Kusch became commander of *U-154* in February 1943 on the eve of the defeat in the Atlantic and quickly made his mark with the crew;

'He showed great sensitivity towards us,' Heinz Kuhlmann recalls. 'I remember the war patrol we did to the tropics when the temperature between the engines was 65 centigrade. He brought us a can of refrigerated mirabelles [plums] to eat and he asked us what we would like to drink. None of the other officers did anything like that.' Sometimes the new commander played records to the crew; one he was particularly fond of was *'Heimat deine Sterne'* by Paul Abraham. 'We liked that very much and no one was troubled by the fact that Abraham was Jewish,' Kuhlmann remembers. Kusch made no secret of his distaste for the Nazis – Hitler was 'insane', a 'megalomaniac'. 'He always spoke his mind freely because he thought he was amongst comrades,' Kuhlmann recalls. 'We knew his views, and the crew felt free to say things like "Hitler has a screw loose."' The official photograph of Hitler that hung in all boats was taken down; there would, the commander observed drily, be 'no idol worship' on *U-154*. By the autumn of 1943 Kusch was openly questioning the wisdom of fighting on with U-boats that were 'obsolescent', especially when Germany's defeat was inevitable. The stream of signals from U-boat Command urging vigorous action was, he told his officers, just useless 'slave driving'.

But not everyone on board *U-154* shared these views. In January 1944 the First Watch Officer, Ulrich Abel, denounced Kusch for expressing opinions 'strongly opposed to the political and military leadership of Germany'. 'Abel was a 300 per cent Nazi,' Heinz Kuhlmann recalls, and he had carefully noted every remark. At the ensuing military trial Kusch was found to have made seditious remarks, some of which 'bore the character of high treason', and was sentenced to death by firing squad. Dönitz made no attempt to intervene or speak to his commander, as he would once have done. One of the charges was that Kusch listened to the BBC and other Allied broadcasts on board his boat; a serious offence in the Third Reich. The same accusation had been levelled at Jürgen Oesten three years before: 'I had a small radio of my own and I listened to enemy broadcasts, but I had a man on board who had been working for the party and he made a report to his superiors that we didn't think much of Herr Hitler and we had the BBC on. Of course this came down from the party to Dönitz, who called me in, and in a case like this you could rely on him. He buried it and the case was closed. I took the man out of my crew, kicked him off and got another one.' Oesten was a member of the old guard, an experienced and highly respected commander, who held the Knight's Cross, and he could count on Dönitz's support. In the first months of the war Dönitz had also been prepared to tolerate the views of his adjutant, Hans-Jochen von Knebel Doeberitz, who made little secret of his family's hostility to Hitler and the Nazis. But by the spring of 1944 Dönitz he stood as a disciple at Hitler's table, a member of his inner circle; a few months earlier he had written that 'anyone who believes he can do better than the Führer is silly', and, he might have added, treasonous.[20]

It did not help Kusch's case that his trial coincided with a low point in the morale of U-boat crews; there were others who shared these views, but were able to count on the discretion of their comrades. 'Whatever the political environment may have been,' Erich Topp later wrote, 'it would still have been in place here for Dönitz to speak to his commander at least once and to stand by him. Or was he so naïve that he did not know what people were saying in the U-boat messes about the party?' Dönitz almost certainly did know; Kusch was to be made an example of, another sacrifice. Appeals for clemency were rejected and on 12 May he was shot. Although no official announcement was made within weeks it was being talked about in the messes. Most of Kusch's crew were to learn nothing of his fate. The new commander of *U-154* was a martinet instructed to restore some National Socialist order; Heinz Kuhlmann counted himself fortunate to be posted ashore. On 2 July 1944 *U-154* was sunk off the Azores; 'I wept. All my best comrades with whom I had spent all those months perished,' Kuhlman recalls.

Dönitz had nurtured an image of the U-boat arm as a fighting elite; he expected its members to be, in the words of Erich Topp, 'the most loyal of the loyal'.[21] In the end the overwhelming majority of commanders and crews were prepared to demonstrate just that. Some were conscious of the privilege conferred by membership of the Freikorps Dönitz; this in Topp's view 'created morale that was strong enough to mask the overwhelming drive of every human being – to survive'. Just as important was the comradeship of the boat – the overwhelming sense that each man shouldered responsibility for the safety of his brothers. In the spring of 1944 the commander of *U-123*, Horst von Schroeter, was ordered to take up a new post ashore: 'I had been on board *U-123* three years. I knew the crew – I had developed a close relationship with them. I didn't want to go. At the beginning of May 1944 I went to see Dönitz and told him I didn't want to leave, and I think this clearly illustrates the relationship between Dönitz and the men he led. He was an admiral of the fleet, I was a lieutenant, and yet I was able to tell him that the boat was no longer up to the demands of the front, but that because of my ties to the boat I would prefer to remain on board. I would find it un-endurable to sit ashore and wait to hear that the boat had been lost.'

Von Schroeter was being offered a chance to survive and return to his wife and family in Germany, and yet he elected not to leave his com-rades. This spirit, the bonds forged by shared danger, kept the U-boats sailing to the bitter end. The crew of *U-123* was to owe its survival in no small measure to the loyalty of its commander; a short time afterwards the boat was decommissioned. It helped, of course, that von Schroeter was a Knight's Cross holder, a man of proven worth; a less able and trusted commander would not have enjoyed as sympathetic a hearing. That much was demonstrated by the events of the following month.

The first news of the long-expected Allied invasion of France reached U-boat Command in the early hours of 6 June 1944. Orders were at once given for 'every available boat' to be flung at the armada in the Channel. 'In this hour of crisis the role of the U-boats was decisive to the outcome of the war,' Staff Officer (Operations) Günther Hessler later wrote. 'Every enemy vessel supporting the landing, even though it may be carrying only fifty men or a tank, is a target,' Dönitz told his men. 'Press home your attack, even at the cost of your boat...a U-boat which inflicts losses on the invasion forces fulfils her highest mission and justifies her existence, even though she herself may be destroyed.'[22]

This was a kamikaze order in all but name; the architect of the U-boat arm, the man still known to some as 'Onkel Karl', was urging its crews to sacrifice themselves. None of Dönitz's commanders were in the end prepared to ask that of their crews. The Allied armada assembled for Overlord numbered more than five thousand ships, supported by nearly six thousand bomber and fighter aircraft; what hope for the U-boat in the face of this huge force? Only U-boats equipped with the *Schnorchel* were capable of operating within striking distance of Allied shipping, and yet those without were also ordered into the Channel. Of the thirty-six boats of group *Landwirt* that sailed from the Biscay ports on D-Day, almost a third were sunk or forced to abort within days; as was to be expected, most of these were non-*Schnorchel* boats caught on the surface by Allied aircraft. It was the same story with the twenty or so boats of group *Mitte* that sailed from Norway to attack shipping at the other end of the Channel. In total twenty-six boats were lost in June 1944; German air and naval forces claimed just nineteen Allied ships in British home waters. So much for Hitler's 'first line of defence'. 'The old spirit of the arm was once again magnificently displayed,' Dönitz logged in his War Diary, and 'the success achieved was satisfactory'.[23] This risible assessment of an utter fiasco only serves to underline how utterly enmeshed Dönitz was in Hitler's world of blind resistance whatever the cost.

Within three months of the D-Day landings the Allied advance had swept the last of the U-boats from their Biscay bases. There was talk of regrouping in Norway, of a fresh Atlantic campaign with the new electro-boats, but only 'true believers' allowed themselves to be convinced. For most of the final months of the war successes in the Atlantic and North Sea barely managed to keep pace with U-boat losses. Dönitz remained resolute in support of his 'beloved Führer'. He was outraged by the attempted assassination of Hitler on 20 July 1944 and castigated the conspirators for believing 'that by the removal of our Führer they can free us from our hard but unalterable struggle of destiny'. In his proclamation to the navy he urged his men to "ruthlessly destroy anyone who reveals himself as a traitor'.[24] The U-boats sailed on to the end; many of those with a command either volunteered or were pressed into service on land. A handful of the Type XXI and XXIII electro-boats were to carry out war patrols in the final weeks. Dönitz cast them at his Führer much as a lifebelt is thrown to a drowning man; 'the mighty sea power of the Anglo-Saxons' was, he reported to Hitler, essentially 'powerless' to combat these new, 'true' submarines.[25] This was just more 'necessary optimism', for Dönitz knew perfectly well that the war at sea had ceased to matter. No one fought harder to ensure that Hitler's mad dream of a Wagnerian twilight for the Reich became a reality. All defeatism was to be ruthlessly stamped out; as late as 20 March 1945, as Soviet troops were advancing on Berlin, Dönitz instructed his officers to 'be hard and strict rather than too soft…if circumstances demand making a quick, horrible example of someone, let us not shrink from the task'.[26] The Kriegsmarine was to stand like 'a rock of resistance' as an example to the rest of Germany.

On 18 April 1945 Jürgen Oesten brought *U-861* safely into the Norwegian port of Trondheim after a year in the Far East and South Atlantic waters: 'We came back from the smiling ease of Far Eastern life and for us the war had finished long ago. But in Trondheim they'd put on the walls, '*Lieber tot als Sklave!*', meaning 'sooner dead than a slave'. The war was not finished here. It was really awful, because if my crew went ashore and went into some bar drinking, they just laughed at some of the others and then the military police came along and arrested them. I had this collar iron [Knight's Cross], and my chief engineer had one as well and that helped – the two of us went from one jail to the other picking up our people.

By the end of April Soviet troops were in the streets of Berlin, within striking distance of the bunker where the broken leader of the broken Reich was 'coordinating' his last-ditch defence of the city. Dönitz and his staff had moved their headquarters to the north German town of Plön. It was here on 28 April that Erich Topp made his last report to Dönitz: 'He was, as ever, optimistic. At no point did he suggest that he no longer believed in a happy, advantageous outcome to the war. It reminded me a little of a picture that was popular in the homes of navy families. It showed "the last man" clinging to the wreck of a ship, fully aware that he is about to die and yet still holding aloft his country's flag, in order to make quite clear that right to the end he still believed in victory.' On 1 May Topp left Kiel in the Type XXI boat, *U-2513*, on his last war patrol; he too had been 'educated' to do his 'duty' to the very end, and that is what he intended to do. On the same day Topp learnt that Hitler was dead and that the 'honourable man' he had named as his successor was Karl Dönitz. It was to be 'the last Führer's' duty to order the unconditional surrender of all German forces; for the second time in his life Dönitz was to witness the humiliation of his country and his navy. Before the surrender took effect he sent one final message to the U-boat arm: 'My U-boat men! We have come through six years of U-boat warfare. You have fought like lions…you are laying down your arms after a heroic battle that knows no equal, unbroken and unimpeachable. We remember with great respect our fallen comrades who sealed their loyalty to their Führer and Fatherland by sacrificing their lives.' Since 'Black May' 1943 at least 450 U-boats and more than fifteen thousand men had been lost waging war against what Dönitz called, 'a crushing material superiority'.[27]

A fortnight after Germany's capitulation Dönitz was arrested and held on war crimes charges, in particular of ordering his U-boat commanders to kill the survivors of torpedoed ships. Lieutenant Commander Colin McFadyean and a colleague from Naval Intelligence visited Dönitz in custody to bring him a message from the Admiralty:

He was being held by the Americans with a lot of other VIP prisoners in a big house outside Frankfurt. We went to this place and asked to see Grossadmiral Dönitz and a nasty, scruffy-looking GI pushed somebody in the room and said, 'Dönitz!', and so we said, *'Guten Tag, Herr Grossadmiral,'* and spoke to him nicely. We were told by the First Sea Lord to tell Dönitz off the record that we reckoned he'd fought a clean war and we had nothing against him, which meant we wouldn't have anything to do with the Nuremberg war crimes trials.

The Admiralty's reluctance to pursue its erstwhile enemy was to count for nothing, the Nuremberg judges found Dönitz guilty of both war crimes and waging aggressive war, and sentenced him to ten years' imprisonment. It was the victors' justice; the U-boat had waged a tough, uncompromising battle in the Atlantic, but there was precious little evidence to suggest that it had been anything other than a 'clean' one. This is not to suggest that Dönitz was guiltless: he had given his whole-hearted support to Hitler; he had spoken publicly, too, of 'the disintegrating poison of Jewry'; above all, he had presided over the sacrifice of thousands of U-boat men.[28] In the last two years of the war there were months in which one in every two U-boats setting out on patrol did not come back. It was no crime to fight on – but to fight on regardless of the cost? The 'self-sacrifice' had, by the summer of 1944 at the latest, ceased to have any sensible purpose. The German U-boat historian, Dr Axel Niestlé believes that more than 60 per cent of those who served in frontline boats lost their lives. Of 859 U-boats that carried out war patrols 648 were lost, one-third of these on their first voyage.[29] The grim grey walls of the U-boat Memorial at Möltenort near Kiel hold the names of more than thirty thousand U-boat men who died in World War II and whose resting place is roughly marked in latitude and longitude.

It had begun on the first day of the war with the sinking of the *Athenia* and ended only on the last; by the time the Battle of the Atlantic had run its course 15 million tons of Allied shipping had been lost, most of it to the German U-boat. In the grim balance sheet of the battle 3500 merchant ships were recorded as sunk in the North Atlantic and British home waters – 70 per cent of all worldwide shipping losses. It is impossible to be sure how many Allied seamen were killed or maimed in those ships; the British merchant service alone lost more than thirty-two thousand men during the war, the Royal Navy 50,758 seamen. This was just a fraction of the total human cost; many thousands of civilians on both sides of the battle were caught in bombing raids on shipyards and ports.

Was Allied victory in the Atlantic ever in doubt? The Royal Navy's official historian, Captain Stephen Roskill, certainly believed so; 'the primary enemy was always the U-boat', he wrote; 'we knew beyond doubt that the peril in which our nation so long stood derived mainly from those utterly ruthless enemies, and that only by destroying them could we survive'.[30] For a short time after the Fall of France in June 1940 the German sea and air assault seemed to threaten Britain's ability to fight on. A handful of well-trained, determined U-boat crews laid siege to the British Isles and inflicted damage on shipping that was quite disproportionate to their numbers. A larger force might have succeeded in cutting the country's Atlantic lifeline, but Dönitz was rarely able to muster more than six U-boats in the operations area at any one time. In the summer of 1941 his fleet began to grow, but by then the Enigma breakthrough had helped turn the tide in the Atlantic. Figures compiled by the American historian Clay Blair suggest that in the first twenty-eight months of war nine hundred convoys – some twelve thousand ships loaded with food and war materials – made the journey to Britain. The U-boat claimed just 2 per cent of this total, less than 300 ships; the convoy had once again proved its worth.[31] Overall losses were much greater, especially amongst ships sunk beyond the umbrella of the convoy. Between June 1940 and December 1941 roughly 36 per cent of the British merchant fleet was lost to enemy action.[32] Imports declined sharply from a pre-war 60 million tons to a little over half that total.

At no point did Britain stand alone in this battle, the Empire rallied round, and Canada in particular played a vital role. By the end of the war more than four hundred ships, almost half the North Atlantic escort force, were Canadian; an extraordinary contribution from a country that could boast only six ships in 1939.[33] Britain could also count on the generous support of the United States, although for two years it was officially neutral. The final victory in the Atlantic was assured with American entry into the war. The USA was able to bring overwhelming military and industrial muscle to bear, enabling the Allies to sweep all before them. Dönitz had enjoyed the briefest window of opportunity in the Atlantic; by December 1941 it had firmly closed. The U-boat was nevertheless to prove, in Roskill's words, 'a source of anxiety to us right to the end'.[34] It was not just a question of Britain's survival; the Atlantic was also continental Europe's lifeline. Only when victory was secured in the Atlantic were the British and Americans free to launch their armies against what Churchill called 'the underbelly of Hitler's Europe'. It was the great land war in the east that sealed the fate of the Third Reich, but victory in the Atlantic helped ensure that the Western allies would be there at the end; and for that Europe should still be thankful.

NOTES ON CONTRIBUTORS

RICHARD AMSTEIN
Born 1918. Joined the Kriegsmarine in 1938 and the U-boat arm in March 1939. Served on nine war patrols with *U-123* as a Leading Control Room Mechanic. After the war he worked as a self-employed electrician.

ADMIRAL JOHN ADAMS
Born 1918. Joined the Royal Navy in 1936. From 1939–42 he served as Sub-Lieutenant HMS *Walker* and First Lieutenant HMS *Cleveland* on convoy escort duty. In1943 he joined the staff of Captain (D) Liverpool, specialising in Anti-Submarine Warfare (ASW). After the war he served in various posts including Captain, 3rd Submarine Squadron 1958–60 and Assistant Chief of Naval Staff 1966–68.

SIR ROBERT ATKINSON
Born 1916. Royal Naval Reserve Officer served in five corvettes from 1940–45 and was commanding officer of three, including HMS *Pink*. Awarded the Distinguished Service Cross and two Bars. After the war he worked in industry and in 1980 became Chairman of British Shipbuilders.

DAVID BALME
Born 1920. Served as a Sub-Lieutenant with HMS *Ivanhoe* and then HMS *Bulldog*. He was decorated with the Distinguished Service Order for his part in the capture of the intelligence materials from *U-110*. He later served with the Fleet Air Arm in the Mediterranean and on the Admiralty Staff of the Eastern Fleet in the Far East. After the war he joined the family firm of woolbrokers in the City of London.

ALBERT BECKER
Born 1923. Joined US Navy Armed Guard 1942. On his first tour of duty his ship, the *City of Flint* was sunk and he spent 46 days in an open boat. He was discharged from the navy in 1944. After the war he worked in quality assurance for IBM; when he retired he bought a motor home and has travelled through every state in the USA.

GRAHAM BENCE
Born 1916. Royal Naval Volunteer Reserve Lieutenant. From 1940–42 served on the corvette HMS *Coreopsis*. Joined HMS *Duncan* as Staff and Navigating Officer in 1943 and later served with the escort carrier *Slinger*. After the war he became a teacher and later took Holy Orders.

PROFESSOR ROBERT HANBURY BROWN
1916–2002. Worked on radar research for the Air Ministry and the Admiralty 1936–42; then in the United States 1942–45. After the war held various academic and public posts including Professor of Physics (Astronomy) at the University of Sydney.

TERENCE BULLOCH
Born 1916. Commissioned in the RAF in 1937. Joined 120 Squadron in 1941 with which he was to become the most successful Coastal Command pilot of the war, sinking three U-boats and seriously damaging three more. Awarded Distinguished Service Order and Bar and Distinguished Flying Cross and Bar. After the war he worked as a pilot with a number of international airline companies.

BRYAN BUTCHARD

Born 1919. Joined the Royal Navy in 1932 as a cadet. Served on convoy escort duty in the Atlantic with the destroyers HMS *Volunteer* and *Vimy*. From 1944 he was the First Lieutenant of HMS *Magpie,* one of the ships of Captain Johnny Walker's 2nd Support Group. Served after the war as Inspector of Naval Ordnance and retired with the rank of Captain.

BILL COFFEY

Born 1919. Joined the Irish Army at the age of eighteen and served as a medical orderly. He later worked as a farm labourer and a fisherman.

DONALD COOMBES

Born 1922. Joined the Royal Navy in 1941 and served as an Able Seaman on HMS *Firedrake*. When she was lost he joined the Merchant Aircraft Carrier *Pretoria Castle*. After the war he worked in sales in the China and Glass industry.

HELMUT ECKE

Born 1918. Trained before the war as a journalist and became a reporter with the Propaganda Ministry in November 1940. His one war patrol was with *U-110*. After the war he worked as a journalist and in the Public Relations Office of the City of West Berlin.

HORST ELFE

Born 1917. Joined the Kriegsmarine in 1936 and the U-boat arm in 1938. Served as a staff officer at BdU (U-boat Command) and then from April 1940 as Second Watch Officer with *U-99* (7 war patrols). In December 1940 he became Commander of *U-139* and then *U-93*. The *U-93* was sunk in January 1942 and he spent five years in captivity. After the war he became the Director of a German steel company and President of the West Berlin Chamber of Commerce.

PETER EUSTACE

Born 1924. Joined HMS *Starling* in 1943 and served as a radar operator and in the ship's office for three years. After the war he became a teacher.

JOHN GUEST

Born 1911. Joined Royal Naval Volunteer Reserve in 1939. Convoy escort duty 1940–43, including HMS *Snowflake*.

From 1943 he was a Lieutenant Commander on the staff of the Western Approaches Tactical Unit in Liverpool. After the war he became a Partner in a firm of London solicitors.

REINHARD HARDEGEN

Born 1913. Joined the Reichsmarine in 1933 and trained as a navy pilot but transferred to the U-boat arm in 1939. He served as Watch Officer on *U-124* and then as Commander of *U-147* (one war patrol) and *U-123* (five war patrols). He sank 25 ships and was decorated with the Knight's Cross with Oak Leaves. He left *U-123* in July 1942 as served at the Torpedo Training School and at the end of the war as a battalion commander in an infantry regiment. After the war he started his own oil trading company.

GEORG HÖGEL

Born 1919. Joined the Kriegsmarine in 1937 and served as a radio operator on 7 war patrols with *U-30* between 1938 and 1940 and on the last war patrol of *U-110*. After the war he worked as an artist and draughtsman.

FRANK HOLDING

Born 1921. Joined the Merchant Navy in 1936. Was serving on the *Beatus* as Assistant Steward when the ship was sunk in October 1940 and as a kitchen porter on the White Star Liner *Laconia* when she was lost in September 1942. After the war he worked on the docks and then as a plasterer.

JOE INSTANCE

1916–2001. Joined the Royal Navy 1933 and HMS *Royal Oak* in 1939 as a Leading Seaman. Later served in destroyers on Atlantic convoy duty. Commissioned after the war, he retired with the rank of Lieutenant Commander in 1959 and became a teacher.

JAKOB ISBRANDTSEN

Born 1922. Joined the US Coastal Picket Patrol in 1942 and commanded the yacht *Edlu II*. From 1944 he served in the Pacific with the USN 5th Fleet. After the war he worked and then ran the family shipping company.

ADMIRAL IAN JAMIESON

Born 1920. Royal Naval College, Dartmouth. Sub-Lieutenant HMS

Windermere 1939–40. Later served on the staff of the Anti-Submarine Warfare Division at the Admiralty, awarded Distinguished Service Cross. After the war served in various posts, including Assistant Director, Naval Intelligence and NATO Commander, Mediterranean.

JAMES KEACHIE
Born 1916. Volunteered in 1939 for the Royal Canadian Navy. Served as Sub-Lieutenant with HMS *Bluebell* before returning to Canada where he directed the new Anti-Submarine Warfare School in Halifax and later ASW operations at HMCS *Naden* on Vancouver Island. After the war he practised law in Toronto.

DON KIRTON
Born 1918. Commissioned HMS *Bluebell* in 1940 and served as a Leading Supply Assistant. He later joined the destroyer HMS *Trafalgar* in the Far East. He left the Navy in 1953 and worked in local government.

DR HANS-JOCHEN VON KNEBEL DOEBERITZ
1918–2002. Joined the Kriegsmarine in 1936 and the U-boat arm in 1938. Staff Officer at BdU and later Dönitz's Adjutant. Three war patrols as Watch Officer on *U-23* and one with *U-99*. Spent nearly six years as a prisoner of war. After the war he became the head of the European subsidiary of an American tobacco company.

VOLKMAR KÖNIG
Born 1920. Joined the Kriegsmarine in 1939 and the U-boat arm in 1941. Served as a midshipman on one war patrol with *U-99*. After the war he ran his own plastics processing company.

HEINZ KUHLMANN
Born 1924. Joined the Kriegsmarine in 1941 and the U-boat arm the following year. Served as a diesel mechanic on five war patrols with *U-105* and *U-154*. After the war he worked as a sales manager for a bird food company.

JOHN LESTER
Born 1925. A Merchant Navy Cadet with the *Richmond Castle*, which was sunk in August 1942. Later joined the *Windsor Castle*, which was sunk in March 1943 with

3000 troops on board. He left the Merchant Navy in 1946 and worked in laundry and textile management and is still the Chairman of his own company.

ADMIRAL HARTWIG LOOKS
Born 1917. Joined the Kriegsmarine in 1936 and the U-boat arm in 1940. Served as First Watch Officer aboard *U-375* and then from May 1942 as the Commander of U-264. He carried out five war patrols and sank three ships. The *U-264* was sunk by the 2nd Support Group on 19 February 1944. After the war he became an Admiral in the West German Navy (Bundesmarine).

SIR DONALD MACDOUGALL
Born 1912. From 1939–40 was a member of the First Lord of the Admiralty's Statistical Branch and then from 1940 the Prime Minister's Statistical Branch. After the war he held various academic and public posts including Head of Government Economic Service and Chief Economic Adviser to the Treasury 1969–73.

HANNS-FERDINAND MAßMANN
Born 1917. Joined the Kriegsmarine in 1936 and the U-boat arm in 1938. After serving as a training officer and then on the staff at BdU (U-boat Command), he joined *U-17* as a Watch Officer and then *U-137*. In December 1940 he became Commander of *U-137* (1 patrol) and in January 1942 of U-409 (6 patrols). He sank four ships before being sunk in the Mediterranean in July 1943. After the war he worked as a sales manager with a number of international shipping companies.

COLIN MCFADYEAN
Born 1914. Joined the Royal Naval Volunteer Reserve in 1939. Served in armed merchant cruisers and destroyers between 1939–42. Joined Naval Intelligence as a Lieutenant Commander in 1943. After the war he was a Partner in a firm of Solicitors in the City of London.

WILLIAM MERTON
Born 1918. Joined the Operational Research Section of Coastal Command in July 1941 and then in 1943 he moved to the office of the Prime Minister's special adviser, Lord Cherwell. After the war he joined Flemings Merchant Bank and eventually became its Chairman.

ERIC MUNDAY
Born 1921. Joined the Royal Engineers in
1941. In December 1942 he was on his way
to Burma on the liner *Ceramic* when it was
torpedoed by the *U-515*. He was rescued by
the U-boat and became a prisoner of war.
After the war he became a surveyor.

JÜRGEN OESTEN
Born 1913. Joined the Reichsmarine in
1933 and the U-boat arm in 1937. Served
as Watch Officer on *U-20* before the war.
He made eight war patrols as Commander
of *U-61* and 3 with *U-106*. From 1941 he
served on the Staff, but returned to sea
in1943 as Commander of *U-861*. He sank
18 ships and was awarded the Knight's
Cross. After the war he worked as a sales
manager with international shipbuilding and
shipping companies.

MARGUERITE PATTEN
Born 1915. Worked as a Home Economist,
with lectures and demonstrations for an
electricity company and the Lincolnshire
Education Authority. From 1942 she was a
Food Advisor with the Ministry of Food.
After the war she became a writer and
broadcaster.

ANTON PLENK
Born 1932. During the war the U-boat
Commander Joachim Schepke was a guest
of the Plenk family. Anton Plenk is the
owner of a wood construction company,
specialising in house building.

SANDY ROBERTSON
Born 1908. Worked before the war as a
diver with Metal Industries raising the
Imperial German Fleet from Scapa Flow.
From 1939 he worked for the Royal Navy
as a diver. After the war he continued to
dive until his retirement in 1963.

ADMIRAL HANS-RUDOLF RÖSING
Born 1905. Joined the Reichsmarine in
1924, secretly trained in 1930 on foreign
built U-boats. In 1935 commissioned the
U-11 and served in Spanish waters during
the Civil War. At the outbreak of war he was
Commander of the Emsmann Flotilla but in
May 1940 he took over *U-48* for two war
patrols and sank 12 ships. He was decorated
with the Knight's Cross. From September
1940 he served in various senior staff
positions, eventually as Führer der U-Boote
West with special responsibility for U-boats

in France. After the war he became an
Admiral in the West German Navy.

LOUIS SCHEICH
Born 1922. Worked for the railway in
Jacksonville until June 1944 when he was
drafted. He won the Purple Heart and
Bronze Star serving with the US 4th
Armoured Division. After the war he
returned to Jacksonville and his job with the
railway.

ADMIRAL HORST VON SCHROETER
Born 1919. Joined the Kriegsmarine in
1937. Served on the battle cruiser
Scharnhorst and then in 1940 transferred to
the U-boat arm. Carried out six war patrols
as Watch Officer of *U-123* before taking
command of the boat in August 1942. In
five war patrols as Commander he sank six
ships and was decorated with the Knight's
Cross. After the war he became an Admiral
in the West German Navy and the
Commander of NATO Naval Forces in the
Baltic.

SIR PETER SMITHERS
Born 1913. Joined Royal Naval Volunteer
Reserve in 1939 and Naval Intelligence in
1940. Served as Assistant Naval Attaché at
the British Embassy in Washington
1941–42. After the war held many national
and international posts, including Member
of Parliament and junior minister; UK
Delegate to U.N. General Assembly
1960–62; Secretary General, Council of
Europe 1964–69.

ADMIRAL ERICH TOPP
Born 1914. Joined the Reichsmarine in
1934 and transferred to the U-boat arm in
1937. Served as First Officer with *U-46* and
then as Commander of *U-57* (two war
patrols) and *U-552* (10 war patrols). He
was the fifth most successful Commander
of the war, sinking 34 ships, for which he
was decorated with the Knight's Cross with
Oak Leaves and Swords. In August 1942 he
left the *U-552* and became the commander
of a training flotilla in the Baltic. After the
war he worked as an architect and then
served as an Admiral in the West German
Navy.

FRANK TRUBISZ
Born 1918. Joined the Merchant Navy in
1941. Served as an Ordinary Seaman on
the *Esso Baton Rouge*, which was sunk by

U-123 in April 1942. He continued to serve
with the US merchant fleet until the end of
the war, when he became a butcher.

MAURICE USHERWOOD

Born 1911. Trained as Anti-Submarine
Warfare specialist in 1937. Served in
destroyers both in the Atlantic and
Mediterranean, where in 1944 he won the
Distinguished Service Cross. After the war
he served on the Staff as an ASW specialist
and retired in 1964 with the rank of
Captain.

JANET WALKER

Born 1913. Followed her husband John's
regiment to the Middle East before being
transferred to South Africa. Janet and her
daughter Doreen were passengers on the
Laconia when the ship was sunk in
September 1942. Doreen was lost. After the
war Janet's husband remained in the army
and she accompanied him on his various
postings. They had two more daughters.

COLIN WARWICK

Born 1912. Served in the Merchant Navy
before the war. Lieutenant in Royal Naval
Reserve, commanding officer HMS *St
Loman* 1940–43, awarded Distinguished
Service Cross and Bar. Between 1944–45
he served as a Lieutenant Commander in
charge of an Escort Group. After the war he
became a marketing consultant in the
United States.

HEINZ WILDE

Born 1919. Joined the Kriegsmarine in
1939 and the U-boat arm the following
year. Served as a radio operator on two war
patrols with *U-110*. After the war he worked
as a sales manager with a large retail chain.

HELMUT WITTE

Born 1915. Joined the Reichsmarine in
1934 and transferred to the U-boat arm in
July 1940. He served as First Watch Officer
on *U-107* and then from October 1941 as
Commander of *U-159*. He sank 22 ships
with the *U-159* and was awarded the
Knight's Cross. He left the boat in June
1943 and served in various staff positions.
After the war he worked in business and
became personnel manager for a German
industrial group.

REFERENCES

CHAPTER 1

1 See p. 32, *Wolf: U-boat Commanders in World War II*, Jordan Vause (Air Life Publishing Ltd 1997)
2 Report of debrief with Lemp – given to British interrogators after the war by Konteradmiral Eberhard Godt – Chief of Operations at (BdU) U-boat Command.
3 Quoted p. 5, *Winston S. Churchill: Finest Hour 1939-41*, Martin Gilbert (Book Club Association 1983)
4 Admiral Canaris as quoted p. 125, *Dönitz: The Last Führer* Peter Padfield (Victor Gollancz 1984)
5 See p. 7, *Memoirs: Ten Years and Twenty Days*, Admiral Dönitz, trans. R.H. Stevens (Weidenfeld and Nicolson 1959)
6 Quoted p. 13, *Memoirs*, Dönitz
7 Ibid
8 Quoted p. 125, *The Odyssey of a U-Boat Commander*, Erich Topp, trans. Eric C. Rust (Praeger, Connecticut 1992)
9 See p. 32, *Wolf*, Vause
10 See p. 165-66, *Business in Great Waters – The U-Boat Wars 1916-1945*, John Terraine (Mandarin Paperbacks 1989)
11 *Seekriegsführung gegen England* Oct. 25 1938, as quoted p. 166, *Dönitz: The Last Führer*, Peter Padfield (Victor Gollancz 1984)
12 p. 67, *Memoirs*, Dönitz
13 p. 68, *Memoirs*, Dönitz
14 p. 29, *Nightmare at Scapa Flow: The truth about the sinking of HMS Royal Oak*, H.J. Weaver (Cressrelles Publishing Ltd 1991)
15 *U-47* War Diary
16 See p. 105, *British Intelligence in the Second World War: Its Influence on Strategy and Operations*, 3 vols., H.F. Hinsley et al. (HMSO 1979-84)
17 See also ADM 290/409 Technical report on torpedo fragments recovered and ADM 199/158 Divers reports on Royal Oak
18 p. 62, *Winston S. Churchill: Finest Hour*, Gilbert

19 p. 50, *Wolf*, Vause
20 As quoted p. 108, *Hitler's U-Boat War: The Hunters 1939-42*, Clay Blair (Weidenfeld and Nicolson 1996)

CHAPTER 2

1 p. 46, *Business in Great Waters*, Terraine
2 p. 163, *The Second World War*, Winston S. Churchill (Cassell 1959)
3 p. 6, *Winston S. Churchill: Finest Hour*, Gilbert
4 As quoted *The Knockout Blow against the Import System: Admiralty Expectations of Nazi Germany's Naval Strategy 1934-9*, Dr Joseph Maiolo, Historical Research vol. 72, no. 178 (Blackwell 1999)
5 59 million as imported in 1937 was taken as the official figure, see p. 144 *Merchant Shipping and the Demands of War*, C.B.A. Behrens (HMSO 1955)
6 p. 23, *Merchant Shipping and the Demands of War*, Behrens
7 See Appendix D, vol. 1, *The War at Sea* (4 vols), Captain S.W. Roskill (HMSO 1954-61)
8 p. 30, *The Defeat of the Enemy Attack on Shipping 1939-45 (Naval Staff History)*, Lt Cmdr D.W. Walters, revised ed. Naval Records Society vol. 137 (HMSO 1957)
9 ASDIC is derived from the initial letters of the committee responsible for the development of a new submarine detector – the Allied Submarine Detection Investigation Committee (of 1917)
10 Churchill Correspondence at Churchill College, Cambridge CHT/4/3
11 Admiral Sir Ernle Chatfield to Churchill 5th May 1936 CHAR 2/272
12 p. 536, vol 2 *Naval Policy Between the Wars* (2 vols) Captain S.W. Roskill (Collins 1976)
13 Quoted p. 38, *Winston S. Churchill: Finest Hour*, Gilbert
14 Churchill papers at Churchill College, Cambridge Char 9/135/173-185

15 p. 106, vol. 1, *The War at Sea*, 4 vols.,
    Captain S. W. Roskill (HMSO 1954-61)
16 Quoted p. 136 *Winston S. Chuchill: Finest
    Hour*, Gilbert
17 p. 16, vol. 1 *German Naval History of The
    U-Boat War in the Atlantic*, 3 vols.,
    Fregattenkapitän Günther Hessler (HMSO,
    London)
18 p. 37, Ibid vol. 1
19 ADM 223/81 OIC Daily reports for
    January 1940
20 p. 130, *The War at Sea* vol. 1, Roskill
21 See *'I believe the Hun is Cheating': British
    Admiralty Technical Intelligence and the
    German Navy 1936-39*, Dr Joseph Maiolo,
    Intelligence and National Security, vol 11,
    no. 1, January 1996
22 p. 248, *Business in Great Waters*, Terraine

CHAPTER 3
1   As quoted p. 356, *Winston S. Churchill:
    Finest Hour*, Gilbert
2   p.164, *Neither Sharks Nor Wolves: The men of
    Nazi Germany's U-Boat arm 1939-1945*,
    Timothy P. Mulligan (Chatham Publishing
    1999)
3   For description of U-boat have drawn on
    information provided by Dr Axel Niestlé
    and pp. 57-64, *The Hunters*, vol. 1, Blair
4   See also ADM 199/2133 Report on *'Jersey
    City'*
5   See p. 54, *The Secret Diary of a U-boat*,
    Wolfgang Hirschfeldt (Orion 1997). The
    crew *U-109* was famously told its patrol had
    been 'crap', it had at least had the courtesy
    to bring its U-boat back.

CHAPTER 4
1   p. 55, *Very Special Intelligence – The Story of
    the Admiralty's Operational Intelligence Centre
    1939-45*, Patrick Beesley (Hamish Hamilton
    1977)
2   Sources for SC 7: ADM 199/1707; Reports
    on SC7 and ADM 199/2057; CB 4050/40
    Monthly ASW Report Sept/October 1940.
    Additional information from *Night of the
    U-boats*, Paul Lund and Harry Ludlam
    (W. Foulsham and Co. 1973)
3   ADM 199/1707 Reports on SC7 – this and
    following report quotes
4   War Diary *U-99*
5   ADM 199/142 Reports HX 79 and
    MFQ1/583 (pt4) Track Chart for HX 79
6   p. 161, *Night of the U-boats*, Lund and
    Ludlam
7   ADM 199/2057 CB 4050/40 (11) Monthly
    ASW Report (November 1940)
8   BdU Diary 20th October 1940, as quoted

p. 52 vol. 1 Hessler
9   p. 107, *Memoirs*, Dönitz
10 p. 213, vol. 1, *Hitler's U-boat War*, Blair
11 p. 117, *Memoirs*, Dönitz
12 p. 207, vol. 1, *Hitler's U-boat War*, Blair

CHAPTER 5
1   p. 398, *The Second World War*, Churchill
2   p. 397, *The Second World War*, Churchill
3   p. 23, *Don and Mandarin – Memoirs of an
    Economist*, Donald MacDougall (John
    Murray 1987)
4   p. 242 *British War Economy*, W.K. Hancock
    and M. M. Gowing (HMSO 1949)
5   As quoted p. 118, *Churchill and the Prof*,
    Thomas Wilson (Cassell 1995)
6   *The Battle of the Atlantic Directive* CHAR
    23/9
7   p. 140, *Merchant Shipping and the Demands
    of War*, C.B.A. Behrens (HMSO 1955)
8   p. 62, *British War Production*, M. M. Postan
    (HMSO 1952)
9   p. 49, *Food and Agriculture in Britain
    1939-45 – Aspects of Wartime Control*,
    R. J. Hammond (Stanford University Press,
    California 1954)
10 *Battle of the Atlantic: Food Problems and their
    Resolution*, Prof. John Raeburn, unpublished
    paper 2001
11 Colville diary 26 February 1941; Colville
    papers as quoted p. 1016, *Winston
    S. Churchill: Finest Hour*, Gilbert
12 p. 65, *The Naval War Against Hitler*, Donald
    Macintyre (B.T. Batsford Ltd 1971)

CHAPTER 6
1   Source pp. 238-9 and 248-254, vol. 1,
    Hitler's U-boat War, Blair
2   pp. 101-105, *U-boat Killer*, Donald
    Macintyre (Weidenfeld and Nicolson 1956)
3   p. 175, *Memoirs*, Dönitz
4   I am indebted to Ralph Erskine for his help
    in understanding the Enigma machine. See
    also *Action This Day: Bletchley Park from the
    breaking of the Enigma code to the birth of the
    modern computer* (Bantam Pres 2001)
5   p. 90, *Count Not the Dead: The Popular
    Image of the German Submarine*, Michael
    Hadley (McGill-Queen's Univeristy Press,
    Montreal and Kingston 1995)

CHAPTER 7
1   Sources: Ralph Erskine and pp. 141-142,
    Enigma: The Battle for the Codes, Hugh
    Sebag-Montefiore (Weidenfeld and
    Nicolson 2000)
2   Source: Ralph Erskine
3   Ralph Erskine says there was generally a

delay of around 12 hours at first, but after August 1941 Hut 8 usually broke Hydra traffic within 36 hours.

4   p. 155, *Operation Drumbeat: The Dramatic True Story of Germany's First U-Boat Attacks Along the American Coast in World War II*, Michael Gannon (Harper and Row 1990)

5   pp. 20-21, *Room 39: Naval Intelligence in Action 1939-45*, Donald MacLachlen (Weidenfeld and Nicolson 1968) Lists 17 sources without mentioning Ultra.

6   pp. 542-5, vol. 1, *The War at Sea*, Roskill

7   Quoted p. 168, *The Battle of the Atlantic*, John Costello and Terry Hughes (Book Club Associates 1977)

8   Ultra seen by the Prime Minister HW1/7, HW1/9 and HW1/42

9   Quoted p. 86, vol. 1, *German Naval History*, Hessler

10   p. 380, vol. 1, *The Hunters*, Clay Blair

11   As quoted Costello pp.181-2

CHAPTER 8

1   p. 69, *Operation Drumbeat*, Gannon

2   ADM 223/15 ff 5-6 as quoted in *The Battle of the Atlantic and Signals Intelligence U-Boat Situations and Trends 1941-1945*, ed. Prof David Syrett for Navy Record Society (Ashgate Publishing Ltd 1998)

3   Admiral Andrews E.S.F. 22 Dec 1941 as quoted p. 176, *Operation Drumbeat*, Gannon

4   As quoted p. 15 vol. 2, *German Naval History*, Hessler

5   ADM 223/15 ff. 11-12, as quoted *U-Boat Situations and Trends 1941-1945*, Professor David Syrett

6   As quoted p. 97, vol. 1, Hessler also ADM 199/1920 HMS/M Clyde Report of attack

7   Source pp. 537, vol. 1, *Hitler's U-boat War*, Blair

8   ADM 223/15, ff. 29-31, as quoted *U-Boat Situations*, Syrett

9   As quoted p. 362, *Operation Drumbeat*, Gannon

10   Source p. 374, Ibid

11   p. 377, Ibid

12   p. 588, vol. 1 *Hitler's U-boat War*, Blair

13   p. 598, Ibid

14   ADM 223/505 Report on penetration of British codes and ciphers and ADM 1/30081 Chart/report showing extent of German penetration of Naval codes and ciphers

CHAPTER 9

1   p. 76, *The Odyssey of a U-Boat Commander*, Erich Topp

2   p. 79, Ibid

3   As quoted p. 25 Hessler vol. 2

4   Ibid

5   p. 124, *U-Boat Command and the Battle of the Atlantic*, Jak Mallmann Showell (Conway Maritime Press Ltd 1989)

6   'German Technical and Electronic Development' by Axel Niestlé in *The Battle of the Atlantic 1939-45: The 50th Anniversary International Naval Conference*, ed. S. Howarth and D. Law (Greenhill Books 1994)

7   p. 240, *Memoirs*, Dönitz

8   See p. 91 *Odyssey*, Topp and 'The German System: A Staff Perspective', Graham Rhys-Jones in *Battle of the Atlantic Conference*

9   pp. 433-42, Axel Niestlé in *The Battle of the Atlantic Conference*

10   pp. 92-99, *Radar Days*, E. G. Bowen (Adam Hilger 1987)

11   Appendix 1 and 2 *German U-boat Losses During WWII: Details of Destruction*, Axel Niestlé (Naval Institute Press, Maryland 1998)

12   p. 420, 'Operational Research in the Battle of the Atlantic', Paul M. Sutcliffe, *The Battle of the Atlantic Conference*

13   p. 425, *The Battle of the Atlantic Conference*, Sutcliffe

14   See also p. 96, *Captain Gilbert Roberts R.N. and the Anti-U-boat School*, Mark Williams (Cassell 1979)

15   Source ADM 1/17621 Report of Western Approaches Tactical Unit Report

16   Appendix 16, *Hitler's U-boat War*, Blair

17   p. 271, *Memoirs*, Dönitz

CHAPTER 10

1   The Admiralty Trade Division Records include gunners aboard merchant vessels list 9,736. p. 181, *Merchant Shipping*, Behrens says 7,978 but this excludes passengers and losses in rescue ships.

2   *U-Boats to the Rescue: The Laconia Incident*, Léonce Peillard (Jonathan Cape 1963)

3   p. 58, vol. 2, *Hitler's U-boat War*, Blair

4   p. 43, *The Laconia Incident*, Peillard

5   p. 59, vol. 2, *Hitler's U-boat War*, Blair

6   p. 61, Ibid. Dönitz had originally directed seven U-boats but this order was countermanded by Hitler who was of the view that no rescue operation should have been mounted at all.

7   p. 159, *The Laconia Incident*, Peillard

8   p. 62, vol. 2, *Hitler's U-boat War*, Blair

9   p. 257, *Dönitz: The Last Führer*, Padfield

10   Two Allied commanders are accused of going further and shooting people in the

water – see case of USS Wahoo and HMS
Torbay. Source: *Submarines at War*, Edwin
P. Hoyt (Stein and Day 1983 and Die
Wehrmacht-Untersuchungsstelle, Munich:
Universitas/Langen-Müller, 1980)
11 p. 104, *The Liners of Liverpool*, part 2, Derek
M. Whale
12 p. 114, *Lone Wolf: The Life and Death of
U-boat Ace* Werner Henke, Timothy P.
Mulligan (Praeger, Connecticut 1993)
13 p. 111, *Liners of Liverpool*, part 2, Whale
14 p. 213, *Neither Sharks Nor Wolves*, Mulligan
15 p. 181, *Merchant Shipping*, Behrens
16 Admiralty Trade Division Records as
quoted Costello and Hughes
17 p. 106, *How to Abandon Ship*, Phil Richards
and John Banigan (Cornell Maritime Press,
Maryland 1942)
18 pp. 10-12, *How to Abandon Ship*, Richards
and Banigan

CHAPTER 11
1 p. 129, vol. 2 *Hitler's U-boat War*, Blair
2 ADM 199/165 '*Loss of HMS Firedrake*'
3 U-boat Trend 30/12/42 ADM 233/17, as
quoted *The Battle of the Atlantic and Signals
Intelligence*, Syrett
4 See also *Coastal Ace: The Biography of
Squadron Leader Terence Malcolm Bulloch,
DSO and Bar, DFC and Bar*, Tony Spooner
DSO, DFC (William Kimber and Co. Ltd
1986)
5 *U-611* was lost with all hands
6 p. 52, *Coastal Ace*, Spooner
7 p. 485, Appendix O, Roskill vol. 2
8 p. 267, Hancock and Gowing, *War Economy*
9 24 December 1942 as quoted p. 128,
Churchill and the Prof, Thomas Wilson
(Cassell 1995)
10 pp. 157-158, *Very Special Intelligence –
The Story of the Admiralty's Operational
Intelligence Centre 1939-45*, Patrick Beesley
(Hamish Hamilton 1977)
11 p. 89, vol. 2, *German Naval History*, Hessler
12 p. 310, *Memoirs*, Dönitz
13 p. 84, vol. 2, *German Naval History*, Hessler
14 UB Command War Diary 23.3.1943 as
quoted p. 95, vol. 2, Hessler
15 p. 367, Roskill vol. 2
16 HS 2/2 SOE Co-operation in the Anti
Submarine Campaign
17 p. 174, *Very Special Intelligence*, Beesley
18 ADM 223/15 ff. 187-188 U-Boat Situation
19/4/43, as quoted *The Battle of the Atlantic
and Signals Intelligence*, ed. Syrett
19 p. 188, *Max Horton and The Western
Approaches*, W. S. Chalmers (Hodder and
Stoughton 1966)

20 p. 272, vol. 2 *Hitler's U-boat War*, Blair
21 As quoted p. 401, vol. 2, *The War at Sea*,
Roskill
22 p. 188, Horton
23 p. 108, *Convoy Escort Commander*,
Vice-Admiral Sir Peter Gretton (Cassell
1964)
24 The convoy had set off from New York but
the escorts joined at St Johns,
Newfoundland from September 1942. HX
convoys departed from New York.
25 As quoted p. 280, *Dönitz: The Last Führer*,
Padfield
26 Sources for following description of ONS 5:
ADM 237/113 – Admiralty file of reports
from ONS 5. Additional sources: *Convoy
Escort Commander*, Gretton; *Black May*,
Michael Gannon (Harper Collins 1998);
The Fiercest Battle, Ronald Seth
(Hutchinsons 1961)
27 p. 144, *Convoy Escort Commander*,
Vice-Admiral Sir Peter Gretton (Cassell
1964)
28 p. 104, vol. 2, *German Naval History*,
Hessler
29 Based on Admiralty Re-assessment October
1991
30 ADM 237/113 Report of Senior Officer
Escort 3rd Support Group
31 Quoted p. 202, *Black May*, Gannon
32 *Black May*, Michael Gannon and *The Defeat
of the German U-Boats – The Battle of the
Atlantic*, Syrett (University of South
Carolina Press, Columbia 1994)
33 ADM/113 Report of Commanding officer
of Tay
34 p. 146, *Convoy Escort Commander*, Gretton
35 Quoted p. 147, Ibid
36 As quoted p. 286, *Dönitz: The Last Führer*,
Padfield
37 As quoted p. 297, Ibid
38 As quoted p. 337, vol. 2, *Hitler's U-boat War*,
Blair
39 p. 340, *Memoirs*, Dönitz
40 As quoted p. 301, *Dönitz: The Last Führer*,
Padfield
41 BdU Diary quoted p. 113, vol. 3, *German
Naval History*, Hessler
42 p. 341, *Memoirs*, Dönitz

CHAPTER 12
1 pp. 406-7, *Memoirs*, Dönitz
2 Dönitz knew nothing about the new XXI
and XXIII boats at this time – they were
still in their initial design period. The ideas
for these were presented to Dönitz in June.
His only hope were the 'Walter' boats and
these were along way from completion – at

this stage he believed the old U-boat types would have to carry the battle for at least another two years.

3   Wolfgang Frank *'Sea Wolves'* p.177 as quoted p.306, *Dönitz: The Last Führer*, Padfield
4   p. 407, *Memoirs*, Dönitz
5   p. 90-91, *Odyssey*, Topp
6   p. 11, vol. 3, *German Naval History*, Hessler
7   p. 379, vol. 2, *The War at Sea*, Roskill
8   p. 629, *Business in Great Waters*, Terraine – an average rate of 42 days per ship
9   p. 676, *The Second World War*, Churchill
10 As quoted p. 421, vol. 2 Blair
11 As quoted p. 425, Ibid
12 p. 420, *Memoirs*, Dönitz
13 ADM 199/2477 *Morale of U-boat Crews*
14 ADM 199/2477
15 p. 189, *Neither Sharks Nor Wolves*, Mulligan
16 p. 254, vol. 3, *The War at Sea*, Roskill
17 As quoted p. 228, *Neither Sharks Nor Wolves*, Mulligan
18 As quoted p. 228, Ibid
19 As quoted p. 227, Ibid
20 As quoted p. 228, Ibid
21 p. 218, Erich Topp paper in *The Battle of the Atlantic 1939-45: The 50th Anniversary International Naval Conference*
22 As quoted p. 70, vol. 3, *German Naval History*, Hessler
23 As quoted p. 423, *Memoirs*, Dönitz
24 As quoted p. 373, *Dönitz: The Last Führer*, Padfield
25 As quoted p. 382, Ibid
26 As quoted p. 696, vol. 2, *Hitler's U-boat War*, Blair
27 Source: *German U-boat Losses During WWII*, Niestlé – total for front boats 269 lost since May but a number were scuttled
28 Quoted pp. 349-51, *Dönitz: The Last Führer*, Padfield
29 p. 4, *German U-boat Losses During WWII*, Niestlé
30 p. 306, vol. 3, pt 2, *The War at Sea*, Roskill
31 pp. 424-26, vol. 1, *Hitler's U-boat War*, Blair
32 p. 250, *British War Economy*, W. K. Hancock and M. M. Gowing (HMSO 1949)
33 p. 585, vol. 1, *The War at Sea*, Roskill
34 p. 305, vol. 3 pt 2, Ibid

OTHER MATERIAL USED

Official histories:
History of United States Naval Operations in World War II, vol. 1: The Battle of the Atlantic 1939-May 1943, Samuel Eliot Morison (Oxford University Press 1948)

Other published works:
Axis Submarine Successes of World War II 1939-45, Jürgen Rohwer (Greenhill Books 1999)
The Battle of the Atlantic – The Corvettes and Their Crews: An Oral History, Chris Howard Bailey (Naval Institute Press, Maryland 1994)
Convoy, Martin Middlebrook (Penguin 1976)
Crisis Convoy: The Story of HX 231, Vice-Admiral Sir Peter Gretton (Purnell Book Services 1974)
The Critical Convoy Battles of March 1943, Jürgen Rohwer (Ian Allan Ltd 1977)
Decoding History: The Battle of the Atlantic Codes, W.J.R. Gardner, (Naval Institute Press, Maryland 1999)
Engage the Enemy More Closely: The Royal Navy in the Second World War, Correlli Barnett (Hodder and Stoughton 1991)
Iron Coffins, Herbert Werner (Bantam Books 1969)
I Sank The Royal Oak, Günther Prien (Grays Inn Press 1954)
The Naval War Against Hitler, Donald Macintyre (B.T. Batsford Ltd 1971)
Really Not Required, Colin Warwick (The Pentland Press Ltd, Bishop Auckland 1997)
Roosevelt and Churchill: Men of Secrets, David Stafford (Little Brown and Company 1999)
Seizing the Enigma: The Race to Break the German U-Boat Codes 1939-43, David Kahn (Random House 1991)
The U-Boat Offensive 1914-45, V.E. Tarrant (Arms amd Armour Press 1985)
U-333: The Story of a U-Boat Ace, Peter Cremer (Bodley Head 1984)
U-Boats under the Swastika, Jak Mallmann Showell (Ian Allen, Weybridge 1987)
The Ultra-Magic Deals: And the Most Secret Special Relationship 1940-1946, Bradley F. Smith (Airlife Publishing Ltd 1993)

Unpublished sources:
U-23 War Diary
U-30 War Diary
U-47 War Diary
U-99 War Diary
U-123 War Diary
Diary of Admiral J. H. Adams (unpub.)
Churchill Papers at Churchill College, Cambridge: CHAR 2/272 CHT/4/3
CHAR 9/135/173-185
CHAR 23/9
ADM 199/2133 Report on Jersey City and Jamaica Progress
ADM 290/409 Technical report on torpedo fragments recovered

ADM 199/158 Divers reports on Royal
Oak
ADM 223/81 OIC Daily reports for
January 1940
ADM 223/83 Summary of Naval Events
382-385 Sept 21-24 covering HX72
ADM 199/1707 and 199/144 Reports on
HX 72
ADM 199/1707 Reports on SC7
ADM 199/2057 CB 4050/40 Monthly
ASW Report Sept/October 1940
ADM 199/2057 CB 4050/40 Monthly
ASW Report Nov 1940
ADM 199/142 Reports HX 79 and
MFQ1/583 (pt4) Track Chart for
HX 79
ADM 199/165 'Loss of HMS Firedrake'
ADM 223/505 Report on penetration of
British codes and ciphers
ADM 1/30081 Chart/report showing extent
of German penetration of Naval codes
and ciphers
ADM 1/17621 Report of Western
Approaches Tactical Unit Report on
interrogation of German Navy
personnel
ADM 237/113 – Admiralty file of reports
on ONS 5
ADM 199/2477 'Morale of U-boat Crews'
ADM 199/2467 SIS Agent reports on
French U-boat bases
ADM 199/1920 HMS/M Clyde Report of
attack
HW 1/7 – HW1/9 and HW1/42 HW5/19
Ultra seen by the Prime Minister
HS 2/2 - SOE Co-operation in the Anti
Submarine Campaign

PICTURE CREDITS
AKG: section A page 2(top), D6(t)
Richard Amstein B 4(t)
Bundersarchiv, Koblenz: A2(below), 3(b),
B2 (both), 3(t), 4(b), 7(b), C1, D2(t)
ECPA: C4
Hulton Archive: A6 (both)
Imperial War Museum: A3(t), 4 (both),5(b),
C2(t), 3(both), 5(t), D8
John Adams: A5(t)
Reinhard Hardegens: B8, C8
John Lester: D3(t)
Library of Congress, Washington: C7, D4
National Archives Washington: C5(b),
6 (both), D1(b), 5(both)
Jürgen Oesten: B7(t)
Popperfoto: A7(centre), C2(b)
Public Record Office: D1(t)
Bibliothek für Zeitgeschichte, Stuttgart: A1,
B7(t left), D2(b)

Submarine Museum Portsmouth: B6(t),
D3(b)
The Art Archive/Imperial War Museum: A7
(both), 8, D7(t)
Erich Topp: B1, 3(t), 5(t), 6(b)
TRH Pictures: D1(c), 6(b)

INDEX